ÉMILE DURKHEIM

ROBERT A. NISBET
WITH SELECTED ESSAYS

GREENWOOD PRESS, PUBLISHERS
WESTPORT, CONNECTICUT

Library of Congress Cataloging in Publication Data

Nisbet, Robert A
    Émile Durkheim.

    Reprint of the ed. published by Prentice-Hall,
Englewood Cliffs, N.J., in series: Makers of modern
social science.
    Bibliography: p.
    1. Durkheim, Émile, 1858-1917. I. Series: Makers
of modern social science.
[HM22.F8D86 1976]   301'.01   75-36358
ISBN 0-8371-8626-9

Originally published in 1965 by Prentice-Hall, Inc.,
Englewood Cliffs, N.J.

Reprinted with the permission of Prentice-Hall, Inc.

Reprinted in 1976 by Greenwood Press, Inc.,
88 Post Road West, Westport, Connecticut 06881

Library of Congress Catalog Card Number 75-36358
ISBN 0-8371-8626-9

Printed in the United States of America

10 9 8 7 6 5 4 3

PREFACE

THE FIRST PART of this book consists of a long essay in which I have tried to set forth in its fullness Durkheim's contribution to modern sociology. The second section is composed of articles on Durkheim by other authors, drawn from the critical literature of the past thirty years, each devoted to a special work or aspect of Durkheim's sociology. Quite apart from the welcome diversity of insight and appraisal that the five articles provide, each of them analyzes in depth in a way that is neither possible nor desirable in the more comprehensive and synoptic approach that I have taken in my own essay.

Regarding my own essay, several prior comments are in order. First, I have felt it necessary to stress the *milieu* of Durkheim's ideas. *Milieu* is a Durkheimian concept, and nowhere is its utility greater than in an understanding of Durkheim's own ideas and emphases. Too many present-day judgments of Durkheim are made as though their authors assumed the same intellectual environment for Durkheim that surrounds them. As a result, the force of his originality and the dimension of his response are lost or distorted. Only by constant reminder of the profoundly, almost obsessively, individualistic age in which Durkheim wrote, and of the deep strains of biologism in the social thought of the nineteenth and early twentieth centuries, can we keep fresh the true magnitude of his contribution and the reason for the relentlessness of his insistence upon *social* explanations of social behavior even when this incurred, as it frequently did, the risk of hypostatization.

Second, I have chosen to present Durkheim's substantive work in terms of several constitutive ideas—unit-ideas, in the late Arthur O. Lovejoy's seminal phrase—rather than in terms of the functional method that Durkheim applied to institutional materials, or the even commoner perspective provided by the bibliographic succession of his major writings. I do not reject either of these approaches to Durkheim's work. They are necessary, and, when one thinks of their yield in the interpretive writings of Radcliffe-Brown, Talcott Parsons, Robert Merton, and Harry Alpert, invaluable. But it is the implicit argument of my essay that there is an equal, and markedly different, yield from the employment of a strictly intellectual approach; that is, dissection in terms of the underlying major constitutive *ideas* that give unity and diversity to his life's work. Five ideas are, I believe, essential; they may fairly be considered the tissues of his sociology: *society, personality, authority,* the *religio-sacred,* and *development.* The value of these ideas lies not alone in their relevance to Durkheim's work; they are the unit-ideas of the central sociological tradition in the nineteenth century—the tradition of Comte, Tocqueville, Le Play, Tönnies, Weber, and Simmel—and through them we are given, I believe, a useful basis of comparison of Durkheim with his fellow titans.

I have quoted often and frequently at length from Durkheim in the pages that follow. I realize that this can be distracting in an interpretive work, but I consider this a small sin beside that posed whenever interpretation succumbs to interpolation—an all too easy vice when one is writing of Durkheim. How often has not his heuristic emphasis on society been converted by the uninformed into a transcendent social monolith? How often has it not been said that concrete human beings are dissolved into mere wraiths of a collective conscience in Durkheim's works? The only answer to all this is, of course, what Durkheim actually wrote.

There is an additional value to frequency and fullness of quotation. It may serve to direct the reader to Durkheim's books and articles. I have deliberately drawn all quotations from Durkheim's principal works, those which are easily available (in English) to the reader. For it is not necessary to go to letters or to obscure or fugitive pieces in Durkheim's bibliography to defend him against charges of "collectivism," "medieval realism," and so on. The defense can be made to rest on what is major and essential to his sociology.

Finally, there is the sense of immediacy and contemporaneity that is drawn only when we are given the opportunity to see Durkheim in his own words. This is important. Despite the fact that many of Durkheim's principal conclusions are by now deeply embedded in the main stream of social science, his books retain a freshness and stimulus that only genuine classics possess. Writing as one who has but recently had the experience of re-reading Durkheim's books, I can freely say that in each there is still to be found that ring of continuing relevance to current problems that alone stamps greatness on an author. Scientist Durkheim was indeed; there has not since been one greater. But he was also moral philosopher and, we need not shrink from noting, artist. In Durkheim the intuitive grasp of the artist is wonderfully assimilated into the framework of scientific design and verification. Durkheim was more than a social scientist. He was, like Tocqueville and Weber, the interpreter of an age. And such was the prescience with which he identified the central themes of industrial and democratic society in the modern West that not even the momentous events of the last half-century have dislodged his relevance.

Since this essay on Durkheim has been drawn, in substantially revised form, from a much longer work on European social thought, written and largely completed during a sabbatical year, 1963-64, I must express warm appreciation to the University of California for salaried leave and to the John Simon Guggenheim Foundation for generous Fellowship assistance that helped make it possible. It is a pleasure to record my further appreciation to Princeton University, and particularly its Department of Sociology, which, through a visiting fellowship, provided the stimulating scene of the writing. Finally, I wish to thank the following publishers for their kind permission to reprint material: Lothrop, Lee & Shepard Co., Inc.; Alfred A. Knopf, Inc.; The Wayne State University Press; Routledge & Kegan Paul Ltd.; The Free Press of Glencoe, Inc.; George Allen & Unwin Ltd.; and The University of Chicago Press.

R.A.N.

CONTENTS

ÉMILE DURKHEIM

INTRODUCTION

MORE THAN ANY other figure in the history of sociology, Émile Durkheim seems to embody what has proved to be conceptually most distinctive in the field and most fertile in its contribution to other modern disciplines. Durkheim, it might be said, is the complete sociologist.

This does not mean, of course, that he was necessarily foremost among the Titans in the field. It would be foolhardy to rank him above Weber or Simmel. He lacked the Renaissance breadth and luster of Weber's learning, which has indeed been unequaled in the social sciences this century. And one will look in vain in Durkheim for the brilliance of Simmel's mind or, for that matter, for the insight into the elements of human behavior that is the hallmark of Simmel's work. Nor can one claim for Durkheim either the intuitive grasp of Tocqueville or the encyclopedic comprehensiveness that made Spencer and Ward notable.

But if one fixes attention upon those sociological elements that are, and have been, unique in the family of social sciences and that have had the greatest influence on other social sciences, Durkheim appears to be first among equals. His reaction to analytical individualism and biologism was more basic and implicative, his elevation of the social into a perspective for understanding human behavior was more systematic, and the uses to which he was able to put this perspective were more varied and fruitful than any that can readily be found among his contemporaries.

There is also the immediacy and directness of his influence. Durkheim's impact upon his students and colleagues bore early fruit. That he was a masterful teacher is witnessed by the long list of important works in almost every field of scholarship—history, economics, psychology, law, government—written by men who acknowledged him as their teacher. Nor was this a personal respect alone. It is impossible to read very far into the works of Gustave Glotz on classical Greece, Hubert on the Celts, De-

clareuil on Roman law, Marcel Granet on China, Maunier on North
Africa, Maurice Halbwachs on memory, or the works of such men as
Davy, Mauss, and Fauconnet—often in the pages of the brilliant review
L'Année Sociologique that Durkheim himself founded—to realize that
his influence was early and very substantive indeed.[1] It was also remarkably consistent: there are no evidences among his followers of the "Oedi-
pal revolt" that the histories of Marxism and Freudianism reveal.

Some might say that this happy fate was Durkheim's because he was
less radical—and, therefore, less likely to arouse either passionate devotion or rebellion. It is true that Durkheim never was, and has not since
become, the kind of charismatic figure that Marx, Darwin, and Freud
shortly became and have remained to this day. But, as the history of
thought documents, philosophers can have powerful—even transforming
—influence on a field of thought and still lack the appeal of a Marx or a
Freud. One thinks of Hobbes in politics, Leibniz in metaphysics, Lyell
in geology, Peirce in modern pragmatism: each possessed extraordinary
originality, but without electrifying influence on either followers or
critics.

If one looks beyond the complex and always unpredictable phenomenon of charisma in the history of thought to the concepts involved and
to their impact upon scholarship, Durkheim appears at least as radical
as Darwin, Marx, or Freud even though, for largely contextual reasons,
his ideas have had nothing like the impact upon civilization that theirs
so plainly have had. Indeed, I am inclined to think that Durkheim's
intellectual break with eighteenth-century ideas was a more fundamental
one than any that can easily be found in Darwin's blend of meliorism and
uniformitarianism, or in Marx's view of man's relation to institutions
and of the progressive course of historical development. Freud, for all
the momentous impact of his explorations of the nonrational, uncon-

[1] The best treatment in English of Durkheim's influence on his contemporaries and
students is Harry Alpert, *Émile Durkheim and His Sociology* (New York: Columbia
University Press, 1939). See especially pp. 47-51 for a discussion of the founding and
epochal significance of *L'Année Sociologique*. In French the most useful work on
Durkheim's significance and influence is C. Bouglé, *Bilan de la sociologie française
contemporaine* (Paris: Alcan, 1935). The most recent comprehensive treatment of
Durkheim's sociology and its influence is Kurt H. Wolff (ed.), *Émile Durkheim,
1858-1917* (Columbus: The Ohio State University Press, 1960). In it, among several
excellent discussions, is a treatment of Durkeim in American sociology by Roscoe C.
Hinkle, Jr., which, though generally valuable, does not allow sufficient importance to
Radcliffe-Brown's influence in breaking ground for the long overdue proper appreciation of Durkheim in the United States. It is a pleasure to express my personal
indebtedness here to a still unpublished study of Durkheim by John M. Foskett,
written in the late 1930's at Berkeley.

scious mind, did not really break with the classic categories of individualism that he inherited from the eighteenth century—nor, for that matter, with biologism, which, through his emphasis on drives (*Triebe*), must be seen as the lingering (if more sophisticated) eighteenth-century fascination with presocial instincts. Durkheim challenges volitional rationalism and sensationism just as Freud did, but he also goes on to repudiate the larger categories of which rationalism and sensationism are parts: to the whole philosophy and methodology of analytical individualism. In fairness to Freud, it must be stressed that—quite apart from his conceptual point of departure—the direction of his analysis was toward the interpersonal and ultimately, therefore, toward the social. But nothing can be found in Freud, at any stage of his theoretical development, that conveys the repudiation of biologism that is the very warp of Durkheim's thinking.

Durkheim's influence upon subsequent scholarship has been as great as that of any one of the three others—perhaps greater than Marx's which, in the long run, has proved to be more cultural, more political, than intellectual. Darwin and Freud have had both cultural impact and continuing scientific influence, the latter to be seen in the unparalleled place Darwin has even today in the field of evolutionary biology and in the position Freud holds in dynamic psychology—not to mention diverse disciplines of the social sciences and humanities in which his theories have, at one time or other, had striking effect.

The case is not perhaps so dramatic for Durkheim. Not even the most ardent Durkheimian could argue any cultural impact of such doctrines as the collective conscience or individual representations—though a case might be made for anomie—but his scholarly influence on the social sciences, starting with sociology and anthropology, has been enormous. In the major studies of moral consensus, social cohesion, social deviation, religion, integration, ritual, and personality that have come forth in almost all the social sciences during the past half-century, Durkheim's manifest as well as hidden influence has been profound. It is no exaggeration to say that Durkheim, in company with Weber and Simmel, has been responsible not merely for the redirection of sociology in the twentieth century but also, as a substantial body of literature gives earnest, for the redirection of much psychology, economics, anthropology, and political science. The three minds are, in a very real sense, the essence of contemporary sociology.

Durkheim's impress upon the American mind was made only slowly; much more slowly than that upon the European mind. Between American sociological thought and the acceptance of Durkheimian perspectives lay the wilderness of homespun individualism, pragmatism, and general suspicion of theory that Europeans, starting with Tocqueville, were so struck by. In retrospect it can be seen that early suspicion and incomprehension of Durkheim in the American scholarly mind were predictable and inevitable. Individualism, as an analytical perspective, was common enough in Europe in the nineteenth century; in America it was a part of the very air men breathed. One may imagine, then, the reaction in this country to such a work as *The Rules of Sociological Method,* with its references to the autonomy of social facts, the independence of social from individual causes, and its relentless insistence upon sociological explanations in terms of superindividual—that is, social—processes. Cooley, whose own insights into the nature of the social bond marked a milestone in American sociology, was perhaps the one most nearly fitted to understand Durkheim, but the scant references suggest that Cooley, like his contemporaries, was generally alienated by what appeared to be Durkheim's reification of the social. The first full study of Durkheim by an American, C. E. Gehlke, in 1915, must be regarded today as nearly useless to an understanding of Durkheim's ideas, whatever its historical value in acquainting American readers with the scope of Durkheim's work.

The turning point from this indifference and neglect was unquestionably A. R. Radcliffe-Brown's coming to the University of Chicago in 1931 and his brilliant demonstrations not only of the meaning of Durkheim's ideas but, more important, of their operational utility and defensibility as hypotheses in the study of social organization. For the first time, Durkheim was made "respectable" in this country as a social scientist. A whole school of social anthropology flourished at Chicago, to a large extent on the basis of Durkheimian insights, a school that established a link between sociology and anthropology that has not been broken to this day.

Before this, as Harry Alpert has put it epigrammatically, Durkheim had been well-known in America but not known well. Now, with Radcliffe-Brown's breakthrough on American sociological consciousness, Durkheim began to receive his due. The perceptive and influential writings of Robert Merton, Talcott Parsons, and Harry Alpert in the middle and late 1930's, the illuminating appendix on French sociology with which Elliott and Merrill concluded their immensely popular textbook on social disorganization in 1934—all had the effect of making American sociologists aware of Durkheim's true worth and his unique relevance to the problems that had largely occupied American sociology for three decades.[2]

The last point is an important one. Durkheim's special contribution to American sociology lies in the fact that, like the Americans, his own sociology began with a conscious recognition of such social problems as crime, suicide, family instability, and social strife. This made for common ground. But what Durkheim added to this recognition of problems was a perspective both theoretical and historical—a perspective that rescued social problems from the empirical atomism, the aimless individualism, that had so dominated the American sociological scene. Durkheim's momentous contrast between mechanical and organic solidarity; his concepts of anomie, altruism, and egoism; his matchless demonstrations of the social elements in personality, religion, and law; and his typology of social integration and disintegration—all of this was, so to speak, manna for American sociology.

Add to substantive contributions such as these Durkheim's profound emphasis on science rather than either uplift or revolution as the avenue to social progress; add also his insistence on delimiting the proper sphere of sociology, on confining it to problems amenable to the kind of treatment of which his own study of suicide is perhaps even today the supreme example, and it is clear that for American sociology—with its unique pattern of individualism, Anglo-Saxon biologism, and Protestant moralism—Durkheim's impact was bound to be more significant, more radically transforming than even the impacts of Simmel and Weber.

Quite apart from the needs of American sociology, the character of American society in the twentieth century, especially after World War I,

[2] Alpert, op. cit.; Robert K. Merton, "Durkheim's Division of Labor in Society," American Journal of Sociology, XL (1934), 319-28 (reprinted in this volume); Talcott Parsons, The Structure of Social Action (New York: McGraw-Hill Book Company, Inc., 1937), Chap. 8-12. The earlier study by C. E. Gehlke is Émile Durkheim's Contributions to Sociological Theory (New York: Columbia University Press, 1915). Sorokin's Contemporary Sociological Theories (New York: Harper & Row, Publishers, 1928), which did so much to make Americans aware of the riches of the European tradition in sociology, gives proper emphasis to Durkeim, but the treatment is largely critical and cannot be said to have advanced Durkheim's influence. It was possible as late as 1923 for a major American sociologist, J. P. Lichtenberger, in a book on the history of sociology— The Development of Social Theory (New York: Appleton-Century-Croft, Inc., 1923)—to ignore Durkheim completely—and also Simmel, Weber, and Tönnies! On Radcliffe-Brown's influence there is no single work to emphasize; nearly all are relevant. In any event, it was his impact upon colleagues and students at Chicago (beginning with visiting lectures in the late 1920's and followed by professional appointment from 1931 to 1937) that did the most to break through the wall of incomprehension and suspicion that had surrounded Durkeim's work in this country and to make him for the first time a social scientist in American eyes.

formed a rich body of materials for the kind of analysis that is at the heart of Durkheim's sociology. The process of social dislocation, the growth of status mobility, the sudden secularization of traditional values, and the recession everywhere of the rural-communal contexts of association that for most Americans had long been the very stuff of society—these and related processes of change made Durkheim's central concepts relevant, not merely in a scientific sense, but in an historic and cultural sense as well. For Durkheim is par excellence the sociologist of anomie, and few societies have offered more abundant and diversified examples of this than America in the twentieth century.

PART ONE

ÉMILE DURKHEIM

ROBERT A. NISBET

ONE

SOCIAL MILIEU AND SOURCES

To UNDERSTAND MAJOR contributions to the history of social thought, one must understand the setting in which these were made—in this case, the ideas and social currents *against* which Durkheim's thought was directed as well as those which exerted a positive force in the shaping of his mind and interests. The history of moral philosophy, from Socrates and Plato to the modern existentialists, reveals the centrality of this truth: that ideas do not, in Sir Isaiah Berlin's vivid phrasing, beget ideas as butterflies beget butterflies. Ideas are dialectical responses, caught up in the logic and circumstance of antithesis. This is, no doubt, as true in the physical sciences, philosophy, and art as it is in the social sciences; but it is more immediately evident and dramatic in the latter. To a striking extent, every major social idea begins as an attack on, a criticism of, or a response to, some other idea. This is not to minimize the importance of data, of fact and experience, which the ideas of social scientists seek to synthesize and clarify. Facts are holy ground indeed, and in science it is the feeling of immediacy of fact and idea that distinguishes the Titans from those lesser mortals who become lost in the penumbra: methodologies, concepts, and systematics.

Nevertheless, in the genesis of thought it is not fact, but idea, that most often provides the challenge, the thesis against which any major idea may be seen as antithesis. It was scholasticism that produced, in powerful negation, the works of Bacon and Descartes at the beginning of the seventeenth century, thus setting the outlines of a whole new age of thought in which atomism replaced organicism, reductionism replaced synthesis, and analytical individualism became the conceptual framework for the study of society. For three hundred years, until the very end of the nineteenth century, the dominant metaphysics of society was individualism.[3]

What is true of social thought generally is vividly exemplified by Durkheim. His work, taken in its largest and most lasting outline, must be seen as a direct response to three main currents of thought in the nineteenth century: analytical individualism, biologism, and the idea of moral progress. Each was a powerful influence in the nineteenth century and each is also a crucial negative context of Durkheim's ideas.

ANALYTICAL INDIVIDUALISM

Nineteenth-century thought, both in Europe and America, was steeped in individualism. It is easy enough today, no doubt, to see this individualism as the final manifestations of a dying concept. Recent scholarship has produced a deep awareness of the nonindividualistic currents in the social and philosophical thought of the century—currents, indeed, which flowed directly into Durkheim's mind.

But if one goes back to the principal works of the time, to the ideas and perspectives which were then cherished and nearly taken for granted, he is aware of little other than the conceptual individualism that pervaded all areas of thought. As a philosophy, as a morality, as a psychology, individualism was dominant—not only as a conclusion but as a methodology. The major principles by which the study of man was carried on did not differ in substance from those that had underlain the Enlightenment. Reality was held to lie, not in institutions or social groups, but in man himself—man the root, man the microcosm—and in the hard, unchanging intraindividual elements of which man was made.

Thus, to take but one example, and it is a weighty one, nineteenth-century economics was built around the assumption that behavior springs ultimately from atomlike forces within the individual, forces which are beyond the power of tradition or law to modify. There was the equally clear assumption that contract—whether between two entrepreneurs or

---

[3] There are many studies of the analytical individualism that dominated European social thought, but the best and most detailed, especially from the point of view of the sociologist, remains Otto von Gierke's *Natural Law and the Theory of Society: 1500-1800,* translated by Ernest Barker (Cambridge: Cambridge University Press, 1934), now available in paperback. Barker's introduction is itself a masterpiece of philosophic and historical insight. The contents were selected by Barker for translation from the much vaster *Genossenschaftsrechts* that Gierke published in the nineteenth century and from which F. W. Maitland, in 1900, had selected and translated key sections on the medieval theory of associations that were to prove so influential in English political thought.

between entrepreneur and worker—is the simple and unmediated consequence of reason and free will, not the by-product of tradition or social code. And perhaps of greatest importance was the assumption that contract, in its wide sense, could be thought of as the very archetype or model of all social relationships—familial, religious, and social, as well as economic and legal.

Even among sociologists, the influence of analytical individualism could be insistent and penetrating. Tarde, whose neglect today conceals a powerful mind and a strong impact on his contemporaries, made the individual the exclusive element and the focus of his sociology; social behavior was simply the consequence of imitation among individuals. Nothing more, Tarde argued, need be premised or concluded.[4]

It was Herbert Spencer, however, who carried individualism to its greatest lengths in sociology. He never questioned the psychology and ethic of individualism and, as Durkheim was to note in many passages, he made contract the very microcosm of society. Although Spencer's likening of society to an organism is the part of his work that today is more often remembered, the philosophy of organism was utterly alien to him.[5] It was alien because, with every element of his theoretical and moral being, Spencer was a utilitarian, in the direct line commenced by the Philosophical Radicals. Spencer's utilitarian individualism was, apart from occasional exaggerations and idiosyncracies, indistinguishable from the main line of thought in the social sciences of his day, and it is for this reason that Durkheim, in all his major works, makes Spencer the protagonist of an age. It is to Spencer specifically—but to individualists in general—that the following words of Durkheim are directed:

> They suppose original, isolated, and independent individuals who, consequently, enter into relationships only to cooperate, for they have no other reason to clear the space separating them and to associate. But this theory, so widely held, postulates a veritable *creatio ex nihilo*. It consists indeed in deducing society from the individual.

[4] Gabriel Tarde, *The Laws of Imitation*, translated by Elsie Clews Parsons (New York: Holt, Rinehart & Winston, Inc., 1903). The controversy between Durkheim and Tarde (more intensely between the students of each) kept French social science in ferment for a quarter of a century. Durkheim's criticisms of Tarde are to be found in his *Suicide;* Tarde's criticisms of Durkheim, in his *Études de psychologie sociale* (1898). Monnerot's more recent criticisms of Durkheim add little to Tarde's. See Jules Monnerot, *Les Faits sociaux ne sont pas des choses* (Paris: Gallimard, 1946), especially Chap. 5.

[5] Spencer himself makes this very clear in his *Principles of Sociology*. See the whole discussion in Vol. 1, Chaps. 2-9.

This, for Durkheim, is absurd—for how would man, assuming that he was actually born an individualist, be able to adapt himself to an existence clashing violently with his fundamental inclination?

> How pale the problematical utility of cooperation must appear to him beside such a fall! With autonomous individualities, as are imagined, nothing can emerge save what is individual and, consequently, cooperation itself, which is a social fact, submissive to social rules, cannot arise. Thus, the psychologist who starts by restricting himself to the ego cannot emerge to find the nonego.[6]

Even Marxism, although resting on an interpretation of human behavior that went far beyond classical economics in its understanding of noneconomic forces, had, at bottom, a view of the individual closer to the Enlightenment than to anything in Durkheim or—for that matter— in Tocqueville, Weber, or Simmel. True, Marx's emphasis on the social conditioning of man, on what he called *the social ensemble,* reveals a recognition of environmental forces in the shaping of ideas, economic behavior, and moral values that stands in momentous contrast to the concepts of the classical economists and most utilitarians of the day. And Marx's sharp ripostes were responsible, above those of any other figure in the century, for rebutting the notion that in bourgeois man lay the timeless reality of human nature.

But when all allowance is made for Marx's insights into the historical and transient character of the social types featured by social development —master, slave, feudal lord, serf, capitalist, worker—two conclusions remain. First, it is class alone—rarely, if ever, local community, kinship, religion, or nation—that Marx endows with the potency Durkheim ascribes to all institutions. Almost invariably in Marx, the phrase *social relations* means *class relations.* By comparison with Durkheim, Marx has a rather attenuated conception of the social. Second, and more to the point here, Marx's view of the nature of man is much closer to that of such utilitarians as Bentham and the elder Mill (men whose visions of society he had little use for) than to anything in Durkheim. For Marx, as for the eighteenth-century *philosophes,* the root is man. In man there may be presumed to be a natural stability, even goodness, and the task confronting socialism is that of emancipating man from the tyranny of institutions and creating a new environment within which man's true nature—from which he had become alienated in the long history of society's oppressions—might reassert itself. This was substantially Ben-

---

[6] Émile Durkheim, *The Division of Labor in Society,* 2nd ed., translated by George Simpson (New York: The Free Press of Glencoe, Inc., 1947), p. 279.

tham's viewpoint, as it had been Rousseau's in the momentous *Discourse on the Origin of Inequality*. Durkheim's view of the nature of alienation is utterly different from Marx's, and so is his conception of the nature of man. Durkheim uses the term *social* in a moral sense; Marx, in an economic sense.[7]

One begins, Durkheim insisted, not with man, not with the individual —either in the abstract or in any of his historical guises—but with society. And society is not reducible to a vast aggregate of individuals in tenuous and shifting assortment by social class or economic category. Neither is society, or any of its components—community, work, religion, law—the consequence of an alienation of what had formerly been vested in man's nature. These, for Durkheim, are primordially, lastingly, and unalterably manifestations of the social. The root is not man, but society. This contrast between Marx's conception of alienation and Durkheim's is itself sufficiently expressive of the gulf between their conceptions of the nature of man. Unlike Durkheim's sociological thought, Marx's image of man must be seen as but a variant form of the same individualism that had activated the works of Rousseau and Bentham.

BIOLOGISM

Closely paralleling individualism as a major context of thought in Durkheim's age was the philosophy that found in physiological or psychophysiological forces the direct causes of human behavior. On the one hand were the racial explanations. Not all of these were of the absurdity which "white supremacy" and Nazism have made of racialism today. There were those in the nineteenth century for whom *Anglo-Saxon, Teutonic,* and *Aryan* were not terms of praise any more than *Negro, Asiatic,* or *Slav* were terms of derogation; those who were simply and neutrally committed to the view that in racial diversity lie the causes of social diversity. Such a conclusion was more tempting then (if still superficial and erroneous to such contemporary minds as Tocqueville, Marx, Mill, and Nietzsche) than it is today, for the relative isolation and historic segregation of non-Western parts of the world made equation of

[7] Durkheim's attitude toward socialism was sympathetic, but wholly aloof. He regarded the Saint-Simonian tradition of socialism as profoundly indicative of the nature of the social problem, but no more scientific, no more diagnostic, than "a cry of grief . . . uttered by men who feel most keenly our collective malaise" (*Socialism,* edited and with an introduction by Alvin Gouldner [New York: Collier Books, 1962], p. 41). Elsewhere, Durkheim classified revolutionary socialism among decadent philosophies spawned by contemporary anomie.

cultural and racial differences seem at least plausible. Even a Gump-
lowicz, much too civilized to succumb to the deductions drawn by a
Gobineau or a Houston Stewart Chamberlain, found in race the fundamental component of history and sociology. Racial hypotheses of human
advancement and retardation, of culture and mentality, were legion. The
very word *race* was commonly used interchangeably with the words *culture* and *nation,* even by those who were not primarily concerned with
racial explanations of progress and society.

Equally widespread was the biopsychological doctrine of individual
instinct. The eighteenth-century search for "sentiments," "passions," and
other intraindividual drives continued into the nineteenth century. The
passion for reductionist hypotheses was universal. Such hypotheses
seemed no more than analogous to the kind of explanations offered by
physicists and chemists. Man's instincts and drives were comparable to
the actions of atoms and molecules in physical matter. If even the racial
hypothesis of cultural differences could be acceptable to men of good
will, the concept of instincts was not likely to be less so. After all, what
was plainer than the universality of such behavior patterns as child-
rearing, economic acquisition, war, and human gregariousness? Why not
then premise presocial instincts in the human race to account for these
uniformities? Such a premise had the advantage of common sense as well
as a precedent in the physical sciences. There was, hence, almost universal acceptance of the proposition that the causes of social behavior lay in
intraindividual complexes and states of the conscious or unconscious
mind.

Freud and Pareto, two giants of the age, are sufficient indication of the
hold that the premise of the intraindividual had upon scholarly minds,
even in the early twentieth century, for the explanation of cultural and
social phenomena. Freud stands clearly in the individualistic tradition:
no matter how far he was finally led to recognize the directive influence
—even the acquired autonomy—of the cultural, he is never very far from
the assumed causal priority of states, drives, or instincts within the individual in discussions of kinship, religion, authority, or civilization. It is
in this sense that one may speak of the "affinity" of Freud and biologism,
though Freud himself chose to regard his all-important doctrine of drives
(*Triebe*) as transitional between biology and psychology.[8]

---

[8] Freud occasionally referred to his "social psychology," but in fact his psychology
was hardly more "social" than that of the utilitarians. Freud, like Marx, was a foster
child of the Enlightenment, and as Philip Rieff has recently written in *Freud:
The Mind of the Moralist* (Garden City, N.Y.: Doubleday Anchor Books, 1961), p. 275,
his concern "remains the individual and his instincts . . .[;] the reference is always

Pareto's thought is built around what he called *residues*. Beyond describing *residues* as "combinations of sentiments"—a characteristic eighteenth-century term—Pareto left the nature of these constants largely unexplored. Although it would be inaccurate to place them without qualification in the category of pure instinct, the primary and even causative role that Pareto assigns them in human behavior, not to mention their universality in human behavior, suggests that in his mind they come closer to intraindividual forces, whether biological or psychological, than to recurrent patterns of merely social or cultural behavior. What Freud assigned to libidinal and aggressive drives, Pareto assigned, in large measure, to residues—residues of combination, integrity, sociability, sex, and so on.[9]

Freud, Pareto, and Durkheim were alike interested in the nonrational, the nonlogical in human behavior. In each there is clear revolt against theories of man that are predicated on the centrality and motivational primacy of rational consciousness. But whereas both Freud and Pareto rested their attacks on forces that are psychogenic or biogenic—forces that are presocial—Durkheim drew his categories of motivation strictly from society and culture.

Durkheim's thought must be judged as the major modern influence responsible for counteracting biologism in the social sciences. This is not to overlook the separate and independent influence of the earlier cultural anthropologists. The work of E. B. Tylor (to name but one), with its transcending emphasis upon culture, was a powerful force in establishing lines of thought that were to culminate in the works of such men as Alfred Kroeber and Robert H. Lowie. Ethnology, by its emphasis on culture as something productive of major differences in human aspect, must indeed be reckoned with in the history of the counteraction of biologism.

Nonetheless, there is reason for counting Durkheim's influence the greater and more diversified in this respect. Durkheim, almost from the beginning, was interested in a theory of the nature of personality, of mind, and of motivations. The ethnologists were not—at least, not until the influence of Durkheim himself began to penetrate the recesses of

---

from society back to the individual, from the manifest public (act) to the latent private (emotion)."

[9] See Pareto, *The Mind and Society*, edited and translated by Arthur Livingston (New York: Harcourt, Brace & World, Inc., 1935). See especially the opening pages of the second volume, where he seeks to clarify the nature of residues. Of the biological character of Pareto's residues, there may be some doubt; but of their intraindividual nature, none.

their field, chiefly through his varied theses on religion. The major ethnological works on culture written before Durkheim's theses appeared —those of Tylor, McLennan, and others, especially in England—contain very little indeed about cultural behavior: that is, about human action as it is affected by cultural values and symbols. They contain instead analyses of culture, considered as something largely independent of concrete human behavior, and a great deal about kinship types, religious ideas and forms, recreational and ceremonial patterns, and so on. But there are no more than scattered and unsystematic hints in this early literature of what has come to be known as the cultural study of personality, of personality-in-culture and culture-in-personality, This, in the anthropological literature, does not appear until the early twentieth century works of A. L. Kroeber and R. H. Lowie, both of whom were admittedly strongly influenced by what Durkheim had already written, especially in *The Rules of Sociological Method,* nearly a full decade before the end of the nineteenth century. Much of what Durkheim placed in the category of the social and collective would be today placed —and, indeed, was so placed by the American anthropologists who read him—in the category of the cultural. The line between the cultural and the social is always a thin one, and never more so than in the works of Durkheim and of the cultural anthropologists who were influenced by him.

The important point at this juncture is, however, simply that Durkheim's generic concept of the social had more to do initially in the dislodgement of biological and psychological explanations of human behavior than the anthropologists' concept of culture. From Durkheim's first major work, *The Division of Labor in Society,* through his influential *The Elementary Forms of Religious Life,* written two decades later, he was obsessed by the thesis of the social nature of mind and personality and of the relation between society and individual conduct. His derivation of mental categories from the constraints of society, his typology of collective and individual representations, and his explanations of psychological integration and disintegration in terms of social and normative integration and disintegration may have found little acceptance at first—even by Kroeber and Lowie—in the precise form in which he stated them. But there is no doubt that from Durkheim's pioneering work came much of the inspiration for concepts like Kroeber's "superorganic" and the refutations of racialism and instinctivism that today are commonly said to derive historically from the ethnologists' culture concept.

THE CRITIQUE OF PROGRESS

The third of the intellectual currents providing background for Durkheim's critical reaction is the whole philosophy of moral progress. Although the idea of progress—especially the developmental theory of change on which it is premised—has roots going all the way back to the Greeks, it is only in the late eighteenth and the nineteenth centuries that it became ascendant and nearly universal as a dogma of moral faith. Durkheim's criticism of progress, although not as sweeping and forthright as his attack on individualism, is nonetheless one of the marks of a certain alienation, a disaffection, with modernism that further separates him from most of his contemporaries.

The idea of progress, as J. B. Bury has succinctly defined it, is a statement of historical synthesis predicated upon the belief that man has progressed, is now progressing, and always will progress.[10] Moreover, progress is not something fortuitous or adventitious, not the benefaction of Providence, but the result of ineluctable forces within the nature of man or his relation to his environment. Fundamental to the Western idea of progress is the premise that some mode of dialectical relation between man and his environment guarantees his gradual improvement; that, however bleak the present may seem, it nevertheless marks a stage of advancement and is the prelude to an even better future. The moral categories of *bad, good,* and *better* are given, so to speak, a rigid historical necessity. And although this succession may be interrupted, retarded, bungled by ill-advised, baneful, or corrupt human efforts, it cannot be offset or reversed. In this view, history is not only irreversible, it is irretrievable in the sense that one may not go to the past for either inspiration or substance.

Deeply implanted in the whole progressive view is a suspicion not only of the past but of those aspects of the present which are most plainly extensions or relics of the past. Hence the distrust of tradition, ruralism, religion, gild, and local community, as well as of aristocracy, monarchy, and military to be found in the thought of men as otherwise different from one another as Bentham, Marx, and Spencer. All three—and they spoke for millions in the nineteenth century—conceived of progress as a release from tradition, a liberation from the sacred dogmas and the communalisms of the past. All three regarded as archaic or reactionary any

[10] J. B. Bury, *The Idea of Progress* (London: Macmillan & Co., Ltd., 1920), p. 5.

theory of reform that did not start with the present, that did not accept the present, whatever its miseries and dislocations, as the sole platform on which the future would be built. Marx, whose view of present and future was assuredly different from that of Manchester liberals of his day, nevertheless joined them in an appreciation of the wonders of capitalism. Even imperialism, as manifested in an East India Company, could be regarded as objectively "good," for—with all its brutalities—it had taken the Indians that much farther along on the road of progress, a road that would lead to capitalism and finally to socialism. And Spencer, whose dismissal of the traditional past could include, just as Bentham's had, the universities, the common law, the church, the Inns of Court, the mutual aid societies, the Poor Laws, and the post office, counted human sufferings and the conflict of economic forces as but short-run manifestations of an inevitable progress.

Although Durkheim's first work began with the effort to show how the division of labor—and modernism in general—reflected a new and higher form of moral solidarity, and although he remained identified, politically, with the "progressive" forces of the moderate left, his work as a whole must be placed among the small minority of the nineteenth century philosophies that questioned, rather than reinforced, the idea of moral progress. He shared the methodology of developmentalism that underlay social science in that century, but his characteristic view of the social and moral scene around him was an alienated one. If he is not as pessimistic about the future as Tocqueville and Weber, the signs of optimism that were so commonplace in the age are altogether lacking in his work. He is less struck by the liberating effects of modern history than he is by the atomizations, insecurities, and anomic withdrawals fostered by industrialization, urbanism, and secularism. Far from hating tradition, convention, and the corporate unities in society, Durkheim repeatedly declared their necessity and lent the force of his entire scholarship to a demonstration that, without these elements of conservatism and integration, no society or social group is conceivable. Far from hailing the spirit of revolt and liberation that had lighted up the intellectual scene in Europe for more than a century, he wrote warningly: "We are living in one of those revolutionary and critical periods where the normally weakened authority of the traditional disciplines can easily give birth to the spirit of anarchy." [11]

[11] Émile Durkheim, *Moral Education: A Study in the Theory and Application of the Sociology of Education,* translated by Everett K. Wilson and Herman Schnurer (New York: The Free Press of Glencoe, Inc., 1961), p. 54.

THE TWO REVOLUTIONS

This leads directly to another aspect of the milieu within which Durkheim's central perspectives evolved: the institutional scene that had been created·in western Europe by the Industrial and the French Revolutions. For all the austerity of his style and his scientific detachment from the issues that directly preoccupied social reformers and welfare workers, Durkheim's sociology is caught up in the momentous changes that were the consequence of these two revolutions. So, for that matter, are the theories of other major sociologists at the end of the nineteenth century —Tönnies, Weber, Simmel, and others. It would be hard indeed to account for the principal themes and emphases of the entire sociological tradition in the nineteenth century without citing the disruptive effect of the two revolutions on European society.[12]

In terms of immediacy and massiveness of impact on human thought and values, it is impossible to find revolutions of comparable magnitude anywhere in human history. The social, cultural, and political changes that began in that period spread throughout Europe and the Americas in the nineteenth century, and to Asia and Africa in the twentieth. The effects of these two revolutions, so closely interwoven as to seem but two sides of the same coin, have been to undermine, shake, or topple institutions which had endured for centuries—even millennia—and, with them, systems of authority, status, belief, and community. What other revolutions in history have produced consequences of such magnitude—measured in terms not only of human effort, authority, and community, but also in terms of human values and aspirations?

Until recently there has been an unfortunate tendency in the writing of history—one that began in the effort to minimize events as well as personages in history and to impose bland continuity everywhere, to depreciate the two revolutions, to bury them in the vistas of a timeless process of development that would have produced, it is said in effect, substantially the same consequences in the modern world had, say, the French Revolution never taken place. This tendency appears, happily, to be waning, and the recent works of such men as Raymond Williams, E. R. Hobsbawm, and E. P. Thompson suggest that the inception of

[12] E. R. Hobsbawm, *The Age of Revolution, 1789-1848* (Cleveland: World Publishing Co., 1962), and Raymond Williams, *Culture and Society, 1780-1950* (New York: Columbia University Press, 1958), have both recently dealt, in fresh and imaginative ways, with the impact of the two revolutions on the scientific and humanistic writing of the age.

modern industrialism and democracy is once again being viewed in a light similar to that in which it appeared to some of the leading minds of the early nineteenth century.

This light was nearly blinding to these minds, and the cataclysmic effects attributed to the two revolutions by those who came immediately afterward may be as easily inferred from the writings of radicals as from those of conservatives. One need but compare the writings of a radical such as William Cobbett with those of conservatives like Bonald, Haller, and Southey. All exhibit the same burning sense of society's sudden, convulsive turn from a path it had followed for millennia. All manifest the same profound intuition of the disappearance of historic values—and, with them, age-old securities, as well as age-old tyrannies and inequalities —and the coming of new powers, new insecurities, and new tyrannies that would be worse than anything previously known unless drastic measures were taken—measures of revolution, reform, or science!

The breakup of the old order—an order that had rested on kinship, land, social class, religion, local community, and monarchy—set free, as it were, the varied elements of power, wealth, and status that had been consolidated for centuries. Dislocated by revolution, scrambled by industrialism's inexorable march, fomented by the new voices of reaction and radicalism, these elements tumbled across the political landscape of nineteenth century Europe in search of new and more viable contexts.

In the same way that the history of nineteenth century politics describes the practical efforts of men to reconsolidate these elements of power, wealth, and status, the history of social thought concerns the various theoretical efforts toward this end: the attempts to put these elements in perspectives that would have philosophic and scientific relevance to the age. The location of power in society, the stratification of wealth and prestige, the role of the individual in the emerging mass society, the reconciliation of sacred values with new economic and political realities—these are themes of the study of society quite as much as they are the themes of practical politics; they are found both in philosophical systems and in the marketplace.

Capitalism, socialism, technology, equalitarian democracy, secularism, political humanitarianism, moral individualism, bureaucracy, and science—ill-assorted though the list may seem—all gained their modern urgency and breadth from the conditions so dramatically ushered in by the two revolutions. Even the categories and words by which these forces were assimilated in man's consciousness were, in large part, the symbolic consequences of the revolutions. How else but in terms of the industrial and democratic revolutions can one account for the coining or modern signification of such words as *democracy, capitalism, ideology, rationalism, bureaucracy, proletariat, middle class, masses,* and *industry?* [13]

What, specifically, did sociology draw from the two revolutions? Foremost, a set of ideas and conceptual antitheses which—from Tocqueville to Durkheim, Weber, and Simmel—have a uniquely constitutive role. Such ideas as *community, status, authority, the religio-sacred,* and their momentous contrasts—*alienation, equalitarianism, power,* and *the secular* —all reflect, through subtle and varied processes, the power of events in giving rise to major ideas. These ideas and their antitheses were not, to be sure, limited to sociology, but in no other field did they have the same unity and intensity.[14]

But the primary concern in this discussion is with Durkheim. What, then, are the specific manifestations of the two revolutions in his thought and writing? More precisely, what are the themes—in his work as a whole—that may be regarded as having been directly communicated to his mind by the experience of living in a period and an environment dominated by the two revolutions? Four themes seem to stand out among all the others.

1. *Gemeinschaft to Gesellschaft.* The famous typology of Tönnies is deliberately used here, for it expresses better than any single phrase in Durkheim's work something that is as fundamental in his thought as it was in that of any other sociologist at the end of the nineteenth century. In strictly social terms, the major consequence of the two revolutions was undoubtedly the increasingly rapid transformation of society from one in which the centuries-old unities of extended family, community, and religion had traditionally been the governing realities in human life to one in which more individualistic, contractual, and money-oriented relationships became dominant. This transition (and the typology to which it gave rise) obsessed nineteenth century social thought; Tönnies did no more than to describe it in the phrase by which it is today best known in sociology. Both the transition and the typology are luminous aspects— whatever the phrase by which they may have been described—of the classic works of Tocqueville, Sir Henry Maine, von Gierke, and many others, not to mention the so-called historical school which included works in all the social sciences. For Durkheim the typology of the two

[13] Williams, *op. cit.,* Introduction, p. xvii.

[14] Sociology in Europe was developed almost wholly around the themes and antitheses cast up by the two revolutions and their impact upon the old order. This is one reason why sociology has had such manifest utility in analyzing the new nations of the present century.

social orders—communal and contractual—is the very substance of his first major work, and from it emerge nearly all of the theoretical and substantive problems that were to engross him for the rest of his life.

2. *Social atomization*. Modern society seemed to give rise to more and more situations in which the individual found himself alone or else caught up in large-scale, relatively impersonal organizations characterized by the psychology of aloneness. With the spread of the democratic franchise, man voted alone as the legally isolated *citizen;* he gained his livelihood as the *worker,* distinct and discrete, bound to others only by what Carlyle called a *cash nexus;* even within marriage and religion, changes in law and custom placed the individual—first the man, then the woman, and finally the child—in a condition of relative separateness that often could conceal anxiety quite as much as it promised freedom. To nearly all minds—conservative, liberal, or radical—the main currents of history seemed to foreshadow a release from tradition and communality, a plunging of the individual into the waters of egoism. This theme, like the first described, fascinated many minds of the nineteenth century—but none more than Durkheim's.

3. *Secularization*. What Weber, quoting Schiller, called *the disenchantment of the world* is but another way of describing the process which involved, on a steadily widening front, the substitution of the values of utility, rationality, and efficiency for traditional norms that, over a period of many centuries, had acquired sacred connotation: monarchy, social class, primogeniture, marriage, property. All of these, along with the concepts of honor, fealty, obligation, and chastity, were losing—or seemed to be losing—the quality of sacredness that had made adherence to them nearly automatic. The jettisoning of sacred values, without the substitution of new ones, appeared to be one of the costs of progress. Tocqueville viewed the onset of modernism as carrying with it the inevitable liquidation of ancient values, and his famous chapter on honor is perfectly expressive of his belief. All the major sociologists of the time made a distinction between the sacred or traditional and the secular or rationalist. Durkheim's momentous typology of the sacred and the profane may be regarded as a conceptual subtilization of a contrast that, in fact, history was making all too real. Inevitably, the individual's relation to moral values was becoming more precarious, more conflict-ridden, than it had been when the moral alternatives were few and the sacredness of traditional values went unchallenged.

4. *Mass democracy*. For many centuries, government in western Europe was concentric, extending from family through parish and neighbor-

hood to class and region. The notion that the individual rather than the group, is the true element of the state appeared, in philosophical terms, prior to the nineteenth century; it came into focus in the writings of Hobbes and Locke, and was broadcast in the next century by the *philosophes*. The same is true of the "general will" theory of authority. Although primarily an eighteenth century concept emphasized most brilliantly by Rousseau, it too has its roots in the seventeenth century. But not until the nineteenth century were the consequences of these theories manifested in institutional terms. However different was the mass electorate in fact from what Rousseau had conceived for a Geneva, it owed much to his thinking—or, rather, to his thinking as translated into administrative and legislative terms by the Philosophical Radicals. In any event, the nineteenth century marks the rise of individuals, en masse, unmediated in their relation to political power by social class or commune. The role of the state becomes ever more positive, advancing into social and cultural areas once reserved for family or church. The large political party becomes, in a sense, the successor of social class in the stratification of power. Mass democracy, with its rationalization and centralization of power, and its general depreciation of intermediate associations and traditional moral contexts, was nearly as vivid as reality in Durkheim's mind as it was in Weber's.

INTELLECTUAL SOURCES:

POSITIVISM AND CONSERVATISM

The discussion has thus far been limited to those ideas and currents which form negative relief for Durkheim's ideas. Of the philosophical currents from which Durkheim drew directly in the fashioning of his social theory, two are particularly crucial: positivism (in its large sense —that of a methodology founded on the rigorous application of scientific values to the study of human nature and society), and conservatism (with reference, not to attitudes, but to certain intellectual perspectives and concepts). Positivism is the lineal descendant of the Enlightenment, and —in all its nineteenth century forms—it shares the Enlightenment's rationalism and secularism. Conservatism, in the modern philosophical sense, is the product of the reaction to the French Revolution and the Enlightenment that took place in Europe early in the nineteenth century.

The spirit of Durkheim's work—scientific, rationalist, positivist—is that of the Enlightenment. Durkheim's constant objective was the establishment of the study of man on foundations as dispassionate, rigorous, and methodologically sound as those of the physical sciences. Much will be said in this essay about the influence of moral philosophy, religion, and moral values on Durkheim's thought, but it is important never to lose sight of his strict and uncompromising desire for a *science* of human behavior; it is reflected in everything he ever wrote. He worked with many of the values of religious and political conservatives, but the methodological essence of his work is that which inspired the minds of the Enlightenment and the whole succession of rationalists in the nineteenth century, for whom the scientific study of society was the major objective. Durkheim is clear on this point, and the following passage expresses his fundamental and unchanging goal:

> Our principal objective is to extend scientific rationalism to human behavior. It can be shown that behavior of the past, when analyzed, can be reduced to relationships of cause and effect. These relationships can then be transformed, by an equally logical operation, into rules of action for the future. . . . It therefore seems to us that in these times of renascent mysticism, an undertaking such as ours should be regarded quite without apprehension and even with sympathy by all those who, while disagreeing with us on certain points, yet share our faith in the future of reason.[15]

But science is content as well as form, ideas as well as method. And the content of Durkheim's sociology reveals a set of concepts that would have been, in many ways, much more understandable to the philosophical conservatives who followed, and condemned, the Enlightenment than to the *philosophes* with whom—on strictly moral and intellectual grounds—Durkheim would have preferred kinship.

For a long time, the positivist objective of Durkheim's thought led those who studied his work to overlook its conservative and religious content. This oversight has been as characteristic of his religious critics (who have found—or have pretended to find—only nonreligion, nonmorality, in his positivism) as it has been of his admirers who, hailing him as scientist par excellence, have therefore limited comment on his sources to those of kindred spirit—such as Montesquieu and Rousseau in the eighteenth century, and Comte and his followers in the nineteenth.

This will not do, however. What is found in Durkheim (and this is not an uncommon phenomenon in the history of thought) is the rationalization, the systematization, and even the secularization of ideas that were, in their first expression in the nineteenth century, emanations

---

[15] Émile Durkheim, *The Rules of Sociological Method*, translated by Sarah A. Solovay and John H. Mueller, and edited by George E. G. Catlin (Chicago: The University of Chicago Press, 1938), Preface.

of philosophical conservatism. It was Durkheim's feat to translate into the hard methodology of science ideas and values that had made their first appearance in the polemics of Bonald, Maistre, Haller, and others opposed to reason and rationalism, as well as to revolution and reform. Ironically, the antirationalist theses of the early conservatives were to become the basis for a science of society that—in Durkheim's view, at least—would gradually replace revealed religion and morality.[16]

Although this discussion cannot deal in detail with all the contributions of philosophical conservatism to Durkheim's sociology, it is important to identify several of the main propositions that originated in the polemical contexts of conservatism and were to culminate as vital perspectives in Durkheim's study of man and society.

The first is the conservative idea of the nature of society. In direct antithesis to the ideas of the Enlightenment, the conservatives had argued the absolute primacy of society. According to this theory, society is not an emanation of presocial forces within the individual; on the contrary, man is a creature of society, and his ideas, language, morality, and relationships are but reflections of the anterior reality of society.

The second idea, flowing logically from the first, is the moral and psychological dependence of man on society. The individual—far from being the self-sustaining, self-stabilizing, and self-directed being that the *philosophes* had premised in their psychologies and reform proposals— is unalterably dependent upon society and its codes. The separation of man from tradition and community, argued the conservatives, led—not to freedom—but to intolerable isolation and anguish.

Third, the conservatives insisted upon the necessity of authority, not only in the state, but in each and all of the nonpolitical relationships which comprise society. Religion, family, community, gild—all of these are forms of authority binding upon man, who owes them duty, and upon the state, which has the responsibility for their just recognition. Human groups are systems of authority; if this authority is dissolved or transferred, the conservatives maintained, the groups cannot survive. The conservatives were as obsessed by the idea of authority as the *philosophes* had been by the idea of freedom.

The fourth conservative idea involves a deep concern with religion and

---

[16] I have touched on this in several articles; among them: "Conservatism and Sociology," *American Journal of Sociology*, LVIII, 2 (September 1952); and "Bonald and the Concept of the Social Group," *Journal of the History of Ideas*, V, 3 (June 1944). See also Lewis Coser, "Durkheim's Conservatism and Its Implications for His Sociological Theory," in *Émile Durkheim, 1858-1917, op. cit.*, for a detailed and penetrating analysis.

with the whole concept of sacred values. In the eyes of the conservatives, the major crime of the French Revolution had been the expropriation of the Church and the general liquidation of religious and sacred authorities. A utilitarian morality, according to the conservatives, is an impossibility, for it is only in the irreducible authority of revealed religion that the imprescriptibility of moral law can have its origin.

Fifth, there is the deeply felt idea of the organismic character of society. In legitimate society, religion, family, state, and community have an articulation of role and function that is organic—and so does the process of change. No society can be made and remade, argued the conservatives. Society has its own laws of development based on the articulation of parts—that is, institutions and groups—and these laws must be respected. The idea of organic development is by no means restricted to conservatives in the early nineteenth century, but it is no exaggeration to say that among them it achieved an almost canonical status.

There is, obviously, a medieval flavor to these ideas. In the same way that the *philosophes* had argued for a natural order—one in which their rejection of feudal and religious institutions might gain legitimacy, as it were—the conservatives appealed to the medieval order in support of their repudiation of modernism. The efflorescence of interest in the Middle Ages that took place in the nineteenth century—the fruits of which ranged from passionate antiquarianism to works of profoundest scholarship—owed a great deal, in strictly historical terms, to the conservative reaction against the democratic and economic revolutions that ushered in that century.[17]

Sociology was caught up in this efflorescence, and although it is manifestly false to attribute common political values to conservatism and sociology, the fact remains that both are to be seen as responses to modernism. There is in sociology a deep substratum of traditionalism—perhaps it would be more accurate to say a sensitivity to traditionalism—that provides the clearest distinction between its characteristic perspectives and typologies of sociology and those of the social sciences (such as economics, politics, and psychology) that drew more directly on the utilitarian-rationalist tradition. To refer to the major sociologists of the

---

[17] The significance to the social sciences of the momentous "rediscovery" of the Middle Ages in the nineteenth century was vast and has been too little noted in the histories. See Williams, *op. cit.*, p. 19; and J. T. Merz, *History of European Thought in the Nineteenth Century* (London: 1914), *passim* but especially Vol. IV. In sociology, the spell of medieval society began with Comte's near adoration and, through gradual denaturation or secularization, became the indispensable image of traditionalism in all sociological typologies of change and differentiation.

age—Tocqueville, Weber, Durkheim, Simmel, Tönnies—is to refer to minds which, though assuredly liberal in practical political orientation, saw Europe's past, present, and future in terms very different from those of the mainstream of liberalism that such historians as Ruggiero and Halévy have identified in such revealing fashion.[18] And this difference lies chiefly in the historical affiliation that sociology, alone among the social sciences, has with conservatism.

It is easy enough to trace this affiliation. Both Saint-Simon and Comte were frank in their praise of what Comte called "the immortal retrograde school." To Bonald alone, wrote Comte, must go credit for having founded the true study of social order. Comte's massive *Positive Polity*— the only work that he expressly subtitled *A Treatise on Sociology*—shows in abundant detail the impress that the conservatives' ideas on family, language, personality, community, and religion had made on him. In Germany, Savigny's notable legal studies and Hegel's vastly influential *Philosophy of Right*—the first major philosophical work deserving the adjective *sociological*—produced effects that were to last throughout the century, culminating, so far as sociology is concerned, in Tönnies's seminal *Gemeinschaft und Gesellschaft* in 1887. No one will today miss the conservative ambience in which Tocqueville thought and wrote. The second volume of *Democracy in America* and the entire *The Old Regime* represent the first systematic treatises on power and stratification in the nineteenth century. Le Play (*"un Bonald rajeuni,"* Sainte-Beuve called him) made the conservative trinity of family-work-community into a methodological framework that produced the supreme piece of sociological field work in the nineteenth century. To these names should be added those of Sir Henry Maine in legal sociology, Otto von Gierke in the study of social and political associations, and Fustel de Coulanges in the introduction of the concept of the sacred to social analysis—major figures responsible for the conversion of the polemical emphases of con-

---

[18] Guido Ruggiero, *History of European Liberalism*, translated by R. G. Collingwood (London: Oxford University Press, 1927); Elie Halévy, *The Growth of Philosophical Radicalism*, translated by Mary Morris (London: Faber and Gwyer, 1928). Curiously, no one has dealt with philosophical conservatism in the nineteenth century in the fashion exemplified by Ruggiero and Halévy. Russell Kirk's fine *The Conservative Mind* (Chicago: Henry Regnery Co., 1953) comes near, but it confines itself almost wholly to England and the United States. The "renaissance" of conservatism between 1791 and 1820 touched every major European country and included some of the first names of thought and letters. It began the "revolt against modernism" that has reached full intensity only in the twentieth century. In a forthcoming work on European social thought, I deal in some detail, though still inadequately, with the the intellectual impact of conservatism in Europe.

servatism into major topics and perspectives for the dispassionate study of society. In their works, as in those of Tocqueville and certain of Le Play's, conservatism undergoes a kind of denaturation.

In Durkheim the process of denaturation is quickened, given catalytic intensity by the distinctiveness of his personal background. Jewish, the son of rabbinical parents, Durkheim had the advantage of being marginal to both the secular-rationalist and the Christian-conservative traditions. That he drank deeply from both traditions is plain enough. Those students who have attempted to measure the relative influence of Saint-Simon and Comte on Durkheim have unduly limited and therefore distorted the sources of Durkheim's thought. His positivism has little or nothing to do with Comte's brand, and his interest in Saint-Simon was chiefly antiquarian. Durkheim's mind was formed by two traditions (he was deeply and widely read), not by two individuals.

There is a certain ironic charm in Durkheim's relation to modern thought. He was a liberal by political choice and action, but his sociology constitutes a massive attack upon the philosophical foundations of liberalism. He was profoundly agnostic in religious matters, distrustful even of Weber because of what he felt to be Weber's undue affinity with religious valuation; but his own sociology of religion is perhaps the most convincing proof ever written of the functional indispensability of religion in one form or other and of the historical primacy of religion among all symbols and modes of thought. He was relentlessly rationalist and scientific in his methodology, yet the substance of his thought is composed almost exclusively of perspectives and insights that have umbilical relation to the early nineteenth-century conservatism that had declared war on rationalism and positivism. Finally, he was committed to a kind of practical social engineering (consider his quasi-syndicalist reform proposals), yet the greater body of his thought suggests the near-impossibility of any disruption of society's normal articulation of function, structure, and meaning.

But the contradictions in Durkheim's thought are neither sharper nor more numerous than those of creative thought in general and, with Whitman, Durkheim might have said: "I contradict myself? Very well, I contradict myself!"

TWO

PERSPECTIVES AND IDEAS

FROM MILIEU WE now pass to content—from a consideration of the background of Durkheim's work to an examination of the specific ideas and researches that form the substance of his contribution to modern social science. The problem of organization is always difficult in such matters, and never more difficult than with respect to so subtle and multifaceted a mind as Durkheim's. There are, of course, various ways of meeting the problem.

The commonest approach involves a consideration of the major works he wrote and published during his lifetime, each providing an important step toward the next work. First, *The Division of Labor in Society* (1893) —the single work in which, it can unexceptionably be said, all of his essential themes and insights are set forth, in tentative fashion at least. Next came the revolutionary methodological treatise, *The Rules of Sociological Method* (1895), in which, working from adumbrations in the earlier work, he laid down the methodological principles that were to guide all his subsequent studies. Then came *Suicide* (1897), proceeding clearly from both earlier works and undoubtedly the first successful treatise in modern sociology to combine theoretical insight with masses of empirical data brought into focus in the form of verifiable hypotheses. Finally came *The Elementary Forms of Religious Life* (1912). This was, if not the first scientific approach to religion, the first systematic fusion of sociological and religious materials in the field of sociology. In it is to be found a distillation of all the best that is associated with Durkheim's unique genius. It is the capstone of his endeavors, and the perfect, logical conclusion of what had begun two decades earlier in *The Division of Labor.*

There is much value in the bio-bibliographical approach, for it makes plain not only the continuity in Durkheim's work but also, and of equal importance, the discontinuities. The discontinuities emerge because, in the process of his intellectual development, Durkheim was led to abandon certain approaches that in the beginning had been crucial. It is sufficient to cite two of these: the distinction between mechanical and organic solidarity, and the equation of social solidarity with juridical repression. These concepts are absolutely fundamental in his first major work, *The Division of Labor;* neither, however, ever again appears in his work: he was led to abandon both. Yet some commentaries on Durkheim deal with each as though it reflected a line of thought as mature as anything to be found in *Suicide* or *The Elementary Forms of Religious Life.* Only by following the development of Durkheim's thought from work to work can this kind of error be avoided.

The bio-bibliographical approach, valuable though it is, has its pitfalls. First, despite the clear continuity of theme and development in Durkheim's successive works, too great an emphasis on this continuity incurs the risk of the genetic fallacy. There is, after all, more to *The Elementary Forms of Religious Life* than what emerges from each of its predecessors. Second, it does not follow that insight into the total nature of a man's work, whether he be scientist or artist, is best gained by merely retracing its development. The one advantage over even so great a mind as Durkheim's is the total view that only time grants, and it is negligent to abandon this advantage for an approach that merely duplicates his own continuity. Finally, some of Durkheim's best works—compiled from his lectures by his students—were published only after his death, and it would be difficult to work these in accurately under the biographical approach.

A second approach, one that is equally valuable when used with imagination and restraint, proceeds from Durkheim's method—or, perhaps more accurately, from that concept which, by its persistent emphasis in his writings, takes on methodological significance: the concept of function. The importance of this concept is clear to anyone who has read even a small part of Durkheim's work or who has been introduced to it through the critical works of Radcliffe-Brown, Talcott Parsons, and others. Indeed, it was the concept of function that Radcliffe-Brown used in his successful effort to extend Durkheim's significance from European to American social science. Whatever one may think of functionalism and its systematic significance, there can be no doubt of the importance of the functional *method* in the works of Durkheim and of his followers.

The importance of the concept of function in Durkheim's work is vividly clear—from *The Division of Labor,* in which he declares the first of his objectives to be the determination of "the function of division of labor, that is to say, what social need it satisfies," through *The Elementary Forms of Religious Life,* which is devoted to a demonstration of the integrative function performed in society, not only by religion as a whole, but also by each of its parts—cult, rite, symbol. In *The Rules of Sociological Method* he makes forthright and didactic what is only implied in his empirical studies. The task of the social investigator has only begun when he distinguishes the efficient causes of any social phenomenon and traces its history; from this he must go on to determine the function of the phenomenon in the system or order of which it is a part. And the function of a social fact, Durkheim declared, must always be sought in the relation of the fact to some social end—an *existing* end, not some defunct belief or norm. It is not difficult to imagine the impact of this concept, once it was understood, in such areas of nineteenth century study as religion and morality, in which—under the influences of utilitarianism, evolution, and diffusion—innumerable traits or aspects of culture were dealt with as "survivals," relics of a defunct past without viable relation either to personality or to the social order.

The concept or method of functional analysis is indeed vital in Durkheim and, as suggested, is fully capable of providing a context for the elucidation of Durkheim's other ideas. The rejection of this approach for one which deals with the concept of function explicitly or implicitly in connection with other topics reflects only a preference for a different type of analysis, not unawareness of this concept's importance.

The approach that will be adopted here is based on the crucial perspectives revealed by Durkheim's work as a whole.[19] Each of these perspectives may be seen as a master thread in the tapestry of Durkheim's thought. Each contains, or is related to, the numerous specific concepts that he contributed to modern sociology. Finally, it will be possible to show, within each of the perspectives, the necessary continuities and discontinuities of his thought.

There are five such perspectives in Durkheim's thought: *society, personality, authority,* the *religio-sacred,* and *development.* Each will be dealt with separately, but an attempt will be made to retain the functional relatedness they so clearly had in his mind.

[19] By *perspective* I have in mind much of what Lovejoy meant by *unit-idea* in his momentous studies in the history of ideas. For a masterly exposition of what is involved, see Arthur O. Lovejoy, *The Great Chain of Being* (Cambridge, Mass.: Harvard University Press, 1936).

All five perspectives possess a scope, a resonance, and a methodological importance that sets them well above most ideas. Each is sufficiently encompassing to make possible generalized insight, not merely into the substance of Durkheim's conclusions, but also into the premises and the methodology which led to these conclusions. This point must be emphasized: a major idea is the very opposite of a static, one-dimensional description; nor is it a mere point in a system. A major idea is, as Howard Mumford Jones has expressed it, "some powerful concept that, refusing to be chained to a closed intellectual system, gets loose, as it were, and ranges widely in time and through human activity, taking on protean shapes as it does so." [20] Rarely is a major idea consistent within itself; in fact, it is usually driven by internal inconsistencies and tensions.

Such are the central ideas and perspectives in Durkheim. Each is powerful and ranging—not only within his own works, but also in contemporary sociology as a whole—and each suffers some of the conflicts of value and premise to which all major ideas are subject. Of the five perspectives, that of society is the most fundamental. From it all the others flow, and the discussion could—with complete justification—be limited to this one perspective. Society, in the distinctive and encompassing sense in which Durkheim uses this word, is the source of both method and content in his theory. Durkheim's functional method and also his treatments of authority, religion, personality, and the nature of change and stability all proceed from the sovereign reality of society.

SOCIETY AS PERSPECTIVE

Durkheim is not merely the sociologist of society, he is also its moral philosopher, metaphysician, epistemologist. For Durkheim, everything human above the level of the manifestly physical or biological begins and ends in society:

> A society is the most powerful combination of physical and moral forces of which nature offers us an example. Nowhere else is an equal richness of different materials, carried to such a degree of concentration, to be found. Then, it is not surprising that a higher life disengages itself which, by reacting upon the elements of which it is the product, raises them to a higher plane of existence and transform them.[21]

[20] Howard Mumford Jones, "Ideas, History, Technology," *Technology and Culture,* I, 1 (Winter 1959), 21.
[21] Émile Durkheim, *The Elementary Forms of Religious Life,* translated by Joseph Ward Swain (London: George Allen & Unwin, 1915), p. 446.

To those who, like Tarde and Spencer, would reduce society to mere interaction rooted in individuals, Durkheim writes:

Society is a reality *sui generis;* it has its own peculiar characteristics, which are not met with again in the same form in all the rest of the universe. The representations which express it have a wholly different content from purely individual ones.

Society expresses itself and becomes known to human consciousness through collective representations, and these are, Durkheim writes (almost in paraphrase of Burke and Bonald):

. . . the result of an immense cooperation which stretches out not only into space but into time as well; to make them a multitude of minds have associated, united, and combined their ideas and sentiments; for them, long generations have accumulated their experience and their knowledge. A special intellectual activity is therefore concentrated in them which is infinitely richer and complexer than that of the individual.[22]

Statements such as these are, of course, the foundation of all the charges—beginning with Tarde's—that Durkheim is guilty of reification, of hypostatization, and so on. It is not strange that these lines—written at a time when Western thought was still steeped in individualism, detached as they commonly have been by readers from the empirical contexts to which they serve as preface—should lead countless readers to deduce from them everything from medieval realism to protofascist totalitarianism. Even the most moderate of criticisms leaves the impression that Durkheim had no real notion of individuality, that he dissolves the identity of the individual in a sea of social facts.

If one confines himself exclusively to the prefatory, generalizing types of statement in Durkheim, of which the quoted passages are examples, the indictments can no doubt be made to seem valid. But Durkheim was not an abstract metaphysician. He was not searching for categorical essences, nor was he seeking truth through the logic of argument or demonstration. He was a scientist, deeply concerned with concrete problems—the nature of personality, of religion, of contract, of morality, and of mental aberration—as these problems are given substance by actual human behavior. To understand what Durkheim meant by *society* and the role he granted it in the analysis of human action, one must eschew abstract statement and look rather to his utilization of the perspective of society.

[22] *Ibid.,* p. 16.

Durkheim's conception of society and of the social bears little relation to that of the utilitarians and most rationalists of the nineteenth century. For Durkheim the word *society* has its roots in the Latin *communitas* rather than *societas:*

> Society cannot make its influence felt unless it is in action, and it is not in action unless the individuals who compose it are assembled together and act in common. [His next sentence is crucial; it may be said to contain Durkheim's very image of society.] It is by common action that it takes consciousness of itself and realizes its position; it is before all else an active cooperation.[23]

From this envisagement of the nature of society proceeds the all-important concept of *the conscience collective* which he defines appropriately in terms of "beliefs and sentiments held in common." Such a view of social organization manifestly has little in common with that of the utilitarians of the nineteenth century. They, like the *philosophes* before them, took as their referent *societas* when they wrote of *society*. For them, Durkheim's image would have seemed intolerably corporate. Durkheim's thinking was deeply affected by the whole revival, in the nineteenth century, of the values and properties of community—community in the sense of groups formed by intimacy, emotional cohesion, depth, and continuity. For Durkheim, *society* is simply *community* written large.

It is interesting and important to note that Durkheim's initial interest in the metaphysical properties of society began with his effort to prove the irrelevance to modern life of the constraints and disciplines embodied in traditional, historical types of social organization. *The Division of Labor* was conceived, quite literally, to prove that the function of the division of labor in modern society is the integration of individuals through their pursuit of complementary and symbiotic specializations, thus making possible—for the first time in history—the termination of traditional mechanisms of social constraint. The function of the division of labor is social: that is, integration. With integration must come new relationships and new laws. The traditional types of relationship and law —based upon repression, mores, and communal sanctions—are gradually expelled. This was the motivation of the book. It was not, however, the conclusion.

In *The Division of Labor,* Durkheim distinguishes between two types of social solidarity: mechanical and organic. The first is that which has existed throughout most of the history of human society. Based on moral and social homogeneity, it is reinforced by the discipline of the small community. Within such a framework, tradition dominates, individual-

[23] *Ibid.,* p. 418.

ism is totally lacking, and justice is overwhelmingly directed toward the subordination of the individual to the collective conscience. Property is communal, religion is indistinguishable from cult and ritual, and all questions of individual thought and conduct are determined by the will of the community. And the ties of kinship, localism, and the sacred give substance to the whole.

The second form of solidarity, which Durkheim calls *organic,* is based on the primacy of division of labor. With the rise of technology and the general emergence of individuality from the restraints of the past, it becomes possible—for the first time in human history—for social order to rest, not on mechanical uniformity and collective repression, but on the organic articulation of free individuals pursuing different functions but united by their complementary roles. Within the framework of organic solidarity there can be a general disengagement of man from the traditional restraints of kinship, class, localism, and the generalized social conscience. Justice will be restitutive, rather than penal; law will lose its repressive character, and there will be a diminishing need for punishment. Heterogeneity and individualism will replace homogeneity and communalism, and division of labor will provide all that is necessary to unity and order.

Such was the initial conception of *The Division of Labor* that may be fairly easily inferred from its opening chapters, especially in light of what Durkheim had written during the three or four years immediately preceding the publication of the book. There is little doubt that the theme of progressive, individualistic rationalism was considerably stronger in his mind at the beginning of the book than it was at the end. The distinction between the two types of society was a familiar one in the nineteenth century and so was the developmental sequence in which Durkheim placed them. Although Tönnies's *Gemeinschaft und Gesellschaft* is the work most commonly thought of (Durkheim had reviewed Tönnies's book shortly after it came out, five years before his own work was published), the distinction between the two types of solidarity had been common in the writings of the historical jurists ever since the beginning of the century, when Savigny's momentous essay on civil law appeared. Tocqueville's differentiation of aristocracy and democracy is presented in terms close to those of Durkheim and Tönnies; so is Lewis Morgan's treatment of "gentile" and "political" society and Sir Henry Maine's notable distinction between societies based on status and those based on contract. Given the essentially progressive nature of the framework of change in which Durkheim first sought to place the two types of society,

his conclusions would have had an amusing similarity to those of Herbert
Spencer—for Spencer's argument, reduced to its essentials, stressed the
progressive ascendancy of ties based on restitutive sanctions and division
of labor over those rooted in tradition and community.

But Durkheim went further. The distinctive contribution of *The Division of Labor* lies in the fact that, even in the process of arguing what he
had conceived as the initial thesis of this work, he saw the inherent weak-
nesses of that argument when pushed to its logical conclusion and, seeing
them, subtly but powerfully altered his thesis. Like Weber, Durkheim
could see that, although the conceptual distinction between the two types
of solidarity or association was a real one, the institutional stability of
the second had to be deeply rooted in the continuation—in one form or
other—of the first. The progressive rationalists of the time argued, rather,
the replacement of the one by the other. What Durkheim, above even
Weber, demonstrated was that such replacement would lead, in fact, to a
sociological monstrosity.

The unraveling of the somewhat tangled threads of Durkheim's demonstration (and it is this that makes the study of *The Division of Labor*
more fascinating than that of any other of his works) is not an easy one.
Indeed, in a sense the book is a kind of palimpsest, and more than a little
ingenuity is needed to discern the point at which the secondary argument
begins to overshadow the initial thesis.

The secondary argument, the argument that close analysis reveals to
be developing from about the mid-point of the book, is best expressed
in the following passage:

> The division of labor can . . . be produced only in the midst of pre-existing
> society. There is a social life outside the whole division of labor, but which
> the latter presupposes. That is, indeed, what we have directly established in
> showing that there are societies whose cohesion is essentially due to a com-
> munity of beliefs and sentiments, and it is from these societies that those whose
> unity is assured by the division of labor have emerged.[24]

The passage is a crucial one, but Durkheim is being a little less than
candid. Although it is true that he has been concerned with the type of
cohesion he has labeled *mechanical*—analyzing its modes of law, custom,
and belief—it is hardly true that he has been stressing the continuing
necessity in modern organic society of sinews of stability that are mechanical in character. The brief analysis of contract and of the indispensable roots of contract in noncontractual forms of authority and relationships may be said to be the watershed of Durkheim's argument.

[24] *The Division of Labor in Society, op. cit.,* p. 277.

It is important to emphasize this aspect of *The Division of Labor:* Durkheim's "reversal" of argument. It is crucial to an understanding of his life's work and is the only way in which his succeeding works can be made congruent with this one. It is a matter of record, of course, that Durkheim never went back, in later studies, to any utilization of the distinction between the two types of solidarity, nor to the division of labor as a form of cohesion, much less to any rationalization of conflict and anomie in society as mere "pathological forms of division of labor." The kinds of society, constraint, and solidarity dealt with in all his later works —either in theoretical or practical terms—have nothing whatsoever to do with the attributes that he had laid down for an organic and (presumably) irreversibly modern society in *The Division of Labor.* On the contrary, society—in all its guises, functions, and historical roles—becomes, for Durkheim, a compound of social and psychological elements that he had first relegated to folk or primitive society. Not only is normal society founded—he would ever after declare—on such traits as collective conscience, moral authority, community, and the sacred, but the only proper appropriate response to modern conditions is the strengthening of such traits. Thus, and only thus, will suicide, economic conflict, and the gnawing frustrations of anomic life be moderated.[25]

In *The Rules of Sociological Method,* which was published in between *The Division of Labor* and *Suicide,* Durkheim transmuted the attributes of mechanical solidarity into the eternal characteristics of social facts in general. This was but a bold heightening of his earlier conclusion that, however one proceeds in the study of human behavior, facts of social exteriority, constraint, and tradition—all of them prime elements of mechanical solidarity—are the only facts that sociologists qua sociologists can be properly concerned with. The fundamental thesis of this small work is that social facts cannot be decomposed or reduced to individual, psychological, or biological data, much less to mere reflections of geographic or climatic substance.

At the time *The Rules of Sociological Method* was published, it must have appeared—in that ultraindividualistic age of social science—as hardly more than a vision of the absolute social mind, a scholastic exer-

---

[25] See the final pages of *Suicide,* translated by John A. Spaulding and George Simpson, and edited with an Introduction by George Simpson (New York: The Free Press of Glencoe, Inc., 1951), where Durkheim first makes his celebrated proposal for the establishment of occupational association which will, he argues, replace the sense of cohesion that has disappeared in religion, local community, and family. These remarks on corporate groups are expanded into a long preface to the second edition of *The Division of Labor* (1902).

cise in reification. As one looks back on that age, it is clear that there were then as few sociologists capable of assimilating Durkheim's central argument into the individualist categories of their minds as there were, a decade or two later, physicists capable of assimilating Einstein's relativity theory into the classical categories of their lectures on mechanics. Today, Durkheim's *Rules,* read carefully and with allowance only for polemical emphases and vagaries of expression, seems to contain little that goes beyond what sociologists regularly assume about the nature of social reality in their empirical studies of institutionalized behavior. Nevertheless, such is the tenacity of descriptive stereotypes in the history of social thought that the criticisms which formed the first response to Durkheim's *Rules* have largely endured—despite the fact that the climate of analytical individualism within which they were made has long since been succeeded by one generally congenial to Durkheim's methodological values.

What was born in *The Division of Labor* and baptized, so to speak, in *The Rules of Sociological Method* received successive confirmations in *Suicide* and *The Elementary Forms of Religious Life.* For too long have students of Durkheim persisted in placing these works in separate intellectual categories, as though they marked discontinuous phases of his life's labors. The opposite is true: the methodology that is emphasized in *The Rules of Sociological Method* has deep roots in *The Division of Labor.* Equally to the point is the fact that the concrete empirical content of *Suicide* and the far-reaching scholarly substance of *The Elementary Forms of Religious Life* both flow clearly and rigorously from the insights and proposals that are stated abstractly in the *Rules.* It will not do, in short, to divide Durkheim's thought into mutant and disconnected phases labeled *evolutionary, metaphysical, empirical,* and *functional-institutional* and to assert that these reflect, in that order, his four major published works.

What all four works have in common—and this applies also to the books posthumously published as well as to the articles that appeared in *L'Année* and elsewhere—is a social metaphysic and a methodology rooted in the conviction that took shape in Durkheim's mind as he wrote *The Division of Labor:* that, however one proceeds to study human behavior, all human behavior above the level of the strictly physiological must be regarded as either emanating from, or else sharply conditioned by, society; that is, by the totality of groups, norms, and institutions within which every individual human being consciously and unconsciously exists from the moment of his birth. Social instincts, prepotent complexes, natural sentiments—all of these may indeed exist in man (Durkheim never denied they do) but viewed against the determinative effects of society on such matters as moral, religious, and social conduct, they are negligible in influence, supplying barely more than the organic base. They are, in any event, impossible to get at—in sociological terms—until all possible consequences of the social have been exhausted. This last point is the major truth so widely overlooked by the individualistic-utilitarian minds of the nineteenth century, as indeed it continues to be overlooked by many even now.

It is easy enough, no doubt, to demolish some of Durkheim's metaphysical constructs, and many critics have so engaged themselves. Considered abstractly, how long can such ideas as *the collective conscience, collective representations,* and *the absolute autonomy of society* stand against the onslaughts of critical empiricism, linguistic analysis, and other manifestations of contemporary philosophy's remorseless hunting down of all that is not conceptually atomic? Let it be conceded immediately: not very long.

But the really important task, logical positivism to the contrary, is not criticism of concept, nor is it definition of concept. As Karl Popper has so wisely emphasized, sciences that make immaculateness of concept the precondition of all empirical and theoretical work never become sciences. Definition breeds only further definition, and the law of infinite regress quickly comes into force. Beyond a certain point it is but a waste of time to seek tidy semantic justifications of concepts used by creative minds. The important and all-too-neglected task in philosophy and social theory is that of observing the ways in which abstract concepts are converted by their creators into methodologies and perspectives which provide new illumination of the world. How often have not such powerful minds as Hobbes, Rousseau, Marx, and Tocqueville suffered as the result of criticism that somehow lost the brilliance of conclusion—of perspective—in the shadows of semantic thickets, justifying itself on the speciously attractive but false ground that if each presupposition is not philosophically aseptic, no value can be attached to the conclusions?

One cannot deal with Durkheim by confining himself to definitions of such terms as *collective representations, individual representations,* and *anomie* any more than he can by seeking to deduce the complexity and subtlety of Durkheim's work from, say, the concepts of structure or function. One must turn to the actual, empirical problems in which Durkheim was interested and which he sought to explain. This is the best way to see the kind of substantive conclusions that are reached on the basis of premises that may indeed be routed in the abstract as metaphysically "meaningless."

Let us look, first, at his analysis of the nature and substance of morality. Durkheim never tired of insisting on the centrality of the moral. All social facts are, at one and the same time, moral facts. He wrote in the final pages of *The Division of Labor:*

> Society is not . . . a stranger to the moral world or something which has only secondary repercussions upon it. . . . Let all social life disappear and moral life will disappear with it, since it would no longer have any objective.

He put the matter even more forcibly in *Moral Education:*

> If there is one fact that history has irrefutably demonstrated, it is that the morality of each people is directly related to the social structure of the people practicing it. The connection is so intimate that, given the general character of the morality observed in a given society, . . . one can infer the nature of that society, the elements of its structure and the way it is organized. Tell me the marriage patterns, the morals dominating family life, and I will tell you the principal characteristics of its organization.[26]

Far from being social morality that is the abstraction, it is individual morality, he emphasizes, that is the abstraction, for where other than within the community can the moral life be seen? "Moral life, in all its forms, is never met with except in society. It never varies except in relation to social conditions. . . . The duties of the individual towards himself are, in reality, duties towards society."[27] Such a statement could seem an exercise in reification only to those nourished exclusively by the milk of abstract individualism! It would have been perfectly understandable to Aristotle, but not to Epicurus; to Montesquieu, but not to Bentham. As a theme, it is indistinguishable from that argued by John Dewey and George Herbert Mead. Finally, it is worth noting that Piaget's brilliant researches into the development of the child's conscience were directly inspired by the impact of Durkheim's thought.

Moral Education provides the opportunity to see in detail how Durkheim utilized the perspective of society in the clarification of morality. (Fully half of this remarkable volume—published posthumously—is taken up with the ways in which moral codes become internalized in the mind of the child. This discussion can deal only with the central proposition of this work.) There are three essential elements of morality.

[26] *The Division of Labor in Society, op. cit.,* p. 399, and *Moral Education . . . ,* p. 87.
[27] *The Division of Labor in Society, op. cit.,* pp. 399-400.

1. *The spirit of discipline.* All moral behavior "conforms to pre-established rules. To conduct one's self morally is a matter of abiding by a norm. . . . This domain of morality is the domain of duty; duty is prescribed behavior." What is the source of this prescriptive element?—not, certainly, the germ plasm. Those who answer "God" have at least the merit of looking outside the individual to an authority capable of command. But for Durkheim, God is but a mythicization of society; his answer, therefore, is "Society." It is society alone—through its kinship, religious, and economic codes, through its binding traditions and groups— that possesses the authority necessary to make the sense of *ought* (which can never be reduced, Durkheim repeatedly contends, to mere interest or convenience) one of the most directive and tenacious forces in human life. It is this unalterable relation of morality to "oughtness," to discipline incapable of reduction to mere inner drive in man, that leads Durkheim to the logical, if dramatic, declaration that "the erratic, the undisciplined, are morally incomplete." [28]

2. *The ends of morality.* Discipline is not enough: for it to become effective, for its function to be made manifest and determining, there must be also ends of morality. These are invariably impersonal, for action oriented to exclusively personal goals—whatever its benefits—is the very opposite of moral action. Whence comes the impersonality that communicates itself, through discipline, to the individual? From society, from the individual's attachment to society:

> [Morality] consists in the individual's attachment to those social groups of which he is a member. Morality begins, accordingly, only insofar as we belong to a human group, whatever it may be. Since, in fact, man is complete only as he belongs to several societies, morality itself is complete only to the extent that we feel identified with those different groups in which we are involved— family, union, business, club, political party, country, humanity.[29]

It is membership in the social group, then, that provides the indispensable context of mediation whereby ends become impersonal ends endowed with the authority that alone makes a reality of discipline.

3. *Autonomy or self-determination.* This third element has nothing to do with Kantian autonomy and Durkheim devotes a good part of his argument to a demonstration of the inadequacies of Kant's individual-oriented categorical imperative. Personal autonomy—that is, self-responsibility—is indeed a crucial element of moral behavior, but this, Durk-

[28] *Moral Education* . . . , *op. cit.*, p. 53.
[29] *Ibid.*, p. 80.

heim argues, is not less a part of society than discipline and group membership. Autonomy is simply the human being's rational awareness of reasons for what he does under the impulsions of discipline and attachment:

> To act morally, it is not enough—it is no longer enough—to respect discipline and to be committed to a group. Beyond this, and whether out of deference to a rule or devotion to a collective idea, we must have knowledge, as clear and complete an awareness as possible of the reasons for our conduct. This consciousness confers on our behavior the autonomy that the public conscience from now on requires of every genuinely and completely moral being. Hence, we can say that the third element of morality is the understanding of it.[30]

With the development of human society, there is a powerful tendency for man's awareness to become ever more acute and sensitive. The need for discipline and attachment remain as great as ever. (This, in answer to contemporary individualists who were proclaiming a new morality— one in which man forever was liberated from social disciplines and attachments and free to govern himself.) But, with his reason, man can know what he is doing and thus achieve a form of intellectual (but not social) autonomy unknown to primitive man.

A second and equally influential use of the perspective of society is the analysis of contract. This begins in *The Division of Labor,* and is made the subject of exhaustive treatment in the later *Professional Ethics and Civic Morals.* In a number of respects, the treatment of contract must rank among the more brilliant *tours de force* of modern social analysis. The point of departure is a refutation of Spencer's position, one in which contract is conceived as the simple, atomic act of two or more individuals achieving union through self-interest supplemented by reason. But it would be an error to limit Durkheim's treatment of contract to this. In proper focus, Durkheim's treatment is a profound attack on a vein of thought that began in the seventeenth century with Hobbes and his contemporaries and continued through the Enlightenment to become, in the nineteenth century, the essence of the utilitarian movement. In this vein, contract is the residual model of all social relationships. Hobbes had endeavored to rationalize even the family tie as an implicit contract between child and parent. In the rationalist-utilitarian tradition of the eighteenth and nineteenth centuries, all that could not be rationalized—legitimatized—by contract, real or imaginary, was sus-

[30] *Ibid.,* p. 120.

pect. The only reality and, therefore, the proper object of scientific attention, is that which emanates from man himself, his instinct and his reason. Social union, however it may appear to simple perception, is in fact the product of some form of contract. In this view, in short, contract is the microcosm of society, the image of human relationships.

This is the image that Durkheim repudiates. Contract, he argues, taken as either historically or logically primordial, is untenable and meretricious. How, Durkheim asks, can men ever be expected to honor a contractual agreement if it rests only on the individual interest or fancy that supposedly brings it into being?

> Where interest is the only ruling force, each individual finds himself in a state of war with every other since nothing comes to mollify the egos, and any truce would not be of long duration. There is nothing less constant than interest. Today, it unites me to you; tomorrow it will make me your enemy. Such a cause can only give rise to transient relations and passing associations.[31]

Contract of any type could not be sustained for a moment, Durkheim argues, unless it was based on conventions, traditions, codes in which the idea of an authority higher than contract was clearly resident. The idea of contract, its very possibility as a relationship among men, appears late in the development of human society. And it comes into existence only in the contexts of already sovereign mores which cannot, by any stretch of the imagination, be reduced to self-interest. These mores have their origin and continuing reality in society, not in states of individual consciousness.

Far from being primary, contract is a derivation of that most sacred and religious of all modes of human relationship: ritual. (The sacred as a perspective will be discussed later; it must suffice here to say only that, for Durkheim, the two most fundamental categories of human thought are the sacred and the profane.) Contract—like private property and the value of individuality, of family, of church, and of state—commands human allegiance only because at an early point in human history it was the reflection of the sacred. And, being sacred, it was ritualized. In ritual, in the sacred and imprescriptible union of man to totem, of man to god, of man to man, lies the origin of contract:

> It is the solemn ritual nature of the undertaking that gives it this characteristic, by sanctifying it and by making of it something that no longer depends on myself, although proceeding from me. The other party is thus justified in

[31] *The Division of Labor in Society, op. cit.,* pp. 203-204.

counting on my word—and vice versa, if the contract imposes mutual obligations. He has morally and legally the right to consider the promise as inevitably about to be kept. If, then, I fail in this, I am transgressing two duties at once: (1) I am committing sacrilege, because I am breaking an oath, I am profaning a sacred thing, I am committing an act forbidden by religion, and I am trespassing on the region of sacred things; (2) I am disturbing another in his possession, just as if I were a neighbor on his land; I am injuring him, or there is danger in it.[32]

It is thus the prior "contract" that man has with his God, with his society, with his neighbor's sacrosanct dominion, that provides the only substratum on which contract—in the sense used by utilitarians and lawyers—can rest. Just as the idea of property itself arose from the conception of sacred things, so the idea of contract arose from the conception of sacred relationships involving things—that is, from ritual. And without the continuing authority of tradition and law, contract could not survive.

Our third example of Durkheim's use of the perspective of society is his famous study of suicide. Here Durkheim's perspective is at its most boldly empirical. To have flung down the gauntlet before the rationalist idol of contract was daring enough. But to take suicide, that most intimate and plainly individual of all acts, and subject it too to the methodology of society—this, surely, must have been more than the utilitarians of that day could easily bear. What had been suggested in *The Division of Labor* about suicide—that is, its relation to periods of social disintegration—was now made the subject of investigation, and precisely in terms of the methodology he had laid down in *The Rules of Sociological Method.*

There are, of course, several motivations behind the work. There is, most obviously, the scientific. Suicide was plainly a problem of interest to many; it had already been studied, and much material of demographic nature was accessible. This Durkheim acknowledges:

> Suicide has been chosen as its subject, among the various subjects that we have had occasion to study in our teaching career, because few are more accurately to be defined and because it seemed to us particularly timely; its limits have even required study in a preliminary work.[33]

But there are also two other motivations behind the work, and these have been less noted. First, Durkheim maintains, the "possibility of

---

[32] Émile Durkheim, *Professional Ethics and Civic Morals,* translated by Cornelia Brookfield (London: Routledge & Kegan Paul, 1957), p. 193. This volume contains lectures not published during Durkheim's life.

[33] *Suicide, op. cit.,* pp. 36-37.

sociology" as a distinct field of study will be made more evident by the discovery of laws affecting suicide that flow directly from the distinctive subject matter of sociology—that is, society and social facts. There is, in short, a practical, professional objective, and that this was never lost on Durkheim is plain in the repeated references to this point in *Suicide*.

> Sociological method, as we practice it, rests wholly on the basic principle that social facts must be studied as things; that is, as realities external to the individual. There is no principle for which we have received more criticism; but none is more fundamental.[34]

For a sociology to be possible, it must have an object distinctively its own. It must take cognizance of a reality that is not already in the domain of other sciences. If no reality exists outside individual consciousness, then sociology lacks any material of its own. For then the only possible subject of observation is the mental states of the individual; these, however, form the field of psychology. From the psychological point of view, the essence of marriage, for example, or of the family, or of religion consists of individual needs to which these institutions supposedly correspond: paternal affection, filial love, sexual desire, the so-called religious instinct.

> On the pretext of giving the science a more solid foundation by establishing it upon the psychological constitution of the individual, it is thus robbed of the only object proper to it. It is not realized that there can be no sociology unless societies exist; and that societies cannot exist if there are only individuals.[35]

Here, plainly stated, is the translation of metaphysics into practical methodology. Rarely has it been done more effectively.

Having justified the study of suicide on demographic and methodological grounds—in each instance, be it noted, stressing the autonomy of the social for what can alone be sociological consideration—Durkheim adds the final justification of his work: a moral one. Suicide, he says, falls in a category that includes economic conflict, crime, and divorce and marks the pathological state of contemporary European society. Remedies must therefore be proposed that might serve to moderate the incidence of suicide, as well as that of other forms of social disintegration. It is in this practical, moral, light that Durkheim refers to "some suggestions concerning the causes of the general contemporary maladjustment being undergone by European societies and concerning remedies which may

---

[34] *Ibid.*, pp. 37-38.
[35] *Ibid.*, p. 38. The continuity of this crucial methodological utterance with the argument of *The Rules of Sociological Method* is, of course, plain

relieve it." Suicide, he emphasizes, as it is found today, "is precisely one of the forms through which the collective affection from which we suffer is transmitted; thus it will help us to understand this." [36]

The conclusions Durkheim reached in this remarkable volume can even today be regarded as a triumphant demonstration of the results he had forecast abstractly in *The Rules of Sociological Method*. His emphasis on society rather than the individual is unremitting in the work, and it is fully sustained by the data and by his verification of hypotheses. His own summarizing words are graphic:

> Wholly different are the results we obtained when we forgot the individual and sought the causes of the suicidal aptitude of each society in the nature of the societies themselves. The relation of suicide to certain states of social environment are as direct and constant as its relation to facts of a biological and physical character were seen to be uncertain and ambiguous.[37]

What are the specific modes by which society becomes the chief determinant of so individual an act as suicide? There are three in particular:

1. *Egoistic suicide.* When cohesion in the groups to which men belong declines to the point of no longer offering the support to ego that is normally given. "Suicide," Durkheim declares in one of his most celebrated propositions, "varies inversely with the degree of integration of the social groups of which the individual forms a part." When society is strongly integrated, it restrains individuals, considers them at its service, "and thus forbids them to dispose willfully of themselves." Among all those in modern populations whose associative ties are relatively weak—Protestants, urban dwellers, industrial workers, professional men—suicide rates are higher than those among aggregates of opposite character.[38]

2. *Anomic suicide.* Paralleling egoistic suicide is anomic suicide, caused by the sudden dislocation of normative systems, the breakdown of values by which one may have lived for a lifetime, or the conflict between ends desired and abilities to achieve them. It is not poverty that impells toward suicide. Durkheim refers to the "remarkable immunity of the poor countries":

> [Poverty] protects against suicide because it is a restraint in itself. Wealth, on the other hand, by the power it bestows, deceives us into believing that we depend on ourselves only. Reducing the resistance we encounter from objects, it suggests the possibility of unlimited success against them. The less limited one feels, the more intolerable all limitations appear.[39]

---

[36] *Ibid.*, p. 37.
[37] *Ibid.*, p. 299.
[38] *Ibid.*, Book 2, Chap. 2.
[39] *Ibid.*, p. 254.

This is, of course, pure Tocqueville. It was in terms of precisely this state of mind that Tocqueville had sought to account for the restlessness, the anxiety, the melancholy he found among the relatively affluent Americans—all of which led, Tocqueville noted specifically, to a high rate of suicide among Americans.

3. *Altruistic suicide.* The third form of suicide is no less social in its governing context than the other two types, but it manifests itself when involvement in a social relationship is so great that the individual is led to take his life because he believes some act of his has brought obloquy upon social relationship. The essence of such suicide, as Durkheim notes, is not escape but abnegation. Although this type of suicide is more likely to be found (but rarely even there) in primitive societies where tribal consensus can be overpowering, it is also to be seen occasionally in those areas of modern society—such as the officer corps of established military organizations—where tradition is dominant and penetrating.[40]

According to Durkheim:

> . . . each human society has a greater or lesser aptitude for suicide; the expression is based on the nature of things. Each social group really has a collective inclination for the act, quite its own, and is the source of all individual inclinations, rather than their result. It is made up of the currents of egoism, altruism or anomie running through the society under consideration with tendencies to langorous melancholy, active renunciation, or exasperated weariness derivative from these currents. These tendencies of the whole social body, by affecting individuals, cause them to commit suicide. The private experience usually thought to be the proximate causes of suicide have only the influence borrowed from the victim's moral predisposition, itself an echo of the moral state of society.[41]

This passage, abstracted from context and approached in strictly analytical terms, might easily be subjected to the same kind of assault that has been visited upon other passages and concepts in Durkheim's works. Can a human society have an "aptitude"—a group, a "collective inclination" —for suicide? Can a social body have "tendencies to langorous melancholy," and so on? The accumulated presuppositions of several centuries of Western individualism would say, emphatically, "No," and said so volubly in Durkheim's own day. Let us not pause, however, to wonder once again at the massive effects on Western thought of an analytical individualism, that paradoxically has prevented more knowledge of man, actual man, than it has made possible, nor pause either to seek to rescue

---

[40] *Ibid.,* Book 2, Chap. 4.
[41] *Ibid.,* p. 300.

Durkheim from familiar charges of reification. Argument is almost always futile and self-perpetuating. Let us instead emphasize this fact only: It was precisely on the basis of the view of society ably summarized in the passage just quoted that Durkheim evolved a methodology and worked by crucial verification to conclusions (very precise conclusions!) on the incidence of suicide in society that have, in only minor ways, been challenged in the seventy years that have elapsed since the publication of *Suicide. Suicide* remains one of the half-dozen great scientific studies in sociology; one need not even lean on the word *classic* to make this judgment.

These three examples—morality, contract, and suicide—will at least suggest the explanatory and illuminative uses to which the perspective of society was put by Durkheim. Through them one can see clearly enough that society, for Durkheim, is neither an inert monolith nor a brooding, ghostly presence epiphenomenal to the individual and discoverable only by the kind of mystic intuition that had produced Rousseau's vision of the general will. On the contrary, as Durkheim repeatedly emphasizes, society is indistinguishable from the observable data of human conduct. What one actually sees are not "individuals," not "instincts," but rather human beings inextricably involved in institutionalized and associative patterns of behavior. Laws, traditions, regularities of expectation and response—these, he had told us in *The Rules of Sociological Method,* form a body of social facts which may be studied in and for themselves. They are clearly visible, even measurable in general terms. It is not necessary to premise internal drives in man, nor to seek explanations in states of individual consciousness, in race, or in geographic and climatic environment. Explanations should be, and can be, drawn from the social data themselves.

What had been stated so metaphysically, so remotely (as it seemed), in the *Rules* was given solid and almost incontestable exemplification in *Suicide.* And it was to be given successive exemplifications during the remaining years of Durkheim's life. Whatever he touched—law, kinship, religion, systems of philosophy, logic, morality—was subjected to the same type of inquiry even though he never again selected a subject as suitable as suicide to expression in the rigorous terms of hypothesis crucially verified.

The three examples chosen—morality, contract, and suicide—do not, therefore, by any means exhaust the list of subjects or problems that are lighted up in Durkheim's work by the perspective of society. Indeed, if one were to proceed in terms of strict logic of organization, the four remaining perspectives could be subsumed under the category *society*. Personality, authority, the religio-sacred—even development—are all regarded by Durkheim as manifestations of society, and his analysis is conducted exactly as it is in the cases of morality, contract, and suicide. His treatment of personality, authority, and religion differs from that of the utilitarians precisely in his derivation of these concepts from the prior reality of society. But in the organizing of a book logic is not enough. Each of these subjects has such manifest importance that it must be dealt with separately as, indeed, a perspective in itself.

PERSONALITY

Durkheim's view of the nature of man follows rigorously and clearly from his conception of the nature of society. Society may be *sui generis* but it is not external to man; indeed, it is inseparable from man and his mind, character, and role. Man and society are fused. Durkheim's theory of personality is first set forth in *The Division of Labor,* in his general attack on utilitarianism and its effort to derive society from presocial individuals:

> The psychologist who restricts himself to the ego cannot emerge to find the nonego. Collective life is not born from individual life, but it is, on the contrary, the second which is born of the first.[42]

What one sees, in rising emphasis throughout the rest of Durkheim's life, is the further argument that, when attention is restricted to the ego, not only cannot the nonego be discovered but even the nature of the ego will remain hidden. Man, Durkheim declares, has a dual nature:

> There are two beings in him: an individual being which has its foundation in the organism and the circle of whose activities is therefore strictly limited, and a social being which represents the highest reality in the intellectual and moral order that we can know by observation. This duality of our nature has as its consequence in the practical order, the irreducibility of a moral ideal to a utilitarian motive, and in the order of thought, the irreducibility of reason to individual experience.[43]

Unquestionably the severest criticism of Durkheim, and the most general, relates to the supposed obliteration of the individual and the ascrip-

---

[42] *The Division of Labor in Society, op. cit.,* p. 279.
[43] *The Elementary Forms of Religious Life, op. cit.,* pp. 16-17. The same specific theme of the "duality" of man had been pursued fifteen years earlier in *Suicide.*

tion to society of a mind and existence independent of individuals. It is easy to draw this conclusion if one limits his reading to those few paragraphs—scattered throughout Durkheim's main works—in which his emphasis upon society becomes virtual apostrophe. Even Durkheim's defenders have found themselves, for the most part, going to merely casual or polemical pieces for evidence of his actual recognition of individuals in society and of the sanctity of their political rights. By friend and foe alike, Durkheim's envisagement of the human being has generally been regarded as tenuous, to say the least.

What is the truth in the matter? What, in fact, is Durkheim's actual view of the relation between society and man? It is—and this must be emphasized—not very different from the view that is today taken for granted in sociological studies of human behavior. It has close affinity with the conception of personality that has come to characterize the social sciences within the past two or three decades. Certainly, it would be difficult to find fault with the statement quoted above. Quite apart from its contemporary acceptability, it has roots in a great deal of the Western tradition. What Durkheim did was to expunge the utilitarian image of man—an image that drew heavily upon the rather narrow view of man as a self-sufficing, discrete, and self-stabilizing being.

Did Durkheim deny the existence of specific creative human beings?— individuals who, by special combination of biological and cultural qualities, towered above their kind? Certainly not. Did he deny the historical importance of such human beings in politics, religion, and philosophy?— again, certainly not. Durkheim was by no means ignorant of or insensitive to history. He had, after all, studied under Fustel de Coulanges. He was certainly not blind to those processes which, at certain times, result in the widespread release of individual minds from tradition, to the consequent enrichment of culture. His posthumously published lectures on education and on citizenship reveal this clearly.

Admittedly, one might wish that Durkheim had given more attention to the specific mechanisms by which collective representations in society are translated, in distinctively individual and often creative ways, into the individual representations that reflect man's relationship to society. But, again, it must be remembered that Durkheim was waging a war against a psychological and biological determinism that it is now all too easy to forget existed. He lived in an age of historiography, when emphasis on discrete individuals, at the expense of contexts and processes, was very common.

Attention to those parts of his work where he is concerned specifically and pointedly with the nature of the bond between society and man reveals a conception of individuality that is familiar enough. Consider, for example, *Moral Education,* which is a treatise not only on morality, but also on social psychology as this field is today understood. Here, especially in the final sections, Durkheim treats in detail the processes through which individuality is formed.

There is no question in Durkheim's mind of the priority of society in these processes. For Durkheim, it must be remembered, *society* includes all that is today more commonly contained under *culture.* It is fundamental and prior but it is neither in conflict with individuality nor external to the individual.

> Individual and society are certainly beings with different natures. But far from there being some inexpressible kind of antagonism between the two, far from its being the case that the individual can identify himself with society only at the risk of renouncing his own nature either wholly or in part, the fact is that he is not truly himself, he does not fully realize his own nature, except on the condition that he is involved in society.[44]

Nor is society something that lies outside man's developed individuality. In each of us lies, Durkheim writes,

> . . . a host of states which something other than ourselves—that is to say, society—expresses in, or through, us. Certainly society is greater than, and goes beyond, us, for it is infinitely more vast than our individual being; but at the same time it enters into every part of us. It is outside us and envelops us, but it is also in us and is everywhere an aspect of our nature. We are fused with it. Just as our physical organism gets its nourishment outside itself, so our mental organism feeds itself on ideas, sentiments, and practices that come to us from society.[45]

But the mental organism feeds itself in unequal ways. Not all individuals assimilate and internalize society's codes in the same way. Conflicts among norms can result in tensions within individuals. Different values are set by society on individuals, and the consequence of this is a tension between individualism and the moral authority of society that is eternal.

Durkheim was well aware of the tension created in society by individual deviation from social norms. Indeed, he recognizes individualism as endemic in all civilizations. In *The Division of Labor* he wrote:

> Individualism, free thought, dates neither from our own time nor from 1789, nor from the Reformation, nor from scholasticism, nor from the decline of

---

[44] *Moral Education* . . . , *op. cit.,* pp. 67-68.
[45] *Ibid.,* p. 71.

Graeco-Latin polytheism or oriental theocracies. It is a phenomenon which begins in no certain part, but that develops without cessation all through history.[46]

Durkheim distinguishes "two extreme and opposed types" of personality in the history of society. On the one hand are those individuals who are notably sensitive to tradition, to rules, and authority. Such personalities "do their duty as they see it, completely and without hesitation, simply because it is their duty and without any particular appeal to their hearts. These are the men of substantial intellect and strong will—Kant is an ideal example—but among whom the emotional faculties are much less developed than those of the intellect." [47]

The opposite personality type is revealed in those individuals characterized "not by self-control and a tendency to withdraw, but by a love of spending themselves, by an outward expansiveness." These Durkheim calls "the loving hearts, the ardent and general souls." If they are capable of great deeds, of flights of brilliance, they yet find it hard to restrict themselves to mundane obligations. One is less sure of these men, Durkheim remarks, for passions, "even the most noble, blow successively hot and cold under the influence of chance circumstances and in the most erratic ways."[48]

The two personality types reflect two types of morality in human history—persisting, universal types—and both personality and moral types are illustrated successively in the various ages of the history of culture. There are the classic ages, such as those of Augustus and of Louis XIV, in which general love of form, rule, and standard brings to the fore discipline and restraint as sovereign values. At such times, the first personality type flourishes. There are, on the other hand, ages—and Durkheim characterizes his own as one—in which standards, rules, and forms become attenuated and flux reigns. In such ages the second personality type becomes more expressive, when there is search for objectives to which men can commit themselves.[49]

It is hard to avoid feeling that Durkheim strongly prefers the first type of personality, morality, and age; but rarely has the second type been portrayed with more sympathy and insight by anyone of this preference.

It would be hard, even by contemporary standards, to find a more exemplary statement of the relation between culture and personality than

[46] *The Division of Labor in Society, op. cit.*, p. 171.
[47] *Moral Education* . . . , pp. 99-100.
[48] *Ibid.*, p. 100.
[49] *Ibid.*, p. 101.

the following, buried in his notable treatment of the elements of religious sacrifice:

> On the one hand, the individual gets from society the best part of himself, all that gives him a distinct character and a special place among other beings, his intellectual and moral culture. If we should withdraw from men their language, sciences, arts, and moral beliefs, they would drop to the rank of animals. So the characteristic attributes of human nature come from society. But, on the other hand, society exists and lives only in and through individuals. If the idea of society were extinguished in individual minds and the beliefs, traditions and aspirations of the group were no longer felt and shared by the individuals, society would die. We can say of it what we just said of the divinity: it is real only insofar as it has a place in human consciousnesses, and this place is whatever one we may give it. . . . [S]ociety cannot do without individuals any more than these can do without society.[50]

These words were written shortly after the turn of the century, though they are clearly presaged by statements in his earlier works, including *The Division of Labor*. Not until John Dewey's *Human Nature and Conduct* and Graham Wallas' *Our Social Heritage* (both of which appeared in the 1920's) can one find a philosophical conception of personality to match Durkheim's in subtlety and relevance.

In tradition and in community, then, lie the essential moral and social sources of what is known as individuality. The utilitarians and critical rationalists had sought to trace what is creative and free in man almost exclusively to processes of separation from institutions and traditions. In release rather than membership, they argued, lie the crucial sources of individuality. There is something in this, of course—more, indeed, than Durkheim was willing to emphasize. But creativeness and innovation cannot be separated from tradition, as every great age in the history of culture witnesses and confirms. The great man of thought and action, however radical, works with materials he has inherited, through ways that are normatively given, and toward ends that are firmly planted in his culture. That the creator rearranges and redirects these, and applies to them energies of uncommon dimension, does not detract from the role of tradition and community.

Plainly, it is personality that Durkheim is concerned with. Reading his works less from the point of view of what he says about the "individual" and more from that of what he says (in *Moral Education*, for example)

<hr />

[50] *The Elementary Forms of Religious Life, op. cit.,* p. 347. The final words in that passage should be required reading for all who charge Durkheim with lacking a sense of concrete human beings.

about the "person," one finds a theory of human nature not different in its essentials from that of Cooley, Mead, and Dewey.

Those who ascribe to Durkheim a purely passive view of the individual in relation to society have not read him carefully. Always he premises the notion of an active, *acting* person. It is well to remember at this point Durkheim's treatment of autonomy as one of the three cardinal elements of morality. Autonomy is, as has been noted, a process by which society's norms and incentives become internalized in the individual, giving rise to self-awareness and self-discipline. The whole idea of personality presupposes for Durkheim what he calls a "self-mastery that we can achieve only in the school of moral discipline."

But the distinction achieved by Durkheim's treatment of the self and self-mastery in the history of social thought lies in its insistent emphasis upon the medium within which the self realizes itself:

> A person is not only a being who disciplines himself, he is also a system of ideas, of feelings, of habits and tendencies, a consciousness that has a content; and one is all the more a person as this content is enriched. For this reason, is not the civilized man a person in greater measure than the primitive; the adult than the child? Morality, in drawing us outside ourselves, and thrusting us into the nourishing milieu of society, puts us precisely in the position of developing our personalities.[51]

Only in society is the individual to be discovered; only in the behavior of individuals is society to be known.

Does all of this mean that the creative activity of specific human beings does not vary from age to age? Does the omnipresence of society's collective conscience assure uniformity? Far from it. Durkheim, as has just been noted, is keenly aware of contrasts among personality types, and he is equally aware that morality is, so to speak, creatively incomplete in some persons whose very obduracy before a given moral code or belief makes them, on occasion, creators of new moral codes and beliefs:

> We have contended that the erratic, the undisciplined, are morally incomplete. Do they not, nevertheless, play a morally useful part in society? Was not Christ such a deviant, as well as Socrates? And is it not thus with all historical figures whose names we associate with the great moral revolutions through which humanity has passed? Had their feeling of respect for the moral rules characteristic of the day been too lively, they would not have undertaken to alter them. To dare to shake off the yoke of traditional discipline, one should not feel authority too strongly. Nothing could be clearer.[52]

[51] *Moral Education* . . . , *op. cit.*, p. 73.
[52] *Ibid.*, p. 53.

But it does not follow from this that an entire moral order may be constructed on the basis of ways of thought and behavior peculiar to the exceptional—to the "erratic, the undisciplined, the morally incomplete." Theories that celebrate the beneficence of unrestricted freedom are, Durkheim says boldy, "apologies for a diseased state." It is only through the practice of moral rules that man develops the capacity to govern himself —that is, to be free.

It is important, Durkheim argues, to keep separate two very different feelings: "the need to substitute a new regulation for an old one; and the impatientice with all rules, the abhorrence of all discipline." The former is a normal and natural feeling, one on which the progress of order—as well as freedom—depends. The latter is, however, always abnormal "since it prompts us to alienate ourselves from the basic conditions of life":

> Doubtless, with some of the great moral innovators, a legitimate need for change has degenerated into something like anarchy. Because the rules prevailing in their time offended them deeply, their sense of the evil led them to blame, not this or that particular and transient form of moral discipline, but the principle itself of all discipline. But it is precisely this that always vitiated their efforts; it is this that rendered so many revolutions fruitless, not yielding results corresponding to the effort expended. At the point when one is rising against the rules, their necessity must be felt more keenly than ever. It is just at the moment when one challenges them that he should always bear in mind that he cannot dispense with rules.[53]

There are ages of tradition and there are ages of individualism. Both are equally "social." The ascendancy of individualism in the history of a society indicates that the society has in some way transferred to values of revolt and liberation the esteem previously accorded values of tradition. Man becomes, through social processes, the heir of what was formerly vested in tradition.

But such ages have their inevitable termination, for in the very process of transferring society's honor from institution to man, Durkheim writes, there arises a false conception of individualism—one in which society's attributes become conceptually transferred to man's biological nature:

> In societies where the dignity of the person is supreme, where man is a God to mankind, the individual is readily inclined to consider the man in himself as a God and to regard himself as the object of his own cult. When morality consists primarily in giving one a very high idea of one's self, certain

[53] *Ibid.*, pp. 53-54.

combinations of circumstances readily suffice to make man unable to perceive anything above himself. Individualism is, of course, not necessarily egoism, but it comes close to it; the one cannot be stimulated without the other being enlarged.[54]

Durkheim's treatment of the relation between individualism and egoism is reminiscent of Tocqueville, who had also put the two in common focus. Egoism, wrote Tocqueville, "is a passionate and exaggerated love of self which leads a man to connect everything with himself and to prefer himself to everything in the world." Individualism, on the other hand, is a mature and calm quality which disposes each member of the community to separate himself from the mass of his fellows. Egoism originates in instinct; individualism proceeds from erroneous judgment —from deficiencies of mind rather than from perversity of heart: "Egoism blights the germ of all virtue; individualism, at first, only saps the virtues of public life; but in the long run it attacks and destroys all others and is at length absorbed in downright egoism.[55]

Tocqueville, too, had been struck by the tendency of the individualistic characteristics of democracies—the drive for wealth, equality, status, and so on—to produce a general malaise and the paradox of men increasingly miserable even in the midst of relative abundance. The essence of the process, for Tocqueville, was the gnawing sense of despair men felt at their inability to reach the heights that were progressively opened to them, new heights that appeared maddeningly on the foundations of what they *were* able to achieve. Tocqueville believed that the frustration caused by constantly receding goals, coupled with the separation from statuses and norms which—however binding they may have been—had at least offered certainty and repose, made democracy and capitalism increasingly traumatic to human sensibility.

Durkheim's view does not differ, basically, from Tocqueville's:

Social man necessarily presupposes a society which he expresses and serves. If this dissolves, if we no longer feel it in existence and action about and above us, whatever is social in us is deprived of all objective foundation. All that remains is an artificial combination of illusory images, a phantasmagoria vanishing at the least reflection; that is, nothing which can be a goal for our action. Yet this social man is the essence of civilized man; he is the masterpiece of existence. Thus, we are bereft of reasons for existence, for the only

[54] *Suicide, op. cit.,* pp. 363-64.
[55] Tocqueville, *Democracy in America,* translated and edited by Phillips Bradley (New York: Alfred A. Knopf, Inc., 1945), Vol. II, p. 98.

life to which we could cling no longer corresponds to anything actual, the only existence still based upon reality no longer meets our needs.[56]

There were others in the nineteenth century—artists, humanists, social philosophers—who could have written those words: Balzac, Nietzsche, Burckhardt, and Simmel, among others. But it is hard to imagine such a passage having been written by anyone in the Enlightenment or by any one of the utilitarian heirs of the Enlightenment in the nineteenth century.

Durkheim refers in this passage to the necessity of "a goal for our action." He then goes on to expand upon this point, with special reference to religious goals. It is not true, he writes, that men must have supramundane ends to give meaning and direction to human life. But there is this much truth in the religious position: social man, in contrast to physical man, requires something that both transcends and reinforces his being. Physically, "man can act reasonably without thought of transcendental purposes. Insofar as he has no other needs, he is therefore self-sufficient and can live happily with no other objective than living." [57] This is not the case with social man, civilized man. He has numberless ideas, feelings, and practices utterly unrelated to organic needs. The function of art, morality, religion, and science is not "to repair organic exhaustion or to provide sound functioning of the organs," and any effort to so reduce them is deceptive. The function is to create sentiments that bind us to others and to expand our social roles: "To play our social role we have striven to extend our intelligence and it is still society that has supplied us with tools for this development by transmitting to us its trust fund of knowledge." [58]

It is interesting to note an apparent contradiction in Durkheim's concept of individualism. At times individualism is made to appear as nonsociety, as the mode of behavior or thought that ensues when man is divorced from society. It is, in this view, the very opposite of the social. But there is another view of the matter, one that arises from his sweeping insistence that everything above the level of physiology derives from society. And in this second view individualism becomes, along with the collective conscience itself, something social in origin. Individualism, Durkheim maintains, is—quite as much as religion itself—the result of society: of society's substitution of what he calls *the cult of the individual*

[56] *Suicide, op. cit.,* p. 213.
[57] *Ibid.,* p. 211.
[58] *Ibid.,* pp. 211-12.

for the traditional religious cult leading to an attribution to man of qualities that were formerly vested in religion. It is the second view that is more consistently Durkheimian—that is, consistent not only with his premises but also with the full body of his work.

Social man is thus, for Durkheim, a precarious unity of two opposed but vital tendencies in history: the collective conscience of society, and individualism. There is even a history of personality to be seen in Durkheim, one represented by an alternation of intensity of these two tendencies. In primitive or folk society, collective conscience is strong; individualism, weak—though not nonexistent. Durkheim does not, like Freud, derive the individualistic, aggressive force from biology, with culture acting as the repressant on this force. For Durkheim, the individualistic element is as "social" as the collective conscience, but its sociality is different, reflecting unlikeness rather than likeness, differentiation rather than homogeneity. Over a long period of time the individualistic element has become stronger as the collective conscience has grown weaker. And this, for Durkheim, is as it should be: it is the basis of freedom. The difficulty lies, however, in the fact that in recent times a disequilibrium has appeared—one in which, under the sway of the cult of the individual, the individualistic element in personality has become relatively hypertrophied, the communal element atrophied. The balance must be somehow redressed by deliberate reinforcements of the collective conscience, but in ways that will not jeopardize either freedom or the democratic nation: hence, his proposal for professional associations.

All of this is a far cry from the total obliteration of the individual and of individual freedom with which Durkheim has so often been charged. It was not personality—not individuality—that Durkheim sought to drive out of sociological consideration; it was, rather, the artificial, abstracted conception of individuality that had come into existence at a time when European philosophers took for granted the massive stability of the social order, seeing in man's biological nature qualities that should have been referred to the institutional and moral order that had been shaped by history. Once one grasps this point, he will find it difficult to charge Durkheim with the annihilation of the individual and deification of society!

But two critical observations must be made, both reflecting Durkheim's failure to carry analysis further. First, he sets his view of individualism more often within its negative or pathological effects (as suicide, divorce, and mental alienation) than within the equally credible, and actual, processes of creativeness in culture. He does not do in any detail what some of his students—notably Gustave Glotz, Maurice Halbwachs, and Marcel Granet—did: carry the identical perspective into an analysis of historical processes of cultural and intellectual efflorescence.

The second point of criticism relates to the actual mechanisms by which individuality is formed through interaction between what Durkheim repeatedly refers to as "the two natures of man": the biological and the social. He provides some promising leads in *Moral Education* —especially the second part, in which he deals with the child in the context of school and related social influences—but little more. Not much can be gleaned from his use of the concepts of collective representations and individual representations: both are descriptive, rather than analytical, concepts and serve to emphasize the role of society and its codes rather than to clarify interactive processes. Nor is there anywhere in Durkheim's writing the kind of analysis of personality in its social elements and states that marks so much of Simmel's microscopic treatment of human nature. Durkheim, in this respect at least, does not even rival Weber. There is in Durkheim a certain reticence about carrying analysis deep into the nature of man. Whether this was the result of personal limitation or a choice dictated by the special mode of positivism to which he dedicated himself is not clear. Above any other thinker of his age, Durkheim was responsible for burying the utilitarian distortion of man's nature and for highlighting the social basis of consciousness; but for clarification of the detailed processes involved one is forced to turn to others. Durkheim sets forth the problem magnificently, but he does not provide the answers.

THE NATURE OF AUTHORITY

The concept of authority runs like a leitmotif through all of Durkheim's works. It is second only to society among the dominant themes of his sociology and philosophy. Durkheim was obsessed by authority, methodologically as well as substantively; indeed, in the beginning he took law as the only real measure of sociality, of solidarity. That he was led to abandon this stringent emphasis did not, however, lessen his insistence on the proposition that true society and true morality exist only when authority over individual mind and behavior is clearly present.

Authority—that is, discipline—is the first of his three elements of morality, and he converts discipline into the single most important constitutive principle of personality:

Ordinarily, discipline appears useful only because it entails behavior that has useful outcomes. Discipline is only a means of specifying and imposing the required behavior. But if the preceding analysis is correct, we must say that discipline derives its *raison d'être* from itself; it is good that man is disciplined, independent of the acts to which he thus finds himself constrained.[59]

Why is discipline good? The answer forms the explicit substance of *Moral Education,* though it could be deduced easily from each of Durkheim's other works. Discipline is authority in operation, and authority is inseparable—even indistinguishable—from the texture of society. Society, as he points out in *The Division of Labor* and in *The Rules of Sociological Method,* is manifest only in the diverse forms of constraint which rescue, as it were, the individual from the void. Authority and discipline form the very warp of personality; without authority man can have no sense of duty, nor any real freedom. Only when traditions, codes, and roles coerce, direct, or restrain man's impulses can a society be said genuinely to exist. Only by constraint, Durkheim could have said, shall one know morality in contrast to anomie, society in contrast to egoism.

He is critical of Bentham and other utilitarians for their false view of the role of authority:

> For Bentham, morality, like law, involved a kind of pathology. Most of the classical economists were of the same view. And doubtless the viewpoint has led the major socialist theoreticians to deem a society without systematic regulation both possible and desirable. The notion of an authority dominating life and administering law seemed to them to be an archaic idea, a prejudice that could not persist. It is life itself that makes its own laws. There could be nothing above or beyond it.[60]

In his *Professional Ethics,* Durkheim continues the theme: "There is no form of social activity which can do without the appropriate moral discipline. . . . The interests of the individual are not those of the group he belongs to and, indeed, there is often a real antagonism between the one and the other." Such interests are only dimly perceived by him: he may fail to perceive them at all. There must, therefore, be some system which brings them to mind, "which obliges him to respect them, and this system can be no other than a moral discipline. For all discipline of this kind is a code of rules that lays down for the individual what he should do so as not to damage collective interests and so as not to disorganize the society of which he forms a part." [61]

[59] *Moral Education* . . . , *op. cit.,* pp. 31-32.
[60] *Ibid.,* pp. 35-36.
[61] *Professional Ethics* . . . , *op. cit.,* p. 14.

Authority, in its relation to man, not only buttresses moral life, it *is* moral life:

> [Authority] performs an important function in forming character and personality in general. In fact, the most essential element of character is this capacity for restraint or—as they say—of inhibition, which allows us to contain our passions, our desires, our habits, and subject them to law.[62]

This last suggests that Durkheim was not unaware of Freudians and others of his day who viewed the rigor of moral authorities as the immediate source of psychological disabilities. The contrast between Durkheim and Freudianism on the matter of discipline is of considerable interest.

Durkheim's views on authority bring him, of course, to the problem of freedom, and he does not hesitate to stress the absolute priority of authority in any situation in which freedom is imaginable:

> In sum, the theories that celebrate the beneficence of unrestricted liberties are apologies for a diseased state. One may even say that, contrary to appearances, the words *liberty* and *lawlessness* clash in their coupling, since liberty is the fruit of regulation. Through the practice of moral rules we develop the capacity to govern and regulate ourselves, which is the whole reality of liberty.[63]

In numerous places, starting with *The Division of Labor* and continuing through his last major work, Durkheim made plain that he considered the present age of European society one in which breakdown of authority was conspicuous and governing. The necessity of moral authority, he writes, is a truth especially to be remembered at the present time:

> For we are living precisely in one of those critical, revolutionary periods when authority is usually weakened through the loss of traditional discipline—a time that may easily give rise to a spirit of anarchy. This is the source of the anarchic aspirations that . . . are emerging today, not only in the particular sects bearing the name, but in the very different doctrines that, although opposed on other points, join in a common aversion to anything smacking of regulation.[64]

It is Durkheim's theoretical concern with authority, in all its breadth and depth, that has so frequently invited charges of "collectivism," "authoritarianism," and "nationalism." Such charges are, however, incorrect and irrelevant. First, such terms have political connotations, and their inevitable effect is to identify Durkheim with the unitary nationalist

[62] *Moral Education* . . . , *op. cit.*, p. 46.
[63] *Ibid.*, p. 54.
[64] *Ibid.*, p. 54.

collectivism that was coming to flower in Europe at that time. Such identification is false. In clear fact, Durkheim's political thought comes close to the opposite extreme. His analysis of the state and its relationship to social order is much nearer to that of the syndicalists of his time than to either the integral nationalism of French conservatives or the more idealized English variety found in the works of men like T. H. Green and Bernard Bosanquet.

In terms of practical politics, Durkheim was a *Dreyfusard*, a term covering beliefs that went well beyond the innocence of Alfred Dreyfus to include such principles as legal equality, civil rights, the rule of law, and political liberty. The term also included anticlericalism, and because of the emotional intensity with which all matters pertaining to the Church in political affairs were then charged, this could sometimes result in a degree of antireligious sentiment sufficient to alienate a few, such as Péguy. Durkheim was never alienated from *Dreyfusard* principles and, given his known religious agnosticism, it was only too easy for supporters of the Church to interpret his views as providing tacit support for the political domination of all religious, intellectual, and moral matters.

Durkheim, one is forced to concede, was easy prey for such distortions. Did he not, in philosophy and sociology, insist upon the absolute priority of authority and of the collective conscience; and did he not deny the existence of "the individual"? Add to this theoretical position his views on what he called *the moral anarchy* of his time, and it was only too easy to suspect him of desiring a reformative authoritarianism.

But however understandable such ascriptions may have been, they are not made the more acceptable. Far from being a monist, a nationalist, or collectivist, Durkheim must be placed among the pluralists who were at that time giving the secular, unitary theory of political sovereignty the first real challenge it had had since Althusius. His ideas are similar to those advanced by such men as Duguit and Saleilles in France, and Maitland, Figgis, and the young Harold Laski in England. Of Durkheim's dedication to society, order, and authority, there can be no doubt whatsoever. But to make this dedication synonomous with unitary nationalism or with centralized economic collectivism, as many critics have, is to miss the very essence of a theory of man's relation to society that culminates in pluralism of authority and rigorous insistence upon what he called *corps intermédiaires*. These *corps intermédiaires*, associations lying intermediate to man and the state and forming the multiple substance of society, are the units of Durkheim's theory of authority—just as abstract individuals were the units of the utilitarian theory. Criticism of individualism, in Durkheim, does not mean repudiation of freedom and acceptance of collectivism. Such criticism is, on the contrary, one of the very salients of any genuine critique of the traditional theory of monistic sovereignty.

A few words on this aspect are useful here. From the time the Western theory of secular sovereignty began to develop—in the writings of men like Marsiglio, Bodin, Hobbes, and, above all, Rousseau—all that was vested by theorists and rulers in the state was taken from such competing groups as the church, the gild, the commune, and the family. Legal centralization necessarily involved a high degree of legal individualism —a relation that had always been clear in the minds of those responsible for the revival of Roman law in medieval Europe. Apart from the legal and conceptual individualism created by the state's absorption of powers from rival groups—apart, in short, from legal atomism—legal monism (that is, monistic sovereignty) was impossible. Hobbes and Rousseau were both brilliantly aware of this and their respective treatises on sovereignty pointed out the inevitable consequences. It was in France, through the writings of Rousseau and the postrevolutionary legislation, that the theory of unitary sovereignty reached its peak; and it was in France, in the nineteenth century, that the reaction against monism began.

Durkheim belongs to this reaction. True, he starts with the centrality of social authority; but for Durkheim authority is plural—manifest in the diverse spheres of kinship, local community, profession, church, school, gild, and labor union, as well as political government. From the premise of the necessity for continuing authority over the individual in each of society's associations, and hence for a limitation on legal and social individualism, Durkheim reaches a critique of the state every bit as pointed as that of the individualists and a good deal more securely grounded in history.

It is important to note that when Durkheim began his work he made juridical rules the only reliable manifestations of consensus in society. That is what is meant by the statement that authority had, for Durkheim, methodological significance. In *The Division of Labor* where, it will be remembered, one of his prime objectives was to show how morality could be studied scientifically, Durkheim chose law as the only clear and reliable means of identifying social solidarity:

> It will be distinctly seen how we have studied social solidarity *through the system of juridical rules;* how, in the search for causes, we have put aside all that too readily lends itself to personal judgments and subjective appreciation,

so as to reach certain rather profound facts of the social structure, capable of being objects of judgment and, consequently, of science.[65]

This is one of the most frequently quoted passages in all Durkheim's work, and although it may be taken properly enough as the motivating aim of *The Division of Labor,* its significance is confined to that work alone. In that work—in principle, at least—Durkheim makes repressive law the identifying attribute of mechanical solidarity, just as he makes restitutive law the essence of organic solidarity. But he did not really restrict himself even there to juridical data alone: he admits that the legalist approach fails to "take into account certain elements of the collective conscience which, because of their smaller power or their indeterminateness, remain foreign to repressive law while contributing to the assurance of social harmony. These are the ones protected by punishments which are merely diffuse." [66]

It is fortunate that Durkheim the scholar and scientist did not let himself be cribbed and confined by Durkheim the methodologist—for if he had not let himself go beyond "juridical rules," there would today be no *Suicide,* no *Elementary Forms of Religious Life,* no *Moral Education,* and even large sections of *The Division of Labor* itself would not have been written.

The main point here is that Durkheim's approach to the study of authority cannot be limited by the processes either of law or of the state. It is in his sharp distinction between society and the state—the distinction made by all pluralists—that it becomes clear how an emphasis on authority is compatible with a political position that, by the standards of that day and this, is incontestably liberal. Only when the individual is securely rooted in a system of social and moral authority is political freedom possible:

> Imagine a being liberated from all external restraint, a despot still more
> absolute than those of which history tells us, a despot that no external power
> can restrain or influence. By definition, the desires of such a being are irre-
> sistible. Shall we say, then, that he is all-powerful? Certainly not, since he
> himself cannot resist his desires. They are masters of him, as of everything else.
> He submits to them; he does not dominate them.[67]

Authority, for Durkheim, is rooted in moral values which ultimately make for legitimacy; otherwise, it is not authority. And freedom is in-

---

[65] *The Division of Labor in Society, op. cit.,* pp. 36-37.
[66] *Ibid.,* p. 110.
[67] *Moral Education . . . , op. cit.,* p. 44.

conceivable save within the context of the rules and norms in which it is defined.

Although the roots of Durkheim's pluralism lie in *The Division of Labor*, his first serious concern with the problem of the individual's relation to social authority and the power of the state is to be found in the final pages of *Suicide*. There he reflects on the measures necessary for a restoration of the kind of authority sufficient to check the moral disorganization of which suicide is a conspicuous manifestation. First to be considered is a possible revival of the extreme penalties which were formerly visited on suicides (e.g., mutilation of the corpse) and their families. But these must be rejected today, for they "would not be tolerated by the public conscience," because suicide "emanates from sentiments respected by public opinion" even if the act itself is not. Given these sentiments, the public would not bring itself to impose harsh measures:

> Our excessive tolerance of suicide is due to the fact that, since the state of mind from which it springs is a general one, we cannot condemn it without condemning ourselves; we are too saturated with it not to excuse it in part.[68]

The family is no solution. It might have been once, but the modern family—the conjugal family—is not only too small to absorb the ills of the human spirit, it has been separated by the forces of modern history from centrality in the economic and political processes that govern man's life and attract his allegiances. The family, far from being a haven for man's fears and inadequacies, is itself in need of the reinforcement that can come only from taking a role in a larger and more relevant form of association—something comparable, functionally, to the ancient but now defunct kindred or extended family. The problem of suicide and the present condition of the conjugal family, Durkheim concludes, are both instances of the modern decline of authority. His treatment of the family and its loss of functional significance must certainly be regarded as among the first—if not *the* first—in what has proved to be a long line of such analyses. Others had distinguished the nuclear family from the extended family, but Durkheim gave it relevance to the problems of contemporary authority and disorganization.

Education is irrelevant to the problem:

> [It] is only the image and reflection of society. It imitates and reproduces the latter in abbreviated form; it does not create it. The evil is moral and deep-seated, and to expect education, which, after all, has but a part of each of its

[68] *Suicide, op. cit.*, p. 371.

students, and for but a short time, to overcome deficiencies in the whole social order is absurd.[69]

The only remedy is

. . . to restore enough consistency to social groups for them to obtain a firmer grip on the individual, and for him to feel himself bound to them. He must feel himself more solidary with a collective existence which precedes him in time, which survives him, and which encompasses him at all points. If this occurs, he will no longer find the only aim of his conduct in himself and, understanding that he is the instrument of a purpose greater than himself, he will see that he is not without significance. Life will resume meaning in his eyes, because it will recover its natural aim and orientation. But what groups are best calculated constantly to reimpress on man this salutary sentiment of solidarity?[70]

Not political society, which is "too far removed from the individual" to affect him uninterruptedly and with sufficient force. The state, in any event, is one of the principal causes of the social atomization and moral emptiness of which suicide is an outcome. Religious society would be hardly more efficacious. Once, yes, but not today when so many currents of secular thought have made it impossible for most persons to return to the dogmatic certitude a religion must have if it is to possess the authority to restrain individuals from suicidal impulses. Roman Catholicism's statistically demonstrable effectiveness in this respect is based on an organizational and intellectual rigidity that would be intolerable, Durkheim thinks, for most persons today. New religions will indeed come into being, but they are certain to be even more liberal in doctrinal matters than the most liberal Protestant sects of the present (and these, as the demographic data show, have virtually no restraining influence).

We are preserved from egoistic suicide, Durkheim concludes, only

. . . insofar as we are socialized; but religions can socialize us only insofar as they refuse us the right of free examination. They no longer have, and probably never will have again, enough authority to wring such a sacrifice from us. . . . Besides, if those who see our only cure in a religious restoration were self-consistent, they would demand the re-establishment of the most archaic religions. For against suicide Judaism preserves better than Catholicism, and Catholicism better than Protestantism.[71]

And, as one is justified in concluding from Durkheim's systematic later study of religion, it is primitive religion—with its total subordination of

[69] *Ibid.*, pp. 372-73.
[70] *Ibid.*, pp. 373-74.
[71] *Ibid.*, p. 376.

the individual—that would be most efficacious of all. In primitive society, where everything is surcharged by the sacred, where all values are set in unremitting contexts of community, suicide—except in its rare, "altruistic" form—is unknown. But modern European society can hardly be supposed capable of returning to this type of religion.

It is in the revival of an adapted form of the gild—that is, in an occupational association specifically adapted to the character of modern industry —that Durkheim finds both the mode of authority and type of membership most likely to supply the social substance now lacking in individual lives. Modern man is encompassed by economic life to a degree unknown in earlier ages. But, at present, "European societies have the alternative either of leaving occupational life unregulated, or of regulating it through the state's mediation, since no other organ exists which can play this role of moderator." [72] Hence, new forms of social organization must be devised to escape the contradiction of a society in which the lives of individuals are regulated but not really ruled by the distant, remote, and impersonal state:

> The only way to resolve this antinomy is to set up a cluster of collective forces outside the state, though subject to its action, whose regulative influence can be exerted with greater variety. Not only will our reconstituted corporations satisfy this condition, but it is hard to see what other groups could do so. For they are close enough to the facts, directly and constantly enough in contact with them, to detect all their nuances, and they should be sufficiently autonomous to be able to respect their diversity. To them, therefore, falls the duty of presiding over companies of insurance, benevolent aid and pensions, the need of which is felt by so many good minds but which we rightly hesitate to place in the hands of the state, already so powerful and awkward.[73]

Such corporations would, in the very relevance of their goals to economic and social needs, wield enough moral authority to restrain the egoistic (and hence suicidogenic) impulses of human beings. Both anomic and egoistic types of suicide would be checked, for the corporation like the medieval gild, would become the center of legitimate moral authority:

> Whenever excited appetites tended to exceed all limits, the corporation would have to decide the share that should equitably revert to each of the cooperative parts. Standing above its own members, it would have all necessary authority to demand indispensable sacrifices and concessions and impose order upon them. By forcing the strongest to use their strength with moderation, by preventing the weakest from endlessly multiplying their protests, by

[72] *Ibid.*, p. 380.
[73] *Ibid.*, p. 380.

recalling both to the sense of their reciprocal duties and the general interest, and by regulating production in certain cases so that it does not degenerate into a morbid fever, it would moderate one set of passions by another, and permit their appeasement by assigning them limits. Thus, a new sort of moral discipline would be established, without which all the scientific discoveries and economic progress in the world would produce only malcontents.[74]

It is important that these new structures be granted a measure of legal authority, for moral authority only follows legal recognition. Historical development, Durkheim writes in a passage of Tocquevillian intensity, has swept away cleanly all older forms of intermediate social organization: "One after another, they have disappeared either through the slow erosion of time or through great disturbances, but without being replaced." [75] Originally kinship, through clan and family, possessed the requisite authority, but it soon ceased to be a political entity and became only the center of private life. Territorial unities—hundreds, villages, communes —gilds, monasteries, and other forms of association followed, but they too have suffered dislocation and atomization:

> The great change brought about by the French Revolution was precisely to carry this leveling to a point hitherto unknown. Not that it improvised this change; the latter had long since been prepared by the progressive centralization to which the old regime had advanced. . . . Since then, the development of means of communication, by massing the populations, has almost eliminated the last traces of the old dispensation. And since what remained of occupational organizations was violently destroyed at the same time, all secondary organizations of social life were done away with.[76]

Only the state has survived the tempest of modern history. (This is the heart of Durkheim's political sociology.) The modern state's action has involved profound paradox. Even as the state has absorbed functions previously embodied in other groups, thus further increasing an already swollen bureaucracy, it has tended—by this very action—to level social ranks and to atomize social groups:

> It has often been said that the state is as intrusive as it is impotent. It makes a sickly attempt to extend itself over all sorts of things which do not belong to it, or which it grasps only by doing them violence. . . . Individuals are made aware of society and of their dependence upon it only through the state. But since this is far from them, it can exert only a distant, discontinuous influence over them; which is why this feeling has neither the necessary

[74] *Ibid.*, p. 383.
[75] *Ibid.*, p. 388.
[76] *Ibid.*, p. 389.

constancy nor strength. . . . Man cannot become attached to higher aims and submit to a rule if he sees nothing above him to which he belongs. To free him from all social pressure is to abandon him to himself and demoralize him. These are really the two characteristics of our moral situation. While the state becomes inflated and hypertrophied in order to obtain a firm enough grip upon individuals, but without succeeding, the latter, without mutual relationships, tumble over one another like so many liquid molecules, encountering no central energy to retain, fix and organize them.[77]

It is in these terms—and they are grand terms: Tocquevillian, Burckhardtian, terms—that Durkheim sets the juridical context for the establishment of his occupational associations. The associations will be units of society—recognized equally by the state, its members, and their families. Being units of society they will have—must have—the grants of legal authority that will render their moral authority sufficient to the necessities of integration and morality.

This aspect of Durkheim's thought has been dealt with at some length for reasons that go beyond the perhaps ephemeral importance of the associations themselves. Irrespective of intrinsic merit, these are now well behind us in terms of historical likelihood. But they have been too often treated as random, more-or-less mutant, fragments of Durkheim's thought. The reverse is true: in these proposals lies the origin and the very essence of his theoretical approach to the problem of authority and power, not merely in modern European society, but in ancient as well as medieval groups, Eastern as well as Western. This was the essence that was to influence a number of brilliant institutional historians. To the works of such men as Gustave Glotz, J. Declareuil, Leon Homo, and Marcel Granet could be added those of others—all of whom found in Durkheim's special conception of individualism and in his dichotomy between social authority and political power a perspective of extraordinary utility in their respective studies. To be sure, the perspective is not original with Durkheim: he inherited it through a continuity that included Tocqueville, von Gierke, and Taine. But it was through the great influence of his own lectures at the Sorbonne and elsewhere that the perspective reached so many.

What is set forth in largely ameliorative context in *Suicide* and in the second edition of *The Division of Labor* is given much more systematic and analytical treatment in the posthumously published *Professional Ethics and Civic Morals*. This is one of the most important of Durkheim's works: *the* most important as far as his political sociology is concerned.

[77] *Ibid.*, p. 389.

The "passion" that it may lack from having been compiled by others is generally compensated for by its breadth, mellowness, and more direct orientation. This book has something of the same relation to *The Division of Labor* in political matters that *The Elementary Forms of Religious Life* has on religious matters. Here, for example, contract is treated in four chapters that greatly broaden and intensify what Durkheim wrote in the earlier work. The same is true of property.

But its greatest importance lies in its sociological treatment of the state in its relation to the person and to the social group. What, for Durkheim, is political society? First, in its normal state, it is pluralistic. Durkheim quotes Montesquieu (the subject of his first dissertation) to the effect that political society involves "intermediary, subordinate, and dependent powers." Without these secondary authorities, the state—except in pathological form—is impossible:

> Far from being in opposition to the social group endowed with sovereign powers and called more specifically the state, the state presupposes their existence; it exists only where they exist. No secondary groups, no political authority—at least no authority that this term can apply to without being inappropriate.[78]

But this is only a part of the picture. For dependent though the normal state is on the secondary authorities that undergird it, there is nevertheless a conflict—sometimes actual, always potential—between the state and these authorities. The individual represents the third point of a triangular relation of forces. His freedom from the state's power, in this perspective, is measured by his absorption in one or more of the secondary authorities—family, church, gild, or whatever it may be. And history shows that, conversely, the individual's protection from the often-overwhelming authorities of these groups is granted and protected by the state through the means of private rights. Private rights are created by the state. This, of course, is an argument that is, amusingly, Rousseauian. "Amusingly," for although the author of *The Social Contract* set the problem of freedom in terms of the state's "emancipation" of the individual from traditional society, he—like others during the Enlightenment, loathed intermediate groups. Durkheim saw in such groups the very basis of a just and stable social order.

This triangular relationship is universal in the history of human societies. In the beginning, it is only latent. Both state and individual

[78] *Professional Ethics* . . . , *op. cit.*, p. 45.

are but dimly conceived realities. It is the social group—clan, tribe, association—that is sovereign:

> In the early stage, the individual personality is lost in the depths of the social mass and then later, by its own effort, breaks away. From being limited and of small regard, the scope of the individual life expands and becomes the exhalted object of moral respect. The individual comes to acquire ever wider rights over his own person and over the possessions to which he has title. . . .[79]

It is interesting to compare this analysis with its roots in *The Division of Labor*. There, in one of the most brilliant paragraphs ever written on power and its relation to individualism, Durkheim reveals an aspect of his mind that is (*mirabile dictu*) as Rousseauian as it is Tocquevillian:

> Rather than dating the effacement of the individual from the institution of a despotic authority, we must, on the contrary, see in this institution the first step made towards individualism. Chiefs are, in fact, the first personalities who emerge from the social mass. Their exceptional situation, putting them beyond the level of others, gives them a distinct physiognomy and accordingly confers individuality upon them. In dominating society, they are no longer forced to follow all its movements. Of course, it is from the group that they derive their power, but once power is organized, it becomes autonomous and makes them capable of personal activity. A source of initiative is thus opened which had not existed before then. There is, hereafter, someone who can produce new things and even in certain measure, deny collective usages. Equilibrium has been broken.[80]

The individual does not break away by his own efforts alone. War and commerce help to create the state, and between state and individual a powerful affinity develops. The history of both Athens and Rome reveals the steady emergence of the individual from tribal society through the help of the also-emerging central state. Indeed, it is the state, historically, that creates the idea of individuality—first in legal terms then, gradually, in economic and moral terms. The famous Cleisthenean reforms in ancient Attica demonstrate this. The individual, released from traditional society, is as necessary to the state's development of jurisdiction and authority as the state is to the individual's achievement of legal, social, and moral identity.

Apart from society (distinguished sharply, be it remembered, from the state), man would not, of course, have the nature that separates him

[79] *Ibid.*, p. 56.
[80] *The Division of Labor in Society, op. cit.*, p. 195.

from the animals. Society has carried man's individual psychic faculties "to a degree of energy and productive capacity immeasurably greater than any they could achieve if they remained isolated one from the other. . . richer by far and more varied than one played out in the single individual alone." [81] But there is another side, a repressive side: "Whilst society thus feeds and enriches the individual nature, it tends, on the other hand, to subject that nature to itself and for the same reason." [82] It is in the nature of every form of association to become despotic unless it is restrained by external forces through their competing claims upon individual allegiance. Until the tight communities of the ancient world were loosened and their members made, in some degree, independent, freedom—as it is known today—was not possible:

> A man is far more free in the midst of a throng than in a small coterie. Hence, it follows that individual diversities can then more easily have play, that collective tyranny declines, and that individualism establishes itself in fact and that, with time, the fact becomes a right.[83]

The only way by which the secondary authorities, old or new, can be restrained from enveloping their individual members and depriving them of the diversity that individualization makes possible is through a greater —a larger—form of association that creates the legal possibility of individual identity, one distinguishable from the social groups to which human beings first belong.

What is taken from the social groups goes in part to the state, becoming lodged in its new system of law, but in part also to individual citizens in the form of prescribed rights. It is in this sense that Durkheim refers to the main function of the state as being "to liberate individual personalities. It is solely because, in holding its constituent societies in check, it prevents them from exerting the repressive influences over the individual that they would otherwise exert." [84]

But Durkheim has not forgotten the quite opposite consequences of the state (emphasized in *Suicide*)—consequences revealed in political hypertrophy and atrophy of society. It is easy for the state itself to become the leveller, the represser, the despot. Unlike the smaller authorities, it cannot, by virtue of its vastness, ever give the individual the sense of community characteristic of the older forms of association—not, that is, without despotic consequences.

[81] *Professional Ethics* . . . , *op. cit.,* p. 60.
[82] *Ibid.,* p. 60.
[83] *Ibid.,* p. 61.
[84] *Ibid.,* pp. 62-63.

The inference to be drawn from this is simply that, if the collective force, the state, is to be the liberator of the individual, it has itself need of some counterbalance; it must be restrained by other collective forces, that is, by those secondary groups we shall discuss later on. . . . . It is not a good thing for the groups to stand alone, nevertheless they have to exist. *And it is out of this conflict of social forces that individual liberties are born.* Here again, we see the significance of these groups, their usefulness is not merely to regulate and govern the interests they are meant to serve. They have a wider purpose; they form one of the conditions essential to the emancipation of the individual.[85]

It is interesting to set this perspective against that put forth a generation earlier by Durkheim's teacher, Fustel de Coulanges, in his brilliant *The Ancient City.* Fustel, though his descriptions of family, clan, and tribe in the early classical city-state reveal matchless sociological insight, failed to sense the historical distinctness of these entities from the state, and was thus prevented—as Glotz has notably emphasized in his study of the Athenian city-state—from appreciating the changing relation of the individual to the two different orders of authority. In Fustel's work, social and political authority are merged, treated as an undiversified manifestation of the absolute state. Fustel is thus blind to the decisive conflict between the social authorities and the political power. He cannot see the latter gradually raising itself from the subordinate, almost negligible, position it occupied in the early history of Athens and Rome to the point where, through its military-based sovereignty, it came to dominate the social authorities and, at the same time, to elevate the status of the individual through its ascription of positive legal rights.

Fustel de Coulanges did not see this, but Durkheim did, and it was largely through Durkheim's recognition of what has been called *the triangular relation* of individual, state, and society that this perspective was to influence a generation of French historians, jurists, and sociologists.

THE RELIGIO-SACRED

Of all Durkheim's perspectives, the most striking—the most radical, given the age in which he lived—is undoubtedly the religio-sacred. His use of religion and the category of the sacred to explain not merely the binding character of the social bond, not merely the origins of human thought and culture, but the very constitution of the human mind, must surely rank as one of the boldest and most brilliant contributions of

[85] *Ibid.,* p. 63.

modern sociology. *The Elementary Forms of Religious Life,* in which
the religio-sacred perspective is given its most detailed expression, is very
probably Durkheim's major work. But the religio-sacred perspective is
by no means limited to this work; it is present also in separate treatments
of property, contract, and authority. The concept of the sacred, like the
concept of authority, is one of the constitutive elements of Durkheim's
analysis of social behavior. That Durkheim regards the sacred as a "trans-
figuration" of society does not mean he considers it a secondary force.
Quite the contrary: in its opposition to the profane, the sacred ranks for
Durkheim as the fundamental state in human thought and morality.

Durkheim shares credit with Weber for having restored religion to a
central role in the study of man. Weber saw religion as an area of
motivation for change in the development of society; Durkheim attributed to it indispensable symbolic and integrative properties in social and
intellectual systems. Each man saw religion as a major and indispensable
area of sociological research. This view marked the culmination of those
nineteenth century intellectual efforts which, beginning with the conservatives, sought to reverse the tide of secular rationalism.

The Enlightenment had regarded religion as little more than a superficial combination of superstition and hieratic tyranny—a part of the
historical past but not an essential aspect of either man's or society's
real nature, and certainly not a necessary hypothesis in the science of
man. Human behavior could be adequately analyzed, the *philosophes*
had argued, by reference to natural elements in man and by impersonal
laws of history; such an analysis had no place for anything as conventional and transient as religious values. The same attitude is to be found
in much nineteenth century thought. The main line of the social sciences
rigorously eschewed religion as either a context or a variable. It accepted
religion as a legacy of the past which would probably endure for a considerable period, but it did not regard religion as relevant to the scientific study of government, economy, or the laws of thought.

A new importance was given to religion and the general area of sacred
values by the conservatives in their reaction to the French Revolution
and the Enlightenment. Their largely polemical and moralistic propositions lead directly to the position that Durkheim took a century later in
his momentous declaration that not only has "religion given birth to all
that is essential in society" but that, apart from a "nonrational, non-
utilitarian scheme of sacred values, no society could possibly hold together." Rarely has religion been so emphatically served as by this anti-
clerical, agnostic, positivist mind!

But although the line of continuity is a straight one, it flows through two intervening figures: Tocqueville and Fustel de Coulanges. Each was responsible for divesting discussions of religion's role in society of their traditional partisan zeal and also for emphasizing the two aspects of religion that were to be given greatest attention by Durkheim. That Durkheim was familiar with the works of Fustel de Coulanges is plain enough from his having sat in the latter's classes as a young man; that he was familiar with those of Tocqueville may be taken for granted: what French moral philosopher was not? From each, Durkheim acquired an important aspect of his own thought on religion and society.

Tocqueville's *Democracy in America* represents the first modern effort to assess systematically and dispassionately the functional significance of religion—not merely in relation to democracy but also in relation to the order and integration of any social system and the structure of the human mind itself. For Tocqueville, the major function of religion is its role as a framework of human belief, one that has enabled man to internalize, in meaningful order, the diversity and empiricism of life:

> In order that society should exist and, a fortiori, that a society should prosper, it is necessary that the minds of all the citizens should be rallied and held together by certain predominant ideas; and this cannot be the case unless each of them sometimes draws his opinions from the common source and consents to accept certain matters of belief already formed. If I now consider man in his isolated capacity, I find that dogmatic belief is not less indispensable to him in order to live alone than it is to enable him to cooperate with his fellows. If man were forced to demonstrate for himself all the truths of which he makes daily use, his task would never end. He would exhaust his strength in preparatory demonstrations without ever advancing beyond them. . . . There is no philosopher in the world so great but that he believes a million things on the faith of other people and accepts a great many more truths than he demonstrates.[86]

Skepticism—even in the provisional, methodological form that Descartes had extolled—is not really possible as a basis of either thought or action. For behind provisional skepticism there must lie conviction regarding the ultimate values of thought—there must lie, indeed, basic patterns of thought that are dogmatic, not methodological. And religion, Tocqueville argues, is the only demonstrable context of this dogma: "When there is no longer any principle of authority in religion any more than in politics, men are speedily frightened at the aspect of this unbounded independence. The constant agitation of all surrounding things

[86] Tocqueville, *Democracy in America, op. cit.*, Vol. II, p. 8.

alarms and exhausts them." From spiritual insecurity, men tend to run
to political refuge, despotism: "As everything is at sea in the sphere of
the mind, they determine at least that the mechanism of society shall be
firm and fixed; and as they cannot resume their ancient belief, they
assume a master." [87] Religion is, then, a structure of belief, one extending
to all aspects of experience, and—far from being an impediment to reason, as the *philosophes* argued—it is the very sinew of reason.

If it is religion's integrative role in thought that Tocqueville stresses,
it is religion's capacity for investing society and culture with a sacred
nature that Fustel de Coulanges so memorably emphasizes. His *The
Ancient City* (1861), an account of the rise and fall of the ancient city-
states of Athens and Rome, was written from a rationalist position nearly
as rigorous as Durkheim's. What made this book unique in that age of
monumental classical scholarship was its single-minded emphasis on religion—and specifically on the sacred—as the prime cause of all that was
foremost in the social, political, and intellectual structure and the vicis-
situdes of these two ancient communities.

It was religion, Fustel de Coulanges concluded in his study, that formed
the foundation of the kinship system: it "established marriage and paternal authority, fixed the order of relationship, and consecrated the
right of property, and the right of inheritance." And from religion came
also

> . . . all the institutions, as well as all the private law, of the ancients. It was
> from this that the city received all its principles, its rules, its usages, and its
> magistracies. But in the course of time, this ancient religion became modified
> or effaced, and private law and political institutions were modified with it.
> Then came a series of revolutions, and social changes regularly followed the
> development of knowledge.[88]

The heart of religion, Fustel emphasized, is not belief or faith or
external authority, but the idea of the sacred; in its first form, the sacred
fire. The sacred fire in each family hearth was, in the beginning, the very
identity of the family:

> The fire ceased to glow upon the altar only when the entire family had
> perished; an extinguished hearth, an extinguished family, were synonomous
> expressions among the ancients. Not everything could be fed into the fire;
> some woods could be, some not. Some stones could be used for preparation
> of the hearth, some not. It was a religious precept that this fire must always

[87] *Ibid.*, Vol. II, p. 12.
[88] Fustel de Coulanges, *The Ancient City*, translated by Willard Small (New York:
Lee and Shepard, Publishers, 1874), p. 12.

remain pure; which meant, literally, that no filthy object ought to be cast upon it, and, figuratively, that no blameworthy deed ought to be committed in its presence.[89]

The essential point of Fustel's work was this: all that was significant in Athenian and Roman social and intellectual history was related originally to the sacred character of the hearth, the sacredness of which, in time, extended to a wider and wider range of objects. When the sacredness of the ancient community declined, sapped by skepticism set in alien contexts of power, the ancient community was no more. Such was Fustel's powerful thesis, one that deeply affected Durkheim.

Durkheim, precisely like Tocqueville, declared religion the origin, not merely of thought, but of the very frame of thought:

> If philosophy and the sciences were born of religion, it is because religion began by taking the place of the sciences and philosophy. But it has been less frequently noticed that religion has not confined itself to enriching the human intellect, formed beforehand, with a certain number of ideas; it has contributed to forming the intellect itself. Men owe to it not only a good part of the substance of their knowledge, but also the form in which this knowledge has been elaborated.[90]

Thus emboldened, Durkheim addressed himself to the ancient problem of the sources of knowledge—specifically, to the problem as it had been brought by the contrasting responses of Hume and Kant in the eighteenth century. How does man acquire his basic categories of thought, his ideas of space, time, causality, and mass? Hume had answered the question in terms of individual experience. Thus—for example—there is, for Hume, no absolute idea of causality, only the additive and experientially acquired notion of "efficient cause" resting on innumerable observations of empirical elements in certain sequence. But, Hume argued, no absolute categorical idea of cause can exist. Kant, radically disagreeing, declared that the categories lie a priori in human thought, that they are the indispensable basis of the assimilation of experience, and that such ideas as causality and time, being a priori, have an authoritativeness that experience alone cannot grant.

Durkheim rejects both views. With Kant, he argues that additive, individual experience alone would never be sufficient to create in a mind the requisite authority over thought that each of these ideas—cause, time, space, and so on—has. But, he would agree with Hume, apriority is not

[89] *Ibid.*, p. 30.
[90] *The Elementary Forms of Religious Life, op. cit.*, p. 9.

so much an explanation as an evasion. Where, then, is one to look?—to
religion, man's oldest and deepest intellectual experience!

Religion, to be sure, is not, for Durkheim, a primary or absolute force.
Society alone has the metaphysical attributes of absoluteness and omni-
potence in explanations of man's conduct and thought. If religion exerts
directive force on the mind, it is only because it is an especially intense
manifestation of the collective mind. Indeed, Durkheim's general conclusion on religion is that religious representations are collective representations, and that what makes religion binding in man's life is not religion
as idea but religion as membership, as communal participation. The
authority of religion is, basically, the authority of society, but it is given
an intensity that no other aspect of social life reveals. Such intensity
emerges from man's ageless division of the world into the sacred and the
profane. Religion is society, but it is a focus of those aspects of society
which are endowed with sacredness. Hence, the nearly limitless influence
of religion on culture and personality, and even on the establishment of
the authority of reason:

> It [the authority of reason] is the very authority of society, transferring
> itself to a certain manner of thought which is the indispensable condition of
> all common action. The necessity with which the categories are imposed upon
> us is not the effect of simple habits whose yoke we could easily throw off with
> a little effort: nor is it a physical or metaphysical necessity, since the cate-
> gories change in different places and times; it is a special sort of moral
> necessity which is to the intellectual life what moral obligation is to the will.[91]

In primitive religious beliefs are found all the principal categories of
thought: cause, force, mass, space, time, and the like. All of them are,
in short, "born in religion and of religion; they are a product of religious
thought." [92]

In what concrete ways is this relation between religion and the categories of thought revealed? Durkheim gives hardly more than a brief
sketch, though it is illuminating. Take, for example, the idea of time.
Everyone is aware of time as something impersonal, binding on his
existence yet clearly transcending it. Everyone has a notion of time in
the abstract and everyone respects its authority over his memory, hopes,
and dreams. How did the conception of abstract, impersonal time arise?
It could not have arisen, according to Durkheim, from simple individual
experience, for then time would have forever remained personal rather

[91] *Ibid.*, pp. 17-18.
[92] *Ibid.*, p. 9.

than impersonal, concrete rather than abstract. The conception of time in the abstract arose—and gained its authority—from the individual's awareness of the intervals marked by communal festivals, by the rites and ceremonies which commemorated events in the life of the community. These imprinted on man's mind the notion of a generalized past, present, and future—and, with it, the notion of a generalized flow of time.

Precisely the same processes operate with the conception of cause. It is in primordial conceptions of the boundless efficacy of society—but made sovereign in man's mind only through religious processes—that the idea of cause as something impersonal, general, and timeless could have arisen. Only in society, Durkheim argues, did there lie something so clearly and incontestably transcending the person and the finiteness of personal experience as to put the stamp of impersonality and imprescriptibility on the idea of cause. What is true of the categories of time and cause is equally true of those of force, mass, space, beauty, the infinite—and all the other conceptions which give structure to human sense data. These conceptions alone make abstract thought possible, and they could never have attained the requisite degree of intellectual authority they possess from individual experience alone.

Even the capacity for classification—the very framework of reflective and abstract thought—comes, Durkheim argues, from the primordial tendency to experience things, not atomistically, as pure sensationism would have it, but within the communal and hierarchical divisions that religion made sacred, made categorical. Classification is, by its very nature, hierarchical: there are "higher" and "lower" orders of fact, value, and proposition. The idea of hierarchy could not, Durkheim thought, have been communicated to man's mind by the raw fact of nature:

> Neither the spectacle of physical nature nor the mechanism of mental associations could furnish them with this knowledge. The hierarchy is exclusively a social affair. It is only in society that there are superiors, inferiors, and equals. . . . It is society that has furnished the outlines which logical thought has filled in.[93]

Considered as epistemology, in the oldest and most fundamental sense, Durkheim's theory of the origins of the categories of thought is no doubt as deficient as any other effort to deal with absolute origins. Critical philosophers—working from either a Humean or a Kantian point of view—have had little difficulty in showing the fallibility not only of Durkheim's own epistemology, but also that of his criticisms of Hume

[93] *Ibid.*, p. 148.

and Kant. But epistemology will be left to the philosophers. What Durkheim's ingenious depiction of the social origins of thought does provide is the groundwork for a sociology of knowledge that has proved very useful, both in the comparative study of cultures—as, for example, Granet on China and Maunier on North Africa—and in the remarkable work of Halbwachs (undoubtedly Durkheim's most brilliant student) on memory. Apart from the impenetrable matter of the ultimate origins of thought and language, Durkheim provides a valuable perspective for the study of historic and comparative representations of the several categories.

To return to the religio-sacred in Durkheim: If religion reduces itself to society, how is this reduction to be seen?—in two ways, Durkheim states. First, by the powerful distinction made by every human group between the sacred and the profane. Here one notes the influence of Fustel's classic work. Durkheim carries the sacred much further, however. Instead of limiting the distinction between the sacred and the profane to primitive or ancient consciousness, as Fustel tended to do, Durkheim makes it crucial and determining for all time. The object, the specific identity, of the sacred may vary from age to age and from people to people, but the category itself is immutable and eternal. Religion, reduced to its essentials, is a society's classification of some things as sacred (beyond the rule of interest and reason) and of other things as profane.

It is important to keep in mind that Durkheim, in distinguishing between the sacred and the profane, is not distinguishing between good and evil. Far from it. There are "sacred" objects limitlessly evil in their conceived relation to man and society, and there are "profane" objects wholly acceptable—even advantageous—to both.

> The division of the world into two domains, the one containing all that is sacred, the other all that is profane, is the distinctive trait of religious thought; the beliefs, myths, dogmas, and legends are either representations or systems of representations which express the nature of sacred things, the virtues and powers which are attributed to them, or their relations with each other and with profane things. But, by sacred things, one must not understand simply those personal beings which are called gods or spirits; a rock, a tree, a spring, a pebble, a piece of wood, a house—in a word, anything—can be sacred. A rite can have this character, in fact, the rite does not exist which does not have it to a certain degree.[94]

Sacred things are, by nature, superior—in dignity and power—to profane things, and particularly is this true in their relation to man himself. Man looks up to them, immolating himself in one degree or other. Man's

[94] *Ibid.,* p. 37.

relation to the sacred is sometimes one of awe, of love, or even of measureless dread; sometimes one of ease and pleasure. Man is not always in a state of expressed inferiority before his gods, for he may joke with and about them, and he may beat the fetish which has caused him mishap. But the superiority of sacred things is assumed nevertheless.

The distinction between the sacred and the profane is absolute:

> In all the history of human thought there exists no other example of two categories of things so profoundly differentiated or so radically opposed to one another. The traditional opposition of good and bad is nothing beside this; for the good and the bad are only two opposed species of the same class, namely morals, just as sickness and health are two different aspects of the same order of facts, life, while the sacred and the profane have always and everywhere been conceived by the human mind as two distinct classes, two worlds between which there is nothing in common.[95]

The absolute and universal nature of the contrast between the sacred and the profane does not mean that things and beings cannot or do not pass from one sphere to the other. The passage quoted, however, highlights the division between the two. Purification rites, as in initiation or eucharistic ceremonies, are the means through which a person or thing passes from the profane state to the sacred. By contrast, the passage from the sacred state to the profane is more often the consequence of an erosion of values or the dislocation of deities and entities by the entrance of new manifestations of the sacred (new religions) or from the spread of skepticism.

The erosion and disappearance of one set of sacred observances is invariably followed by the appearance of new entities or states to which sacred status is granted. There is, Durkheim emphasizes:

> . . . something eternal in religion which is destined to survive all the particular symbols in which religious thought has successively enveloped itself. There can be no society which does not feel the need of upholding and reaffirming at regular intervals the collective sentiments and the collective ideas which make its unity and its personality.[96]

This is also the fate of intellectual and social systems that begin in the most utilitarian or rationalistic circumstances—even those dedicated, in the name of critical reason, to the overthrow of some existing system of sacred values. Durkheim cites the eventuation of political rationalism

[95] *Ibid.,* pp. 38-39.
[96] *Ibid.,* p. 427.

during the French Revolution in worship of the Goddess of Reason, in the establishment of new commemorative festivals.

Durkheim applies the perspective of the sacred and the profane to specific institutions in society in order to show the historical and psychological source of their authority. An example already noted is his use of the sacred with respect to contract. Contract presupposes society, but society gains the authority communicated to the idea of contract only by making contract sacred; hence, the origins of contract lie in ritual. The same applies to property. Whence comes the notion of the right of property?—not, Durkheim argues, from any instinct or sense of self-interest, for these would result only in a desire for aggrandizement, not in a respect for the property of others. And it is this respect which is crucial to the conception of right. Rather, Durkheim concludes, the notion of right of property comes from the sacredness originally diffused in things —some things—and fixed by ritual. His words here are among the finest he wrote anywhere:

> The sacredness diffused in things, which withheld them from any profane appropriation, was conducted by means of a certain definite ritual either to the threshold or to the periphery of the field. It there established something like a girdle of sanctity or sacred encircling mound, protecting the domain from any trespass by outsiders. To cross this zone and enter the little island insulated from the rest of the land by ritual, was reserved to those alone who had carried out the rites, that is, those who had contracted especial bonds with the sacred beings, the original owners of the soil. By degrees, this sacredness residing in the things themselves passed into the persons: they no longer possessed this quality, except indirectly, because they were subject to persons who themselves were sacred. Property, from being collective, became individual.[97]

The idea of the sacred—and, with it, the communal—becomes the basis of Durkheim's interpretation of the character of religion. He rejects the view that religion is defined by belief in gods or transcendent spirits. Nor does he believe its origins can be made synonomous with those of magic. And it is his development of the distinction between religion and magic that forms the heart of Durkheim's theory. Characteristically he makes the distinction between religion and magic in terms of the group and its relative value to each.

Religious beliefs, Durkheim maintains,

> . . . are always common to a determined group, which makes profession of adhering to them and of practicing the rites connected with them. They are

[97] *Professional Ethics* . . . , *op. cit.*, p. 171.

not merely received individually by all the members of the group; they are something belonging to the group, and they make its unit. The individuals which compose it feel themselves united to each other by the simple fact that they have a common faith. A society whose members are united by the fact that they think in the same way in regard to the sacred world and its relations with the profane world, and by the fact that they translate these common ideas into common practice is what is called a church. In all history we do not find a single religion without a church.[98]

Very different is the case with magic. Magic can be—and often is—diffused throughout considerable sections of the populations, and among some peoples it has as many adherents as religion.

> But it does not result in binding together those who adhere to it, nor in uniting them into a group leading a common life. *There is no church of magic.* Between the magician and the individuals who consult him, as between those individuals themselves, there are no lasting bonds which make them members of the moral community, comparable to that formed by the believers in the same god or the observers of the same cult. The magician has a clientele and not a church, and it is very possible that his clients have no other relations between each other, or even do not know each other; even the relations which they have with him are generally accidental and transient; they are just like those of a sick man with his physician.[99]

This distinction between magic and religion has been sharply criticized by ethnologists, chiefly by the late Robert Lowie. Of concern here, however, is not the "rightness" or "wrongness" of Durkheim's views of magic—and whether or not it universally dispenses with the group; rather, it is Durkheim's emphasis on the collective, communal character of religion. The essence of religion is the community of believers, the indispensable feeling of collective oneness in worship and faith. To the possible objection that religion is also, demonstrably, a matter of individual faith—of personal cult—Durkheim replies:

> [T]hese individual cults are not distinct and autonomous religious systems, but merely aspects of the common religion of the whole church, of which the individuals are the members. . . . In a word, it is the church of which he is a member which teaches the individual that these personal gods are, what their function is, how he should enter into relations with them, and how he should honor them.[100]

[98] *The Elementary Forms of Religious Life, op. cit.,* p. 44.
[99] *Ibid.,* p. 44.
[100] *Ibid.,* pp. 46, 425.

The supposition that religion is, as Protestants and secularists alike have argued, something basically individual "misunderstands the fundamental conditions of religious life."

Durkheim is as critical of rationalist explanations of religion as any religious conservative might be:

> The theorists who have undertaken to explain religion in rational terms have generally seen it before all else a system of ideas, corresponding to some predetermined object. This object has been conceived in a multitude of ways: nature, the infinite, the unknowable, the ideal, and so on; these differences matter little.[101]

In such theories, conceptions and beliefs are considered as the essential elements. Religious rites, from this point of view, appear to be "only an external translation, contingent and material, of these internal states which alone pass as having any intrinsic value."[102]

But, Durkheim notes shrewdly, this appraisal of religion, made by outsiders, is very different from that made by individuals who are within the compass of religion and committed to it. For such individuals, the essence of religion is not what it says about things—external or internal—but what it does toward making action possible, life endurable:

> The believer who has communicated with his god is not merely a man who sees new truths of which the unbeliever is ignorant; he is a man who is *stronger*. He feels within him more force, either to endure the trials of existence, or to conquer them.[103]

The first article of belief, where belief is explicit, may well be belief in salvation; but this idea could never have acquired its transforming meaning or profound human sustenance apart from its place in a community of acts, of observances, of rites.

It is, therefore, the cult that is fundamental. According to Durkheim anyone who has ever "really practiced" a religion knows

> . . . it is the cult which gives rise to those impressions of joy, of interior peace, of serenity, of enthusiasm, which are, for the believer, an experimental proof of his beliefs. The cult is not simply a system of signs by which the faith is outwardly translated; it is a collection of the means by which this is created and recreated periodically.[104]

[101] *Ibid.*, p. 416.
[103] *Ibid.*, p. 416.
[108] *Ibid.*, p. 416.
[204] *Ibid.*, p. 417.

Durkheim concludes the long passage (part of which is quoted above) by declaring: "Our entire study rests on the postulate that the unanimous sentiment of the believers of all times cannot be purely illusory." In short, the sociology of religion must begin with religion as it is practiced, as it is experienced, as it *is*—as far as objective observation can convey it. From Durkheim's point of view, the critical rationalists who have sought to dismiss religion as a tissue of superstitions, "expendable" once men are correctly informed, are as much in error as those theologians—especially of the Protestant faith—who have endeavored to express its nature in terms of creed and dogma. Religion is community—cult—or it is nothing but a precarious assemblage of impressions and words with no power to integrate and transfigure.

Every cult presents a double aspect: one, negative; the other, positive. Although the two aspects are inseparable, they can be distinguished. Both aspects flow from the all-important separation of the sacred and the profane:

> A whole group of rites has the object of realizing this state of separation which is essential. Since their function is to prevent undue mixings and to keep one of these two domains from encroaching upon the other, they are only able to impose abstentions or negative acts. Therefore, we propose to give the name negative cult to the system formed by these special rites. They do not prescribe certain acts to the faithful, but confine themselves to forbidding certain ways of acting; so they all take the form of interdictions, or as is commonly said by ethnographers, of *taboos*.[105]

The function of the negative cult is to free man from contamination—or possible contamination—by the profane in order that he may be put in position to achieve the sacred; hence, the value placed upon acts (often extreme) of self-abasement, self-denial, or rigorous asceticism.

> [But] . . . whatever the importance of the negative cult may be . . . it does not contain its reason for existence in itself; it introduces one to the religious life, but it supposes this more than it constitutes it. If it orders the worshipper to flee from the profane world, it is to bring him near to the sacred world. Men have never thought that their duties toward religious forces might be reduced to a simple abstinence from all commerce; they have always believed that they upheld positive and bilateral relations with them, whose regulation and organization is the function of a group of ritual practices. To this special system of rites we give the name of *positive cult*.[106]

[105] *Ibid.*, pp. 299-300.
[106] *Ibid.*, p. 326.

In the positive cult is effected the relationship of god and man that is, Durkheim emphasizes, a reciprocal one. Unlike such observers as Robertson Smith, who defined the chief function of the cult as that of uniting men, Durkheim points out that the cult is as important to the gods as to men themselves—for (and here again is the essence of Durkheim's entire system of sociology) the gods are but manifestations or personifications of society:

> We now see the real reason why the gods cannot do without their worshippers any more than these can do without their gods; it is because society, of which the gods are only a symbolic expression, cannot do without individuals any more than these can do without society. Here we touch the solid rock upon which all the cults are built and which has caused their persistence ever since human societies have existed.[107]

The cult is cellular to religion and constitutive to society as a whole. Without the cult, Durkheim declares, society would weaken. The first effect of religious ceremonies is to put the group's members into action: "to multiply the relations between them and to make them more intimate with one another. By this very fact, the content of their consciousness is changed." Ordinarily, in utilitarian or "profane" activities, there is a strong tendency for individualism—or even divisiveness—to operate among men, thus weakening the web of society. But when the cult exists and rituals are celebrated, men's thoughts are centered upon

> . . . their common beliefs, their common traditions, the memory of their ancestors, the collective idea of which they are the incarnation; in a word, upon social things. . . . The spark of social being which each bears within him necessarily participates in this collective renovation. The individual soul is regenerated, too, by being dipped again in the sources from which its life came; consequently, it feels itself stronger, more fully master of itself, less dependent upon physical necessities.[108]

Here, then, is the context within which religious rites become crucial to the sociologist: they are the visible manifestation of a communion of spirits, of a coalescence of ideas and faiths. Two essential rites are *sacrifice* and *imitation*. The first, through some mode of transubstantiation, symbolically bridges the gap between the profane and the sacred. The second, by focusing upon an ideal conception, be it totem or god, supplies the means whereby men may emulate the ideal and thus be spiritually

[107] *Ibid.*, p. 347.
[108] *Ibid.*, pp. 348-49.

and morally elevated. The idea or category of cause originates in the human mind through the performance and use of imitative rites.

Beyond these are two other types of rite, which Durkheim calls, respectively, *representative* and *piacular*. The primary function of representative rites is to commemorate the group's continuity with past and future, emphasizing—through sacred observances—the links each living member has both with history and with posterity. It is thus that totemic identification with animals or plants is born. Out of these representative rites also come, in time, esthetic and recreational activities—dramatic pageants and games—which give the rites added purpose. The gradual disengagement of these activities from the original religious matrix constitutes one important phase of the secularization of culture. Of them, Durkheim writes:

> Not only do they employ the same processes as the real drama, but they also pursue an end of the same sort: being foreign to all utilitarian ends, they make men forget the real world and transport them into another where their imagination is more at ease; they distract. They sometimes even go so far as to have the outward appearance of a recreation: the assistants may be seen laughing and amusing themselves openly.[109]

Piacular rites introduce another element: the notion of sadness, of fear, of tragedy. All the other rites—sacrificial, imitative, and representative— have one thing in common: "they are all performed in a state of confidence, joy, and even enthusiasm." But there are also rites which are performed in a spirit of unease, of latent pessimism, of apprehension. These Durkheim summarizes under the heading of *piaculum*—that is, "expiation"—the ritual cleansing of man from his sins or his affronts to the sacred powers:

> Every misfortune, everything of evil omen, everything that inspires sentiments of sorrow or fear necessitates a *piaculum,* and is therefore called *piacular.* So this word seems very well adapted for designating the rites which are celebrated by those in a state of uneasiness or sadness.[110]

Between the joyful rites and the piacular, there is, of course, deep affinity. The two poles of religious life correspond to the two states between which any society must oscillate.

> Between the propitiously sacred and the unpropitiously sacred there is the same contrast as between the states of collective well-being and ill-being.

[109] *Ibid.,* p. 380.
[110] *Ibid.,* p. 389.

But since both are equally collective, there is, between the mythological constructions symbolizing them, an intimate kinship of nature. The sentiments held in common vary from extreme dejection to extreme joy, from painful irritation to ecstatic enthusiasm, but in any case there is a communion of minds and a mutual comfort resulting from this communion.[111]

The functional value that Durkheim gives to sorrow in individual life has already been noted. Only in his oscillation between sorrow and joy is man made human. So it is with the oscillation between ritual states of spiritual deliverance and spiritual abasement: each is necessary to the other; both are necessary to religion and to society. The sense of sin (enforced by piacular rites) is as important to social integration as the commission of crimes (in due proportion), which is the only force that can cause the mobilization of moral values—the warp of society and of human conscience.

Precisely as he makes religion into a manifestation of society and its crucial phases, Durkheim makes society, in turn, depend upon a nonrational, supraindividual state of mind that can only be called *religious.* Between religion and society there is a functional interplay. It is only because society attains, through sacred-making processes, a limitless majesty over man that the development of his own distinctive qualities of personality and mind becomes possible. These include man's most profoundly rational, as well as his deepest emotional, qualities. Even logic and its laws are premised upon society:

> It is under the form of collective thought that impersonal thought is, for the first time, revealed to humanity; we cannot see by what other way this revelation could have been made. From the mere fact that society exists there is also, outside of the individual sensations and images, a whole system of representations which enjoy marvelous properties. By means of them, men understand each other and intelligences grasp each other. They have within them a sort of force or moral ascendancy, in virtue of which they impose themselves upon individual minds. . . . Hence, the individual at least obscurely takes account of the fact that above his private ideas there is a world of absolute ideas according to which he must shape his own; he catches a glimpse of a whole intellectual kingdom in which he participates, but which is greater than he. This is the first intuition of the realm of truth. . . . Thus the faculty of conception has individualized itself. But to understand its origins and function, it must be attached to the social conditions upon which it depends.[112]

The cult and its rites form the essential and distinctive elements of religion. But also present in religion are speculative and interpretative

[111] *Ibid.,* pp. 413-14.
[112] *Ibid.,* p. 437.

ideas—ideas that touch upon cosmology, morality, and the nature of society and of man. Here, and here alone, Durkheim says, may conflict between religion and science occur, for science is—by its nature—both a successor and rival of religion in these specific matters. The gradual recession of religion as an explanatory idea may be observed historically in area after area of man's speculative interest. First, it is the physical world—the stars, the mountains, water, subhuman organisms—that is given over to the secular mind of the scientist. His findings, at first inevitably antireligious, are gradually granted exemption from the dominion of religion. Then it is the nature of man—his behavior and his mind—that is relinquished. But this is attended historically by more conflict, for here scientists are dealing with souls and "it is, before all else, over souls that the god of the Christians aspires to reign." That is why the idea of submitting the psychic life to science led for a long time to a feeling of profanation, and is even today repugnant to many minds: "[T]he world of religious and moral life is still forbidden. The great majority of men continue to believe that here there is an order of things which the mind cannot penetrate except by very special ways." [113]

It is the functional similarity of religion and science, so far as man's understanding of—and belonging to—the world is concerned, that insures a certain amount of conflict between religion and science. Religion can never escape a certain speculative function in physical and social matters of cause and substance, even though cult and rite are its true forms. Conversely, science—though the speculative or interpretative function is its primary one—cannot escape a certain degree of ritualization that follows from its institutional character and from its ever-rising position in society's hierarchy of values:

> We have said that there is something eternal in religion: it is the cult and the faith. Men cannot celebrate ceremonies for which they see no reason, nor can they accept a faith which they in no way understand. . . . Science is fragmentary and incomplete; it advances but slowly and is never finished; but life cannot wait. The theories which are destined to make men live and act are, therefore, obliged to pass science and complete it prematurely.[114]

But the authority of science was established, and it has had to be reckoned with:

> From now on, faith no longer exercises the same hegemony as formerly over the system of ideas that we may continue to call religion. A rival power rises

[113] *Ibid.*, p. 430.
[114] *Ibid.*, p. 431.

up before it which, being born of it, ever after submits it to its criticism and control. And everything makes us foresee that this control will constantly become more extended and efficient, while no limit can be assigned to its future influence.[115]

Durkheim's relation to developmentalism is a good deal closer than might be inferred from those treatments that have emphasized his "social statics" or that have placed him squarely among the critics chiefly responsible for the "downfall" of evolutionism in the social sciences. Admittedly, Durkheim's mature work reveals none of the preoccupation with long vistas of evolutionary change that so conspicuously marks the works of Spencer, Ward, Giddings, Hobhouse, and others of his period. And it is also true that his major work gives so much attention to the processes manifest in stability and fixity that its author might easily be thought of as altogether indifferent to social development. But Durkheim's work as a whole presents a very clear picture of the social order regarded as in the process of change and development, and each of his main works deals with a different aspect of this process.

What is meant by *development?* It is a series of changes that proceed in patterned and sequential fashion; that is, it is *process.* But *development* is more than *process.* As the idea has been consistently used for more than two millennia in the West, *development* also means *change that proceeds from internal forces,* through an unfolding of qualities that are resident—or presumed to be resident—in the entity. External agencies may and do affect development—accelerate or diminish it, nourish it —but the essential motive power comes from within, and the actual course followed in the process of development is determined by what is within. Potentiality becomes, in successive stages of maturity, actuality. The essence of development is fulfillment, actualization—the manifestation of that which is latent or germinal.

To assume that a thing is capable of development is to assume that it has life or a state of being analogous to life. Hence, the archetype of development, in logic and in the actual history of the idea in the West, is growth: the growth of a plant or of an organism. Here, clearly and irrefutably, are revealed the essential elements of development: a seed-like origin containing all potentialities of future structure; successive and denotable stages of change; and, finally, an end or a final form that gives

[115] *Ibid.,* p. 431.

meaning or purpose to the whole process. External forces—climate, nourishment, unpredictable events, catastrophes—affect the process, but the fundamental and directive influence comes from within the organism itself. The study of an organism is an examination of its inner nature—an inner nature that is the final explanation of the forms of change revealed in the growth cycle. Thus physiology is, in its literal etymology, the understanding of the nature of a thing—a nature presumed to be in the process of becoming, of realization, through internal forces. Emphases in the idea of development vary from age to age and from writer to writer, especially in the social sciences.

Development, like any major idea, is a perspective. It is a conceptual framework, one in which certain characteristic questions lie ready for the asking, depending upon the special interests of the investigator. Thus, if one assumes that society or any of its institutions is in the process of development, any one or all of the following questions can be asked: (1) What is the origin, or the early conditions or states, from which all succeeding conditions and states have emerged? (2) What are the *stages,* or phases of development, that intervene between original conditions and the present? (3) What are the causes of the process of development? Are they external—to be found in wars, invasions, climate, and so on? Or are they internal—to be discovered in the structure of the thing itself? (4) What is the significance, the meaning, the "direction" of development?

All these questions are integral elements of the perspective of developmentalism. It is short-sighted and incomplete to assume that this perspective is limited to works (such as those of a Spencer or a Marx) that set out to identify unilinear stages in the process. If sociologists today pay little attention to the long, unilinear vistas of the past that marked so many nineteenth century works, they nevertheless have a continuing interest in "stages" of development in such matters as economic growth and in the "causes" and "mechanisms" of change considered internal to social systems. With few exceptions, sociologists deal with the problem of change largely in terms of a search for the self-resident, self-generative forces that the developmental perspective has always emphasized.

How does Durkheim's thought fit the pattern just described? The author of *Suicide* and *The Elementary Forms of Religious Life* could not, certainly, be considered an evolutionist in the ordinary sense of the term, but this does not mean that the assumptions and interests of evolutionism passed him by entirely. Certainly Durkheim himself did not think they had. There is scarcely an institution or group that he does not place within the framework of developmentalism. *The Division of Labor* is only the most obvious example; it is, like dozens of other works written in that period, an effort to explain the present in terms of the development of society: in this instance, the development of moral solidarity. That this work proved to be the point of departure for much more than developmentalism in Durkheim's thought, and in the thought of his students, in no way belies the truth of this statement. Not only social solidarity, but also kinship, property, contract, the categories of the human mind, religion—all are couched in a framework that is as clearly premised on the reality of social evolution as anything to be found in Marx, Spencer, or Ward. In this respect, Durkheim is much closer to the evolutionary tradition in nineteenth century sociology than either Weber or Simmel, each of whom combined social analysis, not with developmentalism (in the strict sense of the term), but with history—comparative history.

Durkheim's achievement is that, although accepting the framework of developmentalism (including its search for origins, comparative stages, and endemic causes), he was yet able to deal with problems of social cohesion, personality, authority, and religion in ways that have left his work as relevant to the interests of our own age as though he had approached these problems directly.

Four points are raised by Durkheim within the perspective of development: (1) the search for origins; (2) the recapitulation of stages; (3) the causes of development; and (4) the trend or direction of the assumed development.

The problem of origins. The first point to emphasize is that Durkheim seems to have accepted, as completely as any social evolutionist in his century, the validity of what had come to be known as *the comparative method.* This, in nineteenth century ethnography, meant much more than simple comparison: it meant that the institutions and norms of coexisting preliterate peoples could be generally regarded as clues to the primitive origins of advanced societies; and it also meant that the logical order of simple-to-complex in which existing peoples could be placed was, in all probability, the actual order of development undergone by advanced societies. The comparative method was not born in the nineteenth century, but it was most widely used and accepted during that period. Almost every social scientist in the age regarded preliterate peoples as, in one degree or another, "living ancestors."

Nowhere in Durkheim's work can one find the kind of exploitation of the comparative method exhibited in the writings of Spencer, Ward, and nearly all the ethnologists. Few were as ingenuous, even childlike, in the telling as Spencer was (in his autobiography he relates how slips of paper, each with an abstracted primitive custom or belief written on it, were arranged in piles on his living-room floor—the arrangement reflecting, in logical order, the assumed development of the institution over an immense period of time). But all of them took for granted the reality of the conclusions drawn from the comparative method. Durkheim was much more sophisticated than most in this respect, but his work too reflects an interest in social origins that remained constant throughout his life.

The interest begins, as has already been seen, in *The Division of Labor*. No purpose would be served here by again reconstructing the argument of this work. It suffices to recall that he viewed mechanical solidarity as the earliest and most primitive form of social organization, and that his illustrations of this phenomenon are drawn from accounts of existing primitive peoples or from studies of the evolution of law based upon "traces" found in earliest legal records. But what is germane here (and too often neglected in the literature on Durkheim) is the fact that he found in primitive life more than simple mechanical solidarity; he found also the beginnings of organic solidarity. Thus, beneath the dominant patterns of early society lie the seeds of modernity. Even in the primitive family, Durkheim notes, there is some degree of division of labor and dim manifestations of restitutive law, of cooperation:

> The history of the family, from its very origins, is only an uninterrupted movement of dissociation in the course of which diverse functions, at first undivided and confounded one with another, have been little by little separated, constituted apart, apportioned among the relatives according to sex, age, relations of dependence, in a way to make each of them a special functionary of domestic society. Far from being only an accessory and secondary phenomenon, this division of familial labor, on the contrary, dominates the entire development of the family.[116]

In the same work, Durkheim attacks the problem of origins even more fundamentally, and in a way that leads directly to his later systematic treatment of this problem in *The Rules of Sociological Method:*

> There are in each of us . . . two consciences: one which is common to our group in its entirety which, consequently, is not ourself, but society living and acting within us; the other, on the contrary, represents that in us which is personal and distinct, that which makes us an individual. . . . There are, here, two contrary forces, one centripetal, the other centrifugal, which cannot flourish at the same time. We cannot, at one and the same time, develop

---

[116] *The Division of Labor in Society, op. cit.,* p. 123.

ourselves in two opposite senses. If we have a lively desire to think and act for ourselves, we cannot be strongly inclined to think and act as others do. If our ideal is to present a singular and personal appearance, we do not want to resemble everybody else.[117]

Conflict between these "two consciences," both of which are aboriginal, is to a very large extent what motivates the whole process of social development.

In *The Elementary Forms of Religious Life* Durkheim gives a nearly matchless account of the need for study of origins and, for that matter, of the evolutionary perspective. In the following passage, he justifies utilization of the materials of primitive religion (specifically, Australian totemism):

> In the first place, we cannot arrive at an understanding of the most recent religions except by following the manner in which they have been progressively composed in history. In fact, historical analysis is the only means of explanation which it is possible to apply to them. It alone enables us to resolve an institution into its constituent elements, for it shows them to us as they are born in time, one after another. On the other hand, by placing every one of them in the condition where it was born, it puts into our hands the only means we have of determining the causes which gave rise to it. Every time that we undertake to explain something human, taken at a given moment in history—be it a religious belief, a moral precept, a legal principle, an esthetic style, or an economic system—it is necessary to go back to its most primitive and simple form, to try to account for the characterization by which it was marked at that time, and then to show how it developed and became complicated little by little, and how it became that which it is at the moment in question.[118]

It would be hard to find, even in the nineteenth century, a more forthright defense of the evolutionary study of origins. Yet it remains true that the long-run significance of Durkheim's study of religion—and that which seems to have impressed itself on his own consciousness—is not so

[117] *Ibid.*, pp. 129-30.
[118] *The Elementary Forms of Religious Life, op. cit.*, p. 3. As I explain in the next paragraph of the text, there is a logical, or taxonomic, as well as developmental, justification given by Durkheim for his interest in primitive forms, but the developmental cast of his thought cannot be disregarded. In an excellent critique of this aspect of Durkheim's thought, Claude Lévi-Strauss appreciatively quotes Mauss as having once said, with Durkheim's approach in mind: "It is easier to study the digestive process in the oyster than in man; but this does not mean that the higher vertebrates were formerly shellfishes." See Lévi-Strauss, "French Sociology," in *Twentieth Century Sociology*, edited by Georges Gurvitch and Wilbert E. Moore (New York: The Philosophical Library, Inc., 1945), p. 527.

much developmental, in the ordinary sense of the term, as it is what can best be thought of as microsociological. In Durkheim's mind, the totemism of the aborigines in Australia was important, not so much for its assumed exemplification of religion in its earliest form, as for its exemplication of religion in its simplest form. It was not so much the primitive origins of religion that interested him, but the discovery of its constitutive elements. Yet it remains true that the idea of development, of unfolding, was a vivid one in his mind.

Stages of development. There is little in Durkheim's work to compare with the imposing sequences of stages that are to be found in the writings of such men as Westermarck, Hobhouse, Frazer, and others who dealt with religion and morality in Durkheim's time. The middle chapters of *The Division of Labor* give some indication of the phases involved in the development of social solidarity. And, after all, this book was conceived as a kind of evolutionary treatise—one in which the relation between mechanical and organic types of solidarity in human history is shown to be genetic as well as sequential. Durkheim provides brief glimpses into the transitional or intermediate types of solidarity that may well have intervened between these two major stages. Durkheim's interest in stages is to be seen in other works, as in the sections of *Professional Ethics and Civil Morals* concerned with the development of contract and property. Contract, for example, is explained in terms of stages: ritual contract, real contract, consensual contract, and finally just contract. The usual illustrations, drawn from preliterate and ancient peoples, are provided. The same approach characterizes his treatment of property. Durkheim was, in short, no stranger to the nineteenth century's fascination with stages of social evolution.

But the fact remains that, for Durkheim, analytical and taxonomic concerns triumph over those of genetic succession. He accepted, in large measure, the nineteenth century's ethnographic concern with stages, but it is essential to recognize his conceptual conversion of stages into types. The contrast between past and present is a major aspect of Durkheim's methodology, but in most of his work this contrast has background, rather than foreground, importance. More to the point, Durkheim even denies the reality of developmental continuity in the history of social types. In this he was exceptional in his age.

The causes of development and change. The nineteenth century search for causes took two main forms: external and internal. Not often—indeed, if ever—are these completely separated in the works of a single writer, but they have to be distinguished from one another. In the main line of sociology—from Comte, through Tocqueville and Marx, to Durkheim and Weber—it is the effort to descry internal causes of change that is foremost: to find in the structure, in processes of common and continuing nature, the real motive forces of change.

Here Darwin's *Origin of the Species* took greatest effect—not, certainly, in establishing the idea of evolution (for this had been deeply embedded in social thought long before 1859), but in increasing the scientific prestige of a single principle of explanation of long-run change. Change was expressed in terms of processes ("variations," in Darwin's case) that are to be found in the present as well as in the past and may also be confidently assumed for the future. Attention is directed—not toward external events and impacts never to be repeated—but toward internal processes that are inalienable aspects of the structure itself—be it the biological species, the family, or the society as a whole.

Durkheim's reference to the two consciences in man—the collective and the individual—and the conflict between them has already been noted. It is this type of cause, rather than that embodied in his not-very-successful effort to deal with demographic and social density in *The Division of Labor*, that became of increasing interest to him and that was to register greatest effect on subsequent sociological and ethnological thought. The conflict between the two consciences is not, to be sure, a mode of psychological explanation. In his important chapter on the explanation of social facts in *The Rules of Sociological Method*, Durkheim is emphatic on this point. Social evolution, he insists, does not have its origin in the psychological constitution of man, for "we would then have to admit that its motivating force is some inner spring of human nature." He dismisses both Comte and Spencer on this matter, finding in each man an appeal to what is no more, no less, than instinct. Hence, the famous principle: *"The determining cause of a social fact should be sought among the social facts preceding it and not among the states of the individual consciousness."*

And, further, "the function of a social fact ought always to be sought in its relation to some social end." The emphasis here, in context, is on the word *social*. Any misplaced psychological effort to reduce social function to psychogenic has no support from Durkheim:

> Psychological training, more than biological training, constitutes . . . a valuable lesson for the sociologist; but it will not be useful to him except on the condition that he emancipate himself from it. . . . He must abandon psychology as the center of his operations, as the point of departure for his excursions into the sociological world to which they must always return.

This leads directly to the crux of the problem of origins in the study of social change: "The first origins of all social processes of any importance should be sought in the internal constitution of the social group." It is clear, Durkheim argues, that "the impulsion which determines social transformations can come from neither the material nor the immaterial, for neither possesses a motivating power." What is important to the sociologist is what Durkheim calls *the social or human milieu*. The principal task of the investigator ought to be that of discovering "the different aspects of this milieu which can exert some influence on the course of social phenomena." *Milieu* must be understood as comprising human beings and cultural patterns, as well as strictly social processes of interaction.

Because a number of sociologists have interpreted this—both in their commentaries and in their empirical work—as sanction for confining attention to what lies solely within the group, one point should be emphasized: Durkheim makes plain that the milieu goes beyond the simple structure of the group. The group has, to be sure, a milieu of its own (Durkheim calls it *a special milieu*), and study of this milieu—whether in a family or a profession—is vital:

> Nevertheless, the action of these particular milieux could not have the importance of the general milieu, for they are themselves subject to the influence of the latter. We must always return to the general milieu. The pressure it exerts on these partial groups modifies their organization.[119]

What is the relation of the social milieu to history? Durkheim is somewhat ambiguous on this point. *The Division of Labor*—not to mention his studies of religion, contract, and property—suggests the importance he gave to examining past stages of development for the causal light they throw on the present. But *The Rules of Sociological Method* provides an incisive critique of this. Durkheim denies the possibility of discerning any "inherent tendency which impels humanity ceaselessly to exceed its achievements," and he denies with equal emphasis that there is any filiative relation among past stages: "The antecedent state does not produce the subsequent one; the relation between them is purely chronological." If all principal causes of social events lay in the past, "each society would no longer be anything but the prolongation of its predecessor, and the different societies would lose their individuality and would become only diverse moments of one and the same evolution." It can indeed be said, Durkheim goes on,

[119] *The Rules of Sociological Method, op. cit.*

. . . that certain conditions have succeeded one another up to the present, but not in what order they will henceforth succeed one another, since the cause on which they are supposed to depend is not scientifically determined or determinable. Ordinarily, it is true, we admit that evolution will take the same direction as in the past; but this is a mere postulate. Nothing assures us that the overt phenomena express so completely the nature of this tendency that we may be able to foretell the objective to which this tendency aspires as distinct from those through which it has successively passed. Why, indeed, should the direction it follows be rectilinear? [120]

It is this brilliant analysis that has often led to the supposition that Durkheim's thought is totally removed from the developmental perspective. Clearly, it is not. The approach he takes in some of his empirical studies cannot be overlooked, but his critique of the hypothesis of filiation—of each stage regarded as bearing the seeds of its successor—strikes at the heart of the whole philosophy of change found in such diverse minds as Comte, Marx, Spencer, and Ward. Had Durkheim chosen to follow up this critique in more intensive detail, had he chosen to elaborate on the concept of milieu, we should be the richer today in our studies of change and also freed of the common but baseless interpretation of Durkheim that is used as sanction for the extraction of efficient causes of change from intragroup relations alone.

The direction of development. Among the major currents of thought that Durkheim opposed by the nature of his conclusions was the concept of moral progress. The nineteenth century was, as many historians have stressed, pre-eminently an age of optimism about man's moral development, his happiness, his capacity for living with others and with himself. Today it is clear that, along with the massive optimism of the age, there were also expressions of thought in which pessimism was the reigning note. Tocqueville, Burckhardt, and Weber could regard the future with dark misgiving. There were others: Lamennais, Dostoievski, Heine, Nietzsche, Kierkegaard, and—across the Atlantic—Melville and Hawthorne. Diverse and distinctive though these minds were, they had in common a view of the present, in relation to the past and to the future, that separated them sharply from most of their contemporaries and that marks them as precursors of the twentieth century.

In European sociology a certain somberness of mind is notable. Tocqueville, in his *Democracy in America* (not to mention letters written in late life), takes a view of the future that is anything but sanguine. Weber

[120] *Ibid.* The quotations on causation and explanation are drawn from the section between pp. 109 and 120.

and Simmel reveal, in explicit statement as well as emphasis, a distrust of, or unease with, modernism. Without succumbing to defeat or total renunciation, they nevertheless display an alienated quality in their work. They saw, or could see on frequent occasions, in the present a tragic inversion of the very forces that had ushered in the modern world, that had liberated man from centuries-old oppression and superstition. It was a subversion in which individualism was becoming atomism and democratic will a new despotism (Tocqueville); in which rationalism was producing a new, bureaucratic type of regimentation (Weber); in which the urban-pecuniary economy was bringing about a displacement of man's own self (Simmel). For the major European sociologists of the period, the direction of Western social development was mixed, to say the least.

Durkheim falls very clearly in the company of Tocqueville, Weber, and Simmel in this respect. Modern development, he writes, "has swept cleanly away all the older forms of organization. One after another they have disappeared either through the slow erosion of time or through great disturbance, but without being replaced." Class, kindred, parish—all have disappeared or weakened under the massive forces of modern individualism and political centralization. Durkheim sees no likelihood of either kinship or religion becoming vital forces in human life once more, and he specifically disavows the state as the means of restoring moral or social organization. According to Durkheim, it is in the establishment of occupational organizations alone that hope lies, but it is a mark of his melancholy view of history that he explicitly places this mode of reform against the tides of "progress" and concedes it to have somewhat more relation to the medieval and ancient worlds than to anything that contemporary history seemed to be spawning. There is a broad gulf between the view of history found in the progressive writings of his day—a view resting on faith in history's capacity to resolve all organizational problems —and Durkheim's almost melancholy envisagement of the modern age.

A host of passages in Durkheim's works supports the conclusion that he considered the cohesive and stabilizing forces of European society to be undergoing disintegration—transitory, perhaps, in the longest view, but not the less real and ominous. Suicide is taken by Durkheim as the index of a very deep flaw in the social constitution; that is, "the general unrest of contemporary societies." In moderate degree suicide is normal, but in contemporary civilization "the exceptionally high number of voluntary deaths manifests the state of deep disturbance from which civilized societies are suffering, and bears witness to its gravity." [121]

---

[121] *Suicide, op. cit.,* p. 391. Lewis Coser has suggested that Durkheim's view of his

He refers to the "currents of depression and disillusionment emanating from no particular individual but expressing society's state of disintegration." Such currents "reflect the relaxation of social bonds, a sort of collective asthenia, or social malaise, just as individual sadness, when chronic, in its way reflects the poor organic state of the individual." Such currents are collective; that is, social. And because they are social "they have, by virtue of their origin, an authority which they impose upon the individual and they drive him vigorously on the way to which he is already inclined by the state of moral distress directly aroused in him by the disintegration of society." [122] Admittedly, a certain incidence of suicide, like a certain incidence of crime, is inherent in the conditions which also produce high culture—the arts, letters, and the liberal professions. But suicide has come to mark in our society, Durkheim concludes, "not the increasing brilliancy of our civilization, but a state of crisis and perturbation not to be prolonged with impunity." [123]

Durkheim's melancholy does not rest on the incidence of suicide alone. In *The Division of Labor,* he had noted the nearly inverse relation between the development of culture and human happiness. States of boredom, anxiety, and despair are relatively unknown in a primitive or simple society, he observed, for the common causes of these states are largely absent. In civilized societies they mount and, with them, endemic unhappiness. One should not conclude, Durkheim emphasizes, that progress causes these states; more likely they are concomitant: "But this concomitance is sufficient to prove that progress does not greatly increase our happiness, since the latter decreases, and in very grave proportions, at the very moment when the division of labor is developing with an energy and rapidity never known before." [124]

Durkheim's attitude toward happiness has little in common with the reigning notions of his day. Far from seeing in happiness the proper goal of individual and social energies, he deprecates it: "Too cheerful a morality is a loose morality; it is appropriate only to decadent peoples and is found only among them. . . . From certain indications it even seems

---

age may not be different from what Saint-Simon (a prophet of progress nonpareil) termed *a critical age* in contrast to *organic ages*. Coser's insight is a valuable one, even though I do not relinquish my belief that there is more in common between Durkheim's and, say, Burckhardt's view of the future than between Durkheim's and Saint-Simon's. The cultural malaise that enveloped much of European thought in the late nineteenth century—touching both Weber and Durkheim—seems to me a context significantly different from that within which Saint-Simon wrote.

[122] *Ibid.,* p. 214.
[123] *Ibid.,* p. 369.
[124] *The Division of Labor in Society, op. cit.,* p. 250.

that the tendency to a sort of melancholy develops as we rise in the scale of social types." There is a functional necessity in sadness, as there is in crime:

> Man could not live if he were impervious to sadness. Many sorrows can be endured only by being embraced, and the pleasure taken in them naturally has a somewhat melancholy character. So, melancholy is morbid only when it occupies too much place in life; but it is equally morbid for it to be wholly excluded from life.[125]

One can imagine such a sentiment coming from Tocqueville or Weber, but not from Mill or Spencer.

Historical periods like ours, Durkheim observes, are necessarily filled with anxiety and pessimism. For our objectives are Faustian in scope.

> What could be more disillusioning than to proceed toward a terminal point that is nonexistent, since it recedes in the same measure that one advances? . . . This is why historical periods like ours, which have known the malady of infinite aspiration, are necessarily touched with pessimism. Pessimism always accompanies unlimited aspirations. Goethe's Faust may be regarded as representing par excellence this view of the infinite. And it is not without reason that the poet has portrayed him as laboring in continual anguish.[126]

This is precisely the condition that had led Tocqueville to see increasing frustration and unhappiness as the consequence of democracy, and it is the background that Durkheim sees for the general breakdown in social and moral discipline. That he regarded this breakdown as critical is plain enough:

> Indeed, history records no crisis as serious as that in which European societies have been involved for more than a century. Collective discipline in its traditional form has lost its authority, as the divergent tendencies troubling the public conscience and the resulting general anxiety demonstrate.[127]

There are still other ways of assaying the intensity of the modern malaise that has gripped European society: through the proliferation of philosophical systems based on skepticism and materialism. Durkheim compares the modern age in this respect with periods of decadence in ancient Greece and Rome when, similarly, belief-systems arose that reflected loss of faith and membership in society:

> The formation of such great systems is . . . an indication that the current pessimism has reached a degree of abnormal intensity which is due to some

[125] *Suicide, op. cit.,* pp. 365-66.
[126] *Moral Education . . . , op. cit.,* p. 40.
[127] *Ibid.,* p. 101.

disturbances of the social organism. We well know how these systems have recently multiplied. To form a true idea of their number and importance is it not enough to consider the philosophies avowedly of this nature, such as those of Schopenhauer, Hartmann, and so on? We must also consider all the others which derive from the same spirit under different names. The anarchist, the esthete, the mystic, the socialist revolutionary, even if they do not despair of the future, have in common with the pessimist a single sentiment of hatred and disgust for the existing order, a single craving to destroy or to escape from reality. Collective melancholy would not have penetrated consciousness so far if it had not undergone a morbid development. . . .[128]

Such is Durkheim's reaction to an age that his contemporaries—secularists, individualists, Protestants, and progressives alike—were hailing as the onset or at least the harbinger of a new order, a new freedom, a new morality. Durkheim's is clearly an alienated view of modern culture. He is too much the child of modernism himself, too deeply devoted to science and to liberal democracy, to seek refuge in any of the traditionalisms that vain and reactionary politics sought to impose upon France and on Europe in general. But—unlike a great many of his fellow rationalists, fellow liberals, and fellow democrats—he knew that no stable order could be built directly on the intellectual pillars of modernism: until the values of science and liberal democracy were rooted in social contexts as secure and binding as those in which religion and kinship had once been rooted, and until they were endowed with the moral authority —the sacredness—that these more ancient institutions had once known, European society would continue in the state of crisis that would subvert each and every proposed political remedy.

Durkheim's reaction to the sanguine atmosphere of moral progress in his time was, thus, as complete as his reaction to individualism and biologism. Indeed, his concepts of the collective conscience, of the eternal cult, of anomie, and of the functional role of discipline are predicated upon this reaction. To overlook the moral in Durkheim's thought is to overlook the social: they are but two faces of the same coin.

[128] *Suicide, op. cit.,* p. 370.

PART TWO

SELECTED ESSAYS
ON DURKHEIM

DURKHEIM'S
DIVISION OF LABOR IN SOCIETY

ROBERT K. MERTON

DURKHEIM'S *De la division du travail social* has been accorded a belated English translation, forty years after its initial publication.[1] This testimony to the continued esteem with which Durkheim's work is regarded provides the impetus for a reconsideration of the first magnum opus of this hegemonic protagonist of the sociologistic school. The value of such an examination is twofold: it permits a re-estimation of the role played by Durkheim in the development of modern sociological thought, and it brings to a focus several conceptions fundamental to much of contemporary research.

An analysis of the theoretical context in which this work was written is of moment in appreciating its contributions. Deep in the current of the positivistic thought which stemmed from Comte, Durkheim's *Division* embodies many of its characteristic features. It seeks to adopt the methods and criteria of the physical sciences for the determination of those mechanically induced social laws which, under given conditions, obtain with an ineluctable necessity. Explicit in this procedure is, of course, the assumption of the feasibility of so doing and of the susceptivity of social phenomena to such study. The fact that the concept of causation, more markedly perhaps in the social sciences than in the physical, is an epistemologic assumption, a matter of imputation and not of observation, is ignored. Within this positivistic tradition the *Division* is further classifiable as instancing the anti-individualistic, anti-intellectualistic approach. It is an avowed revolt from the individualistic-utilitarian positivism which, finding its prototypes in the systems of Hobbes

From *The American Journal of Sociology*, XL (1934), 319-28. Reprinted by permission of the author and the publisher.

[1] George Simpson, *Émile Durkheim on the Division of Labor in Society* (New York: The Macmillan Company, 1933). Subsequent citations refer to this edition.

and of Locke, characterized so much of English social thought. A radical sociologism seemed to Durkheim to be the one way of maintaining the autonomy of sociology as an independent discipline, and it is to this dominant preoccupation that many of his conceptions are due. Of special significance is the fact that the *Division,* although it adumbrates many ideas which Durkheim subsequently developed in some detail,[2] presents an objective approach, with implicit reservations, from which he later diverged sharply, notably in his *Formes élémentaires de la vie religieuse.*

The peregrinations of the ideas expressed in the *Division* have included this country, but a brief summary is nonetheless desirable to establish the basis of this discussion. The source of social life, maintains Durkheim, is twofold: the similitude of consciousnesses and the division of social labor. In one society-type, which he calls *primitive,* solidarity is induced by a community of representations which gives birth to laws imposing uniform beliefs and practices upon individuals under threat of repressive measures. These repressive laws are external—that is, observable in the positivistic sense—indexes of this "mechanical solidarity." The division of social labor, on the other hand, while it enhances—nay, compels—individuation, also occasions an "organic solidarity," based upon the interdependence of cooperatively functioning individuals and groups. This type of solidarity is indexed by juridical rules defining the nature and relations of functions. These rules may properly be termed *restitutive law,* since their violation involves merely reparative, and not expiatory, consequences. Historically, the movement has been from mechanical to organic solidarity, though the former never disappears completely. The determining cause of this trend is found in the increased size and density of populations with the usual, if not invariable, concomitant, increased social interaction. This so intensifies the struggle for existence that only through progressive differentiation of functions is survival possible for many who otherwise would be doomed to extinction. This continuous trend occurs mechanically through a series of disturbed and re-established social dynamic equilibria.

Now, as previously suggested, Durkheim seeks to combat individualistic positivism which ignores the relevance of social ends as partial determinants of social action. He is, hence, faced with a perturbing dilemma: as a positivist, to admit the irrelevance of ends to a scientific study of society; as an anti-individualist, to indicate the effectiveness of social aims

---

[2] The starting-point of *Le Suicide* is explicit in Book II, Chap. 1, of the *Division; Les Règles de la méthode sociologique,* pp. 349 ff.; and *Les Formes élémentaires . . . ,* pp. 288 ff.

in conditioning social action, and thus in effect to abandon radical positivism. For, if, as positivism would have us believe, logic and science can deal only with empirical facts, with sensa, then a science of social phenomena, on that score alone, becomes impossible, since this attitude relegates to limbo all ends—i.e., subjective anticipations of *future* occurrences—without a consideration of which human behavior becomes inexplicable.[3] Ends, goals, aims, are by definition not logico-experimental data but rather value judgments; and yet an understanding of social phenomena requires a study of their role.[4] This does not involve a determinism-teleology embarrassment, but simply notes the fact that subjectively conceived ends—irrespective of their recognition of all the pertinent data in a given situation—as well as "external conditions," influence behavior. To ban ends as "improper" for scientific study is not to exempt sociology from metaphysics, but to vitiate its findings by a crude and uncriticized metaphysics.[5]

At the time of writing the *Division*, Durkheim was too much the positivist to acknowledge explicitly the full force of this position, but his conscious methodologic doctrines notwithstanding, he surreptitiously slips between the horns of the dilemma and salves his anti-individualistic conscience by dealing with *social* ends. Thus, he indicates quite clearly that if society were simply a resultant of juxtaposed individuals brought into temporary contractual relationships for the satisfaction of their respective immediate interests, that if the typical social relation were the economic, then we should no longer have a society but Hobbes's "state of nature":

> For where interest is the only ruling force each individual finds himself
> in a state of war with every other since nothing comes to modify the egos,

[3] Strangely enough, this position is admitted by the positivist, V. Pareto. See his *Traité de sociologie générale* (Paris, 1917), II, pp. 1349 ff. Cf. Talcott Parsons, "Some Reflections on 'The Nature and Significance of Economics.'" *Quarterly Journal of Economics*, XLVIII (1934), 511-45. I am deeply indebted to Dr. Parsons for much of the viewpoint here expressed.

[4] Compare Heinrich Rickert, *Kulturwissenschaft und Naturwissenschaft* (Tübingen: Mohr, 1921), pp. 99 ff. Léon Duguit, whose conceptions of solidarity by similitude and through division of labor closely resemble those of Durkheim, presents a brilliant exposition of the significance of ends for interpretation. This, in spite of his ultra-positivism. See his *L'État, le droit objectif et la loi positive* (Fontemoing, 1901), pp. 33 ff. In this country, the most exact statement of this position is to be found in W. I. Thomas and F. Znaniecki, *The Polish Peasant in Europe and America* (Chicago: University of Chicago Press, 1918-20), particularly in the discussion of social attitudes and "definition of the situation."

[5] Compare C. Hartshorne and P. Weiss (eds.), *Collected Papers of Charles Sanders Pierce* (Cambridge, Mass.: Harvard University Press, 1931), Vol. I, pp. 52 ff.

and any truce in this eternal antagonism would not be of long duration.[6]

This corresponds to Durkheim's description of anomie. But the fact is, he continues, that even in such highly contractual and "individualized" societies as our own, this brutish state of nature does not obtain. What, then, obviates this condition which, were the individualistic approach valid, one would expect to find characterizing a contractual society? It is the "consensus of parts," the integration of individual ends, the social value-complex.[7] This is clearly seen in the legal regulation of contracts between individuals, for although it is true that these contracts are initially a voluntary matter, once begun, they are subject to society as the omnipresent and controlling "third party." Through a system of law, an organ of social control, the accord of individual wills is constrained for the consonance of diffuse social functions. Moreover, in this process, society plays an *active* role, for it determines which obligations are "just"— i.e., [in] accord with the dominant social values—and which need not be enforced. With this incisive analysis, Durkheim refutes one of the basic doctrines of an atomistic sociology, for he finds in the very relation which had been regarded as individualistic par excellence the significant interpenetration of social factors.[8]

His conception is similar to Sumner's "strain toward consistency" and autonomy of the mores and to Goldenweiser's notion of the limit to the discrepancies between the various aspects of a culture. This view of society is linked to an acknowledgment of the previously mentioned role of social ends and to an acceptance of the doctrine of emergence. That social behavior cannot be explained through reference to the behavior of individuals in mere juxtaposition is maintained by both Durkheim and Pareto,[9] and it is precisely this view which is held to justify sociology as a distinct discipline.

In Durkheim's discussion of social ends is a latent antimechanistic trend. For when instruments are fashioned for the attempted attainment

[6] *Division* . . . , pp. 203-204; cf. p. 365.

[7] *Ibid.*, p. 360. Cf. Parsons, *op. cit.*, p. 517.

[8] The distinction between Durkheim's analysis and the social contract theories should thus be quite clear. As Durkheim himself remarked: "*Il n'y a qu'un critique singulièrement superficielle qui pourrait reprocher à notre conception de la contrainte sociale de rééditer les théories de Hobbes et de Machiavel.*" *Règles* . . . , p. 151.

[9] It is particularly striking that Pareto, with his leanings toward empiricism, should adopt this view. *Traité* . . . , Vol. I, p. 26. "*Notez qu'étudier les individus ne veut pas dire que l'on doit considérer plusieurs de ceux-ci mis ensemble, comme une simple somme; ils forment un composé, lequel, à l'égal des composés chimiques, peut avoir des propriétés qui ne sont pas la somme des propriétés des composants.*" This conception is, of course, marked in all of Durkheim's words, but an exposition of it was first given in his *Règles* . . . , p. 126.

of ends, by this very fact conditions are evolved which act not only in the direction of the goals, but react upon and frequently change the value estimations. These new valuations may relieve man from the necessity of accepting the "conditions of existence"—Durkheim's milieu—and acting in the previously determined manner. His "definition of the situation" having changed, his behavior has a new orientation, and mechanistic determinism—based on a knowledge of the *objective* factors—no longer adequately accounts for this behavior. But as is frequently characteristic of mechanistic theorists, Durkheim does not properly distinguish his abstract conceptions, in this instance the external conditions of existence, from the concrete situation, which includes the usually suppressed elements of man's selection of objectives. The ineluctable conclusions derived from his abstract delineation of the situation he thinks to represent actual facts, in all their empirical variety.[10] To put it in another way, Durkheim neglects to treat his conceptions as advisedly ideal constructions demanding appropriate alteration before they can adequately describe concrete social phenomena.

In his presentation of societal evolution, Durkheim professes to trace genetically a transition from mechanical to organic solidarity, and it is here that his defective ethnographic data lead him astray. With Maine and Steinmetz, he affects to note the preponderance, even the exclusive existence, of *penal* law in primitive society. In point of fact, as recent field studies have demonstrated, primitive societies possess also a corpus of restitutive, civil law, involving rights and duties between individuals, and kept in force by social mechanisms.[11] The existence of such essentially contractual relations among primitive peoples detracts from the plausibility of Durkheim's theory of unilinear development. Moreover, in affirming the preponderance of organic solidarity in modern societies, Durkheim tends to depreciate unduly the persistent factor of community of interests. This bias warps his analysis of the elements of social cohesion. Such group-integrative factors as conceptions of honor, *Ehre,* and the subsumption of individual under collective interests during periods of war and of conflict generally, which are significant elements in the

[10] Hume had long since perceived this confusion of mechanistic science. Professor A. N. Whitehead denotes the error by the descriptive phrase, "The Fallacy of Misplaced Concreteness." See his *Science and the Modern World* (New York: The Macmillan Company, 1931), pp. 75 ff. A keen psychological description of the basis of this error is to be found in Richard Avenarius' *Kritik der reinen Erfahrung* (Leipzig: Reisland, 1907-8), Vol. II, pp. 376 ff.

[11] Bronislaw Malinowski, *Crime and Custom in Savage Society* (New York: Harcourt, Brace & World, Inc., 1926), pp. 55 ff. Contrast Durkheim's statement that "in primitive societies . . . law is wholly penal." *Division* . . . , p. 76.

cohesion of contemporary societies,[12] are unwarrantably ignored by Durkheim in his endeavor to find in the division of labor the sole source of modern solidarity. The inviolate unity of a group becomes imperative during intersocietal conflicts, and this unity is largely achieved through appeals to common sentiments. Likewise, is the nonjuridical notion of honor a powerful, if not always effective, regulatory device making for social cohesion. The fact that such forms of mechanical solidarity still subsist suggests additional grounds for rejecting Durkheim's argument of unilinear development.

Durkheim's conception of this unilinear evolution must, moreover, be reconsidered in the light of what has been appropriately termed the "principle of limits" of development.[13] Development in a given direction may continue until it becomes self-defeating, whereupon reaction occurs in an opposite direction. Were it not that Durkheim attempts to extrapolate beyond the universe of his data, he might have found in the ever more frequently occurring states of anomie accompanying the increase of division of labor an index of this reaction. In the economic world, one need but note movements of reconsolidation after optima of differentiation have been passed, to realize that the process is not necessarily unidirectional.

To arrive at his conception of evolution, Durkheim does not, as has been alleged, abandon his sociologistic position. It is true that he finds the "determining cause" of increased division of labor in the growth and heightened density of populations, which is primarily a biological factor, but it is only insofar as this demographic change is associated with increased social interaction and its concomitant, enhanced competition, that the stipulated change will occur. It is thus this social factor—the "dynamic density," as he terms it—which Durkheim finds actually determinant. In a subsequent work he makes this point even more definitely by noting that population density and dynamic density are not always associated—in China, for example—and that in these instances the increase in division of labor is considerably inhibited.[14] Hence, the facile formula

---

[12] Cf. Georg Simmel, *Soziologie* (München and Leipzig, Duncker & Humblot, 1923), pp. 202, 404 ff.

[13] Cf. A. A. Goldenweiser, "History, Psychology, and Culture," *Journal of Philosophy, Psychology, and Scientific Methods*, XV (1918), 593; P. A. Sorokin, "The Principle of Limits," *Publications, American Sociological Society* (1932), 19-28.

[14] *Régles* . . . , *op. cit.*, p. 140. "*Nous avons eu le tort, dans notre Division du travail, de trop présenter la densité matérielle comme l'expression exacte de la densité dynamique.*" Paul Barth manifestly errs in ascribing to Durkheim an unmodified materialistic interpretation of history. Durkheim's shift to idealism became marked in his work on religion. Cf. Barth's *Die Philosophie der Geschichte als Soziologie* (Leipzig: Reisland, 1922), pp. 628-42.

which attributes an increased differentiation of function solely to demographic changes must be revamped. To the extent that this differentiation is generalizable as a social process, it may be said to be associated with competition between individuals and between groups, whatever the factors leading to such competition.

If we abandon Durkheim's unilinear theory, we are left with an acute characterization of the two societies, mechanical and organic, taken as ideal-types or as heuristic fictions. These may then be considered as limiting cases, never obtaining in empirical reality, which may be fruitfully employed as poles of reference toward which empirical data are theoretically oriented. Durkheim's work thus provides a conceptual scheme which may be used to advantage in the interpretation of processes of differentiation, integration, competition, and the like.

Another aspect of Durkheim's methodology, which characterizes not only the *Division,* but also his later works, is his use of "indexes" which he considers the "external," measurable translation of the "internal," not directly observable social facts. Just as the physicist measures heat and electricity through certain objectively observable and easily measurable phenomena, such as the rise and fall of mercury in a glass tube and the oscillation of the needle of a galvanometer, so Durkheim hopes to use repressive and restitutive law as indexes of mechanical and organic solidarity, respectively.[15]

At this point, a fundamental difficulty arises. If the observed facts (L) are to be significant and relatively accurate indexes of the types of solidarity (S), the following relationships must hold true. Let L $(x, y \ldots .)$ be written for a function of measurable quantities $(x, y \ldots)$ (statistics of penal or restitutive law) and let it be so related to S $(x', y' \ldots)$ (the social fact—social cohesion) that these postulates are satisfied. When L varies in a determinate fashion, S varies correspondingly. When there are successive increases in L, the first changing L from L_1 to L_2 and the second from L_2 to L_3, so that the first increase is greater than the second, then the first increase in S (solidarity) is greater than the second. This postulate must still obtain when *less* is written for *greater*.[16] This affords a concomitant variation between the social facts and their indexes, the variations of the former being directly unmeasurable and relative to the directly measurable variation of the latter.

It is precisely this sort of relationship which Durkheim fails to demonstrate. He does not establish with any precision the perfect associations

---

[15] *Division* . . . , p. 66.
[16] Compare A. L. Bowley, *The Mathematical Groundwork of Economics* (Oxford: Clarendon Press, 1924), pp. 1 ff.

which he assumes obtain between his types of solidarity and of law. For example, organic solidarity may be regulated by customary usages and mores without ever becoming definitely translated into civil law. This was notably the case during a great part of the Middle Ages.[17] Furthermore, as has been suggested, much of mechanical solidarity in contemporary society—that evidenced by "honor," for example—finds no expression in repressive law. These necessarily brief indications must suffice to signify the debatable premises on which Durkheim bases his system of indexes.[18]

In his generally brilliant chapter on the division of labor and happiness, Durkheim evidences another fundamental weakness of his method. He eliminates certain possible explanations of a particular set of social phenomena by demonstrating that the logical consequences of the rejected theories are not in accord with observed facts. He assumes that the possible number of explicative theories is determinable, x, and that having eliminated x-1 explanations he is left with the necessarily valid solution. Thus, he holds that "the desire to become happier is the only individual source which can take account of [the] progress [of the division of labor]. If that is set aside, no other remains." [19] This method of projected experiment was brought into prominence by Descartes (to whom Durkheim was avowedly indebted), who maintained that in approaching reality one will find that many consequences result from initially adopted principles and that rational consideration will decide which of these consequences is realized.[20] But the fallacy of this method lies in the initial assumption that one has exhausted the totality of possible explanations. The elimination of alternative theories in no wise increases the probabilities of the other alternatives.

Of Durkheim's *Division*, one may say in general that it presents an incisive and suggestive analysis of a determinate social process and its structural correlates. If its conclusions are too sweeping, if its method is at times faulty, one may yet acknowledge from the vantage point afforded by four decades of subsequent research that it remains one of the peak contributions of modern sociology.

[17] Cf. Paul Vinogradoff, "Customary Law," in *The Legacy of the Middle Ages,* edited by G. C. Crump and E. F. Jacob (Oxford: Clarendon Press, 1927), pp. 287-319.

[18] The same sort of criticism may be leveled against the indexes of group cohesion and disintegration employed by Durkheim in *Le Suicide.*

[19] *Division* . . . , p. 251. That this is an extreme statement is clear, for Duguit, *op. cit.,* pp. 50 ff., suggests an individualistic, and noneudemonic, explanation.

[20] René Descartes, "Discours de la méthode," *Œuvres* (Paris, 1902), Vol. VI, pp. 64 ff.

DURKHEIM'S *SUICIDE:*
FURTHER THOUGHTS ON
A METHODOLOGICAL CLASSIC

HANAN C. SELVIN[1]

SIXTY-EIGHT YEARS after it first appeared in print, Émile Durkheim's *Suicide*[2] is still a model of social research. Few, if any, later works can match the clarity and power with which Durkheim marshaled his facts to test and refine his theory. The stature of this work is even more impressive when one remembers that Durkheim lacked even so rudimentary a tool as the correlation coefficient. Yet the methodology of *Suicide* is important to those now engaged in empirical research, not merely to historians of sociology. Durkheim recognized and solved many of the problems that beset present-day research. Others he formulated so lucidly—perhaps because he did not exile his methodology to appendixes—that their solution is relatively simple with the tools now available.

Methodology has several meanings to sociologists. To some it means questionnaires, interviews, punched cards—the tools of research. To others, such as Durkheim himself and Parsons,[3] it means the assumptions and concepts used in constructing a theory. Here it will be used to mean the systematic examination of the procedures, assumptions, and

---

[1] An earlier version of this paper appeared in the *American Journal of Sociology,* LXIII (1958), 607-19. The major differences are in the treatment of replications. Both versions owe much to Robert K. Merton, who taught me how new knowledge can come from restudying the sociological classics, and to Paul F. Lazarsfeld, who showed me that methodology can be exciting as well as useful.

[2] Émile Durkheim, *Suicide,* translated by John A. Spaulding and George Simpson (New York: The Free Press of Glencoe, Inc., 1951).

[3] Émile Durkheim, *The Rules of Sociological Method,* translated by Sarah A. Solovay and John H. Mueller (New York: The Free Press of Glencoe, Inc., 1950); Talcott Parsons, *The Structure of Social Action* (New York: The Free Press of Glencoe, Inc., 1949), pp. 20-27 and Chap. 9.

modes of explanation used in the analysis of empirical data.[4] This focus
on Durkheim's methodology is not meant to minimize the importance of
his theoretical insights; the value of methodological investigations, after
all, is that they lead to more effective theorizing about social behavior.
But Durkheim's theoretical development has been discussed by many authors, notably the others in this book, while his analytical procedures
have not received the attention they deserve.

MULTIVARIATE ANALYSIS

Central to Durkheim's methodology is his use of what has been called
multivariate analysis: "the study and interpretation of complex interre-
lationships among a multiplicity of characteristics."[5] Much of the empirical analysis in *Suicide* can be viewed as the progressive introduction
of additional variables. It will be useful to examine one of these analyses
in detail, for it includes several of the procedures to be considered in this
paper.

The first chapter on egoistic suicide (Book II, Chap. 2) begins with
the relation between religion and suicide rates for three groups of countries—the predominantly Protestant, the mixed Protestant and Catholic,
and the predominantly Catholic.[6] But, as Durkheim points out, this comparison includes countries with radically different social conditions and
therefore requires consideration of the relation between religion and suicide within each country. Thus Bavaria, the German state with the lowest proportion of Protestants, has the lowest proportion of suicides. And,
in what may seem a mere piling-up of instances, the provinces within
Bavaria also exhibit this same relation: "Suicides are found in direct
proportion to the number of Protestants and in inverse proportion to
that of Catholics." Prussia and the Prussian provinces are the site of a
similar analysis. Then the analysis is repeated for a third country: Switzerland. Here Durkheim takes advantage of the fact that both French-
and German-speaking areas contain some cantons that are largely Catholic and others that are largely Protestant. This allows him to hold constant the effect of language as well as of nationality ("race") while examining the effect of religion on suicide.

[4] Paul F. Lazarsfeld and Morris Rosenberg (eds.), *The Language of Social Research*
(New York: The Free Press of Glencoe, Inc., 1955), p. 4.
[5] *Ibid.*, p. 11. *Multivariate analysis* has a somewhat different meaning in statistical
theory.
[6] This and the following two paragraphs are taken from *Suicide, op. cit.*, pp. 152-56.

All the preceding analyses are based on data for large aggregates: Durkheim here classifies nations or provinces according to their rates of suicide and their proportions of Protestants, rather than according to the proportions of Catholics and Protestants in these countries who kill themselves each year. The implications of this procedure will be considered later; here it is enough to note only that Durkheim recognized the difference between relations based on aggregate data and those based on individual data, for he goes on to say that "in a fairly large number of cases the number of suicides per million inhabitants of the population of each confession has been directly determined." He then presents data on the suicide rates of individuals by religion for twelve periods of time in five countries, as well as some fragmentary data for France.

After disposing of the "deviant" case of Norway and Sweden, Durkheim considers the low suicide rate among Jews. Compared with Protestants and Catholics, Jews are more likely to live in cities and to pursue intellectual occupations—both conditions that are associated with higher suicide rates. Therefore, Durkheim reasons, if the reported rate of suicide among Jews is lower despite these conditions, the "true" Jewish rate must be even lower than the figures reveal it to be.

As this passage makes plain, multivariate analysis meant more to Durkheim than simply considering the separate relations between suicide and the several independent variables—religion, nationality, and language. Each new variable is progressively incorporated into the preceding analyses, so that several variables are considered jointly. The methodology of multivariate analysis is most clearly seen in the case where a relation between one independent variable (say, religion) and the dependent variable (suicide) is "elaborated" by the introduction of a third variable or "test factor" (say, nationality). Lazarsfeld, Kendall, and Hyman have defined three major types of elaboration: *explanation, interpretation,* and *specification.*[7]

Explanation is the attempt to "explain away" the apparent meaning of an observed relation. For example, the association between religion and suicide might have been a manifestation of nationality, inasmuch as some countries, like Germany, have both a high suicide rate and many Protestants. Looking into this possibility, Durkheim finds that the original association between religion and suicide persists when national differences are taken into account; nationality is, therefore, not an explanation of this relation.

[7] The most complete discussion is in Herbert H. Hyman, *Survey Design and Analysis* (New York: The Free Press of Glencoe, Inc., 1955), Chaps. 6 and 7.

Once convinced that nationality and language do not explain away the association between religion and suicide, Durkheim turns to the interpretation of this relation: What is the chain of variables connecting two such disparate phenomena as Protestantism and suicide? A spirit of free inquiry, according to Durkheim, is the most important link in this chain: Protestanism fosters free inquiry, and free inquiry in turn leads to a higher rate of suicide.

Although Durkheim lacked the statistical techniques to develop these ideas rigorously, he saw their central place in theoretically oriented research.[8] The relation between two variables ". . . may not be due to the fact that one phenomenon is the cause of the other but to the fact that they are both the effects of the same cause, or, again, that there exists between them a third phenomenon, interposed but unperceived, which is the effect of the first and the cause of the second." [9]

Specification, the third mode of elaboration, identifies the conditions under which a relation holds true in greater or less degree. For example, the effect of religion on suicide is less in the German cantons of Switzerland than in the French. Specification leads to the development of multivariate theories of behavior in a way that is not true of explanation and interpretation. The aim of specification is to construct a three-variable relation—to say that, as in the example just cited, the effect of religion on suicide is greater in one place than in another. Note that this statement cannot be decomposed into a set of two-variable relations. Explanation, on the other hand, involves a three-variable association only as an intermediate step, either toward rejecting the apparent finding or toward affirming its provisional meaning; in either case, the result is not a three-

[8] The statistical tools that Durkheim needed were developed by Karl Pearson and G. Udny Yule during the 1890's, most notably in Yule's use of multiple regression to study "panel" data on poverty: G. Udny Yule, "An Investigation into the Causes of Changes in Pauperism in England, Chiefly During the Last Two Intercensal Decades": Part I, *Journal of the Royal Statistical Society*, LXII (1899), 249-86. Neither the Durkheim group in France nor the students of poverty in England (Charles Booth, B. Seebohm Rowntree, and A. L. Bowley) seem to have known of this and other papers in which Yule applied his newly developed statistical tools to social phenomena. Social research is only now beginning to replace tabular analysis with multiple regression and other powerful statistical techniques. (I have developed these ideas in a study sponsored by the National Science Foundation, which is now being revised for publication.) Had Durkheim, Booth, and their followers recognized the importance of Yule's work, survey research might have been further advanced than it is now. A Senior Postdoctoral Fellowship from the National Science Foundation in 1963-64 enabled me to study the reasons for which this intellectual innovation did not diffuse into social research during the period from 1890 to World War I; an account of this research is in preparation.

[9] *Rules . . . , op. cit.,* p. 131.

variable relation. Interpretation, likewise, uses the three-variable association only to produce a series of two-variable relations, to show that these relations are linked by the variables they have in common.

This greater complexity of specification, its essential three-variable nature, leads to more complex problems in analysis. Durkheim's successes and failures in coping with some of these problems are instructive. Three problems will be considered: (1) the joint effects of group and individual characteristics on individual behavior; (2) the theoretical problems stemming from the statistical concept of "interaction"; and (3) the question of when to stop an empirical analysis.

CONTEXTUAL ANALYSIS

The variety of analyses that come under the heading of *specification* is suggested by Hyman's classification; among other ways, one can specify a relationship according to the interest and concern of respondents, the time and place at which it occurs, or the conditions and contingencies on which it depends.[10] Durkheim's analysis provides still another type based on *units of analysis*. This type of specification, of which there are several varieties, has been called *contextual analysis:*[11] it involves the joint effects of an individual characteristic and a group characteristic on rates of individual behavior. In discussing the lower suicide rate among married people, Durkheim points out that in France the difference between the married and the single (as measured by his "coefficient of preservation") is greater among the men, while in the Grand Duchy of Oldenburg it is greater among the women.[12] That is, the social and cultural differences between France and Oldenburg are manifested in two essentially different ways: (1) They exert a *direct* effect (the over-all suicide rate is noticeably higher in France than in Oldenburg); (2) they exert an *indirect* effect (the *relation* between sex and suicide is different in France and in Oldenburg). In other words, national characteristics have a differential impact on the sex-suicide association in the two countries, the difference between the sexes being greater in France than in Oldenburg and in the opposite direction.

[10] Hyman, *op. cit.*, pp. 295-311.

[11] My first use of this idea was in the research reported in Hanan C. Selvin, *The Effects of Leadership* (New York: The Free Press of Glencoe, Inc., 1960). The same idea has been developed in different ways by Peter M. Blau in "Structural Effects," *American Sociological Review*, XXV (1960), 178-93, and by James A. Davis, Joe L. Spaeth, and Carolyn Huson in "A Technique for Analyzing the Effects of Group Composition," *American Sociological Review*, XXVI (1961), 215-25.

[12] *Suicide, op. cit.*, p. 179.

Methodological devices such as contextual analysis are more than in-genious ways to manipulate data. As Merton has emphasized, they are important in opening new directions for theory.[13] Durkheim's contextual analysis raises questions about the ways in which group and individual characteristics interact to affect behavior. For example, under what con-ditions do national characteristics produce such a marked reversal in the association between individual attributes and behavior?

The negative side of this case can also be found in *Suicide:* where Durkheim lacked adequate statistical techniques, he was occasionally led into theoretical contradictions. At one point he asserts that "the relation between the aptitude for suicide of married persons and that of widowers and widows is identically the same in widely different social groups, from the simple fact that the moral condition of widowhood everywhere bears the same relation to the moral constitution characteristic of marriage." [14] But Durkheim's data on Oldenburg and France lead to the opposite con-clusion—that the relation between the suicide rates of married persons and widows and widowers was *not* the same in the two countries. What Durkheim lacked and what has since become available is a precise con-ception of statistical interaction, the ways in which the association be-tween two variables depends on the values of a third variable.[15]

Durkheim's treatment of statistical interaction and of the theoretical relations that it measures is notably inconsistent. Sometimes, as here, he ignores the presence of interaction in his data. Elsewhere, he correctly notes its presence, remarking, for example, that seasonal differences in suicide are less pronounced in cities than in rural areas.[16] And in another place he assumes, without any evidence, that the interaction of tempera-ture and location is zero: ". . . if the temperature had the supposed in-fluence, it should be felt equally in the geographical distribution of sui-cides." [17]

One possible reason for Durkheim's inconsistency is that he had not formalized his analytical procedures. In effect, each time he came to a

---

[13] Robert K. Merton, *Social Theory and Social Structure,* revised and enlarged ed. (New York: The Free Press of Glencoe, Inc., 1957), Chap. 3.

[14] *Suicide, op. cit.,* p. 307.

[15] The phenomenon of statistical interaction has been given many different names (e.g., specification, conditional relationship, differential impact, differential sensitivity, and nonadditivity of effects).

[16] *Suicide, op. cit.,* p. 120.

[17] *Ibid.,* p. 113.

case of specification, it had to be reasoned through from the beginning. Formalizations such as the Lazarsfeld-Kendall-Hyman types of elaboration enable the analyst to recognize the same principle at work in different instances and therefore to treat them similarly.

WHEN TO STOP AN EMPIRICAL ANALYSIS

The idea of elaboration also illuminates the seemingly unrelated problem of deciding when further analysis is needed. Durkheim's treatment of "race" and suicide provides a case in point.[18] Arguing that the high rate of suicide in Germany "might be due to the special nature of German civilization," he decides to "see whether the German retains this sad primacy outside of Germany." To this end he examines the suicide rates in the provinces of Austria-Hungary, in which German-speaking people . . . [form] from 1.9 to 100 per cent [of the population], and finds "not the least trace of German influence" on the suicide rate.[19] However, a close examination of Durkheim's data—particularly of the five provinces that have high proportions of Germans and disproportionately few suicides—leads to quite different conclusions. These provinces —Upper Austria, Salzburg, Transalpine Tyrol, Carinthia, and Styria— comprise the western part of present-day Austria. If these five contiguous provinces are removed, the Spearman rank correlation for the remaining ten provinces is 0.95, indicating an almost perfect relation between the suicide rate and the proportion of German-speaking people.

The important point here is not substantive but methodological. Durkheim stopped his analysis as soon as he found a "zero" relationship. This procedure is perhaps more common in research today. Small associations are considered a signal to turn to other matters, especially when the associations are not statistically significant. The reasoning behind this assumption is never made explicit, but it would seem to be that, if two variables are not associated when other items are left free to vary, they will not be associated when these other items are "held constant." That is, if the total association between two variables is zero, the partial as-

---

[18] *Ibid.*, pp. 86-87.

[19] This table is a good example of the consequences of Durkheim's lack of a quantitative measure of association. Durkheim apparently regarded anything much less than perfect concomitant variation (i.e., a rank correlation of 1.0) as "independence." By modern standards the Spearman rank correlation for this table is actually very high— 0.57! Unknown to me at the time I discovered this was Yule's discovery of the same mistake in Booth's work: "On the Correlation of Total Pauperism with the Proportion of Out-relief," *Economic Journal*, V (1895), 603-11.

sociations will be zero. Sometimes this is true; often it is not. Hyman's passage on the "elaboration of a zero relationship" [20] indicates that this may happen when the two partial relations are approximately equal in size and opposite in sign. For example, a surprisingly small association between job satisfaction and participation in community organizations resulted from a positive association between participation and satisfaction among members of the working class and a negative association of approximately the same size in the white-collar class.

To my knowledge, Hyman's is the only published discussion of this problem. It may be useful, therefore, to make two further points suggested by Hyman's brief treatment. First, he implied that this kind of relation is uncommon and even accidental. Actually, it may occur frequently under certain conditions—for example, in the kind of contextual analysis in which individuals are assigned to groups instead of being born into them or choosing them themselves. A study of leisure-time behavior in army training companies found that many small or zero associations between behavior and an individual characteristic, such as marital status, resulted from opposite and approximately equal associations in companies with different "leadership climates." [21]

Second, still another type of elaboration of a zero relationship may be ranged alongside the two identified by Hyman. A zero association between two variables may occur even when both partial associations are in the same direction. The hypothetical example in Table 1 shows that this case would interest the student of political behavior. At both levels of education, the people with more information tend to choose the Democratic Party, yet the "collapsed" table of information and party affiliation without regard to education will show that, among both the more informed and the less informed, 50 per cent are Democrats. The two partial associations are positive (and about the same size); the total association is zero. Unrealistic as this example may be (although it could describe a university town with a Democratic newspaper), it does demonstrate the importance of looking into those zero associations that theory or previous research suggests should not have been zero. A zero association between two variables may therefore result from any one of three different conditions in the partial relations: zero associations in both partials, equal and opposite associations, or associations in the same direction. Only the first of these is a signal to stop the analysis.

[20] Hyman, *op. cit.*, pp. 307-10.
[21] Selvin, *op. cit.*, Appendix E.

Table 1

Information and party affiliation, education held constant
(Hypothetical Data)

	LESS EDUCATION		MORE EDUCATION	
	MUCH INFORMATION	LITTLE INFORMATION	MUCH INFORMATION	LITTLE INFORMATION
Per cent Democratic	38	24	74	63
N	(200)	(100)	(100)	(200)

TYPES OF REPLICATION IN EMPIRICAL RESEARCH

Another multivariate procedure that is conspicuous in *Suicide* and that deserves intensive inquiry is *replication,* the systematic restudy of a given relation in different contexts. In the first chapter on egoistic suicide, the original table relating religion and suicide is followed by no fewer than *seventeen* replications in three pages. Now these replications are examples of elaboration and they serve to clarify the meaning of the original relation. But why so many of them? Durkheim's answer is not altogether clear. He does demand that the facts cited to support a thesis be "numerous enough not to be attributable to accidental circumstances —not to permit another explanation—to be contradicted by no other fact." [22] But these principles are not systematically explained. This section will therefore examine some of the types of replication in *Suicide* and will consider what functions replications may serve in current research.

Durkheim's lavish use of replications is in sharp contrast to modern survey research, where a relation usually appears only in a single table. One reason that Durkheim used so many replications is undoubtedly that his data came from official records; it cost him little more to study suicide in six countries than in one. On the other hand, in contemporary surveys the researcher must gather his own data, often at great expense, so that one community is a practical limit. (However, as will be seen, this is no longer as true as it once was.) A second reason for examining a hypothesis in only one table is the belief that a close adherence to modern techniques of statistical inference—tests of significance and confidence intervals—guarantees the statistical soundness of the conclusions. This point

[22] *Suicide, op. cit.,* p. 95.

of view has recently been vigorously attacked and staunchly defended.[23] The points at issue may be clarified by examining the different kinds of replication and their functions in survey analysis; one type of replication will turn out to provide an effective alternative to conventional tests of significance.[24]

Of the several kinds of replication in *Suicide, unit replications* are the most frequent; in these the original finding is re-examined in different groups of subjects—for example, the excess of military over civilian suicides is confirmed for eight different countries of Europe.[25] Durkheim further replicates this finding within the Austro-Hungarian Empire; the military-civilian difference persists in the various military areas.[26] These two examples suggest that unit replications may be divided into two subtypes: *external replications* and *internal replications*.

In external replications, the conclusions of one study are tested independently in another study, usually conducted by a different investigator.[27] Cross-cultural comparisons are a familiar example. Demographers and others who work with official records also conduct external replications as a matter of course.

[23] The controversy in sociology began with Hanan C. Selvin, "A Critique of Tests of Significance in Survey Research," *American Sociological Review*, XXII (1957), 519-27. The full list of relevant works that appeared after this article is too long to present here. In my judgment some of the most important are: Leslie Kish, "Some Statistical Problems in Research Design," *American Sociological Review*, XXIV (1959), 328-38; Lancelot Hogben, *Statistical Theory* (New York: W. W. Norton & Company, Inc., 1958); Hanan C. Selvin and Alan Stuart, "Data-dredging Procedures in Survey Analysis" (forthcoming). The first and third of these contain references to other relevant works.

[24] To judge from the language of some of the reactions, my original article on tests of significance was seen as an attack on the received doctrines of scientific method, or, what is apparently the same to some critics, as being against statistical inference. For what it is worth, my intention was to criticize the *misapplication* of accepted principles and the *misuse* of tests of significance. As nearly as I can tell now, the only significant mistake in the original article was the claim that all variables correlated with the independent variable must be held constant before the test can be properly interpreted. As John W. Tukey and Robert McGinnis have pointed out to me, to remove all the concomitants of a variable is to destroy the variable itself. What I should have said, in consonance with Lazarsfeld's discussion of "explanation," is that one must hold constant all known variables that are *causally prior* to both the independent and the dependent variables. For an additional and more serious problem in interpreting probability statements in survey research, see Selvin and Stuart, *op. cit.*

[25] *Suicide, op. cit.*, p. 228.

[26] *Ibid.*, p. 235.

[27] For a collection of external replications and an interesting treatment of the factors making for successful replications see Robert C. Hanson, "Evidence and Procedures Characteristics of 'Reliable' Propositions in Social Science," *American Journal of Sociology*, LXIII (1958), 357-70.

In internal replications, a finding is restudied for smaller groups within the original set of subjects. In the passage on military and civilian suicides there are several external replications, based on the different countries, and several internal replications for areas within one country.[28] Although these replications have a geographical basis, a finding may be replicated in groups formed on any set of variables. In the chapter on anomic suicide (Book II, Chap. 5), Durkheim presents a table of suicide rates by occupation for eight countries. Here the various countries act as external replications for his original finding on occupations and suicide. But the same table could also serve as an internal replication of the national differences considered in the earlier chapter on egoistic suicide, the comparisons between over-all national suicide rates being replicated for the comparable occupational groups within the countries.[29]

In its statistical form an internal replication must be *stratified* or *conditional:* the original relation is re-examined in a set of higher-order relations, according to the values of one or more additional variables. This is not true for external replications. A relation originally found for one country may be externally replicated in a series of different countries; the original relation and the replications have exactly the same form. However, if the analyst has access to more detailed tables, he can produce stratified external replications that are identical in form to the internal replications; Durkheim's re-examination of the military-civilian difference in suicide within the provinces of Austria-Hungary is an example. When one is working with official statistics, the possibilities of this kind of replication are limited by the variety of tables . . . available. The full possibilities of this form of replication appear only when one has access to individual data, preferably on punched cards or some other form of record that allows for rapid tabulation. Consider, for example, the relation between occupation and voting for the "liberal" or "left-wing" party. This relation may be externally replicated in as many countries as there are comparable voting studies—perhaps as many as two dozen. But each of these replications may be stratified according to the values of at least two or three variables taken together—say, for young Protestant men, for young Protestant women, for middle-aged Protestant men, and so on.[30] In Durkheim's day, before punched cards were introduced, such tabulations would have been impossibly expensive. Today,

[28] *Suicide, op. cit.,* pp. 228-39.
[29] *Ibid.,* p. 258.
[30] For many examples of external replications in voting studies, see Seymour Martin Lipset, *Political Man* (Garden City, N.Y.: Doubleday & Company, Inc., 1960).

the wide availability of "libraries" of punched cards and of tabulating or computing machinery means that such complex replications cost very little.[31]

Properly conducted, replications may serve at least three important functions in survey research: to broaden the scope of the hypothesis under study, thus generalizing it beyond the limits of the original sample; to lessen the seriousness of the ecological fallacy, in which relations between properties of individuals are wrongly inferred from relations between properties of groups; and to provide a more valid test of statistical significance when the conventional tests cannot be validly applied. The treatment of these functions in the following three sections does not pretend to offer anything new in statistical techniques but, rather, takes a new look at some existing problems and techniques.

REPLICATIONS AND INDUCTIVE INFERENCE

Is there a statistical technique for inferring valid general statements from a particular sample? Some statisticians would extend the logic of drawing a sample from a finite, existing population to the assumption that a sample already drawn has come by a random process from an infinite hypothetical universe.[32] There are many differences between the two situations; perhaps the most important has to do with the possibility of testing the inferences derived from the probability calculations. One can test conventional sampling theory by comparing the outcomes of an appropriately designed series of sampling experiments on populations whose parameters are known. Nothing remotely comparable is possible for samples drawn from infinite hypothetical populations. There is no way to *demonstrate* that the sample provides any guide to statements about the population. Instead of trying to warp the demonstrable principles of statistical inference into an undemonstrable canon of inductive inference, it seems better to agree with Karl Popper that there is no such

---

[31] The oldest and largest "library" of punched cards is the Roper Public Opinion Center at Williams College in Williamstown, Massachusetts. There are several smaller collections elsewhere in the United States and in Europe, and, of course, every large survey organization has its own library of completed studies—i.e., of potential external replications.

[32] For an explicit equating of inductive inference and statistical inference see Kenneth R. Hammond and James E. Householder, *Introduction to the Statistical Method* (New York: Alfred A. Knopf, Inc., 1962), pp. 235-37 and 340-41. Perhaps no amount of argument can convey the bizarre quality of statements based on this position as well as the following quotation from a study of delinquency: "The use of statistical tests of significance was considered justified as 1952 is a sample of years and San Diego a sample of cities which might have been used."

thing as a technique of inductive inference or, what amounts to the same thing, that one can never "prove" a general proposition.[33]

All that one can do, according to Popper, is to try to *disprove* the proposition. The more stringent the tests that are not failed and the greater their number, the higher one's level of confidence in the truth of the generalization. Sooner or later, every proposition will be disproved. The creative theorist then formulates a new proposition that meets the last test and that, he hopes, will survive many new tests. Popper's argument, in short, is that science moves toward generality by trying to replicate and that the credibility of the general proposition increases in proportion to the stringency of the tests.

Durkheim's use of external and internal replications illustrates two ways in which one can make tests more stringent. In external replications one searches for a new context that has certain desirable properties, as when Durkheim tests his hypothesis of egoistic suicide on the deviant case of England.[34] An unstratified external replication like this one extends the scope of the generalization to new contexts. Stratified replications, whether internal or external, increase the stringency of the test by specifying more precisely the nature of the independent variable. Thus the first few pages on egoistic suicide are a progressive discarding of irrelevant national and local differences until the effect of religion is seen as purely as possible.

REPLICATION AND THE ECOLOGICAL FALLACY

Robinson first called the attention of sociologists to the fallacy of assuming that associations computed from group means or group proportions are valid estimates of the associations that would be obtained from individual data.[35] Most of Durkheim's analysis is based on such fallacious reason-

---

[33] Karl Popper, *Conjectures and Refutations* (New York: Basic Books, Inc., 1963). Popper had formulated these ideas as early as 1935 in his *Logik der Forschung*, an English translation of which has recently appeared as *The Logic of Scientific Discovery* (London: Hutchinson & Co. [Publishers], Ltd., 1959). As so often happens, Popper's ideas were independently discovered by others at about the same time; I first heard them in a series of lectures by Robert K. Merton in 1948-49 on the relations between sociological theory and empirical research.

[34] *Suicide, op. cit.,* pp. 160-61.

[35] William S. Robinson, "Ecological Correlations and the Behavior of Individuals," *American Sociological Review,* XV (1950), 351-57. This problem seems to have been discovered and treated independently in psychology and statistics, although not so fully as in Robinson's paper. See Edward L. Thorndike, "On the Fallacy of Imputing the Correlations Found for Groups to the Individuals or Smaller Groups Composing Them," *American Journal of Psychology,* LII (1929), 122-24; G. Udny Yule and Maurice G.

ing. Thus he reports that the rate of suicide in departments of France varies according to the proportion of "persons of independent means." [36] This result is consistent with either of the following hypotheses: *none* of the people who commit suicide has independent means, or *all* of them have independent means. The ecological association between characteristics of departments reveals nothing about the individual association between a person's wealth and whether or not he commits suicide.

Not every case of ecological association entails the ecological fallacy. Menzel has shown that ecological associations are not only permissible but necessary when the unit of analysis is a group rather than the individuals in it.[37] However, Durkheim never theorizes about wealthy and poor departments, only about wealthy and poor individuals. And if he were interested in group characteristics—at the level, say, of departments or provinces—why would he replicate for successively finer subdivisions within these groups, in two cases carrying the replications down to individuals.[38] It is clear that Durkheim was guilty of the ecological fallacy.

To say that Durkheim's procedures were fallacious is not necessarily to invalidate his conclusions. The conclusions may be true, even if they do not follow from his data. In effect, Durkheim recognized this problem and attempted to solve it in the only way open to him: the systematic use of internal replications. When he was able to carry the replications down to individual data, there is, of course, no ecological fallacy: the hypothesis stated for group data is confirmed for individual data. However, even when Durkheim did not have individual data, the procedure of replicating in smaller units may lead, as Duncan and Davis have shown,[39] to useful estimates of the individual association.

Durkheim's data cannot be used to illustrate this procedure, for a reason to be stated shortly. Consider, instead, the following ecological data from a hypothetical city in which there are twenty election districts of one hundred voters. Each of the first ten districts has 10 per cent

Kendall, *An Introduction to the Theory of Statistics*, 14th ed. (New York: Hafner Publishing Co., Inc., 1950), pp. 310-15. The most complete discussion of ecological correlations from a sociological point of view is in Otis Dudley Duncan, Ray P. Cuzzort, and Beverly Duncan, *Statistical Geography* (New York: The Free Press of Glencoe, Inc., 1961).

[36] *Suicide, op. cit.*, p. 245.

[37] Herbert Menzel, "Comment on Robinson's 'Ecological Correlations and the Behavior of Individuals.'" *American Sociological Review*, XV (1950), 674; see also the discussion of the "modifiable unit" in Yule and Kendall, *op. cit.*, pp. 310-13.

[38] *Suicide, op. cit.*, pp. 154, 175.

[39] Otis Dudley Duncan and Beverly Davis, "An Alternative to Ecological Correlation," *American Sociological Review*, LVIII (1953), 665-66.

Republicans and 20 per cent voting for Goldwater. (These are group attributes; nothing is said about the number of individuals who are both Republicans and for Goldwater.) The other ten districts are 80 per cent Republican and 90 per cent for Goldwater. However one chooses to measure association—by product-moment correlation, by percentage differences in a fourfold table, or by any other index—this is a perfect ecological association: all the districts with many Republicans are for Goldwater, as against none of the districts with few Republicans. This is formally the kind of relation studied by Durkheim.

Now consider any one of the first ten districts. The number of Republicans for Goldwater [there] is not known, but it is easy to see that it must lie between a maximum of 10 and a minimum of zero. The corresponding values for the other ten districts are 80 and 70. If each district had the maximum possible number of Republicans for Goldwater, the total for the city would be $(10 \times 10) + (10 \times 80) = 900$; the minimum total for the city would be $(10 \times 0) + (10 \times 70) = 700$. Table 2 shows the maximum and minimum values for the four cells of the individual association. If the association between Republicanism and preference for Goldwater is the maximum in each district, then, for the city as a whole, 100 per cent of the Republicans and 18.2 per cent of the Democrats prefer Goldwater—a difference of 81.8 per cent. This is something less than the perfect ecological association; there, every Republican district was for Goldwater and every Democratic district for Johnson. Similarly, if the within-district associations are as small as possible, then 77.8 per cent of the Republicans and 36.4 per cent of the Democrats are for Goldwater—a difference of 41.4 per cent.

The ecological data for the districts thus lead to bounds for the in-

Table 2

Party affiliation and candidate choice
(Hypothetical Data)

INDIVIDUAL CANDIDATE CHOICE		INDIVIDUAL PARTY AFFILIATION		
		Republican	Democratic	Total
Goldwater	*Max.*	900	200	1100
	Min.	700	400	
Johnson	*Max.*	0	900	
	Min.	200	700	900

dividual association in the city as a whole. Durkheim's procedure of replicating in successively smaller units would, likewise, seem to generate bounds for the individual associations on which his analysis is really based. In fact, Goodman has shown that the smallest units give the closest bounds; nothing would be gained in the example above by aggregating the districts into larger areas.[40] Durkheim's reason for replicating at several levels instead of going directly to the smallest units is probably that his data were uneven (i.e., he did not have comparable figures for the provinces in all his countries).

The only difficulty in applying this procedure to Durkheim's data is that it will not work. Goodman's analysis indicates that bounds can be inferred only when the points in the ecological scatter plot are located

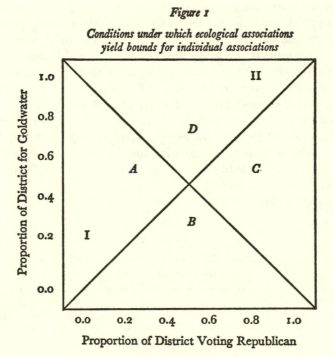

Figure 1

*Conditions under which ecological associations
yield bounds for individual associations*

Proportion of District Voting Republican

---

[40] Leo A. Goodman, "Ecological Regression and Behavior of Individuals," *American Sociological Review,* XVIII (1953), 663-64; and "Some Alternatives to Ecological Correlation," *American Journal of Sociology,* LXIV (1959), 610-25.

in at least two of the four regions in Figure 1. The two sets of points for the hypothetical election data are located in Regions *A* and *D*, as shown. But if the proportion for Goldwater is replaced by the suicide rate and the proportion of Republicans by any one of Durkheim's independent variables (say, the proportion of Protestants), then all Durkheim's data are located in Region *B*. (This is the region in which the suicide rate is lower than the proportion of Protestants and also lower than the proportion of non-Protestants.) No amount of replication, therefore, will lead to bounds for the individual association between suicide and Protestantism or between suicide and any of Durkheim's independent variables. Suicide is too rare an event, compared with the rates of the other variables he used.

Ecological reasoning in *Suicide* is not limited to geographical data. "A proof of the slight effect of marriage [on suicide] is the fact that the marriage rate has changed very little since the first of the [nineteenth] century, while suicide has tripled."[41] Here, again, the real question is whether married people are more or less likely than single people to commit suicide. With these data, however, a positive, negative, or zero individual association is possible. Data aggregated over time can lead to false interpretations, just as can data aggregated over geographical units. In both cases the difficulty is removed by studying the data within units rather than ecologically. There is no ecological fallacy when the independent variable and suicide are examined for individuals within each geographical area or for individuals within each time period. In other words, both versions of the ecological fallacy can be considered as cases of "spurious association." This, it will be recalled, is an erroneous inference that is "explained away" by holding constant a variable that accounts for the variations in both items being studied. The associations between region and religion and between region and suicide may account for the ecological association between religion and suicide; holding region constant removes any possibility of a false inference from this association. Similarly, the association between suicide and the marriage rate may lead to false inferences unless it is examined within relatively short time periods. There is thus a close methodological connection between problems of ecological association and procedures of multivariate analysis.[42]

[41] *Suicide, op. cit.,* p. 185.
[42] This is an explanation in which the "ordering principle" is not "time" but "level of aggression" or "level of complexity." Cf. Patricia Kendall and Paul F. Lazarsfeld, "Problems of Survey Analysis" in Robert K. Merton and Paul F. Lazarsfeld (eds.), *Continuities in Social Research: Studies in the Scope and Method of "The American Soldier"* (New York: The Free Press of Glencoe, Inc., 1950), p. 196.

Part of the attack on the use of significance tests in theoretically oriented survey analysis has rested on the difference in the ability of the survey investigator and the experimenter to deal with "extraneous" causal factors. In addition to experimental "control" of the environment and of the materials with which his subjects deal, the experimenter has the invaluable tool of *randomization*, the assignment of his subjects to one or another "treatment" by some random procedure, such as tossing a coin or using a table of random numbers. It is this alone that lies at the basis of the modern theory of experimental inference.[43]

In principle, then, the means of the dependent variable in the experimental and control groups should differ only because of two classes of phenomena; the effects of the independent variables included in the design of the experiment and the totality of random phenomena that affect individual scores (random errors of response and of processing as well as of assignment). Estimating the effects of the random errors makes it possible to say something about the probable role of the independent variables. In surveys, however, a third source of observed variation is present: nonrandom errors in measuring the variables. For example, in research comparing samples of delinquents and nondelinquents, it is possible that the two groups may differ in several nonrandom ways. It is usually difficult to find and interview the delinquents, and some of them have extreme scores on the independent variable; thus there will be nonrandom errors of sampling and of response. Again, the delinquents who agree to be interviewed may be less likely to give honest answers; the differences between their answers and the truth are certainly not random.

The presence of such nonrandom errors of unknown sign and magnitude makes it impossible to draw valid conclusions about the effects of the independent variables from a test of significance, regardless of whether the test shows a "significant" or a "nonsignificant" difference: a "significant" difference may as well be the result of the nonrandom errors as of the independent variables, and a "nonsignificant" difference can appear when large differences produced by the independent variables are masked by nonrandom errors of approximately the same magnitude and opposite sign.

[43] See any statistical treatment of the design of experiments—e.g., Oscar Kempthorne, *The Design and Analysis of Experiments* (New York: John Wiley & Sons, Inc., 1952).

The supporters of significance tests in survey analysis have generally agreed with the logic of this position, but some have discounted its importance, arguing that experienced survey researchers usually have some idea of the size and direction of their nonrandom errors. As long as this argument rests on knowledge of the nonrandom errors (even on crude estimates), it is sound. Such knowledge is most likely in organized research, where techniques are standardized and where data on the operation of these techniques can be accumulated over a series of studies; it is hard to see how it can be found in those who do not work in organized research centers and who conduct surveys infrequently.[44] Furthermore, and this point cannot be stressed too strongly, acting *as if* one had such knowledge of the nonrandom errors is *not* the same as actually having it. The argument of the preceding paragraph shows that one must know the direction and approximate size of the nonrandom errors in order to draw valid inferences from significance tests.

Better survey techniques and more knowledge of how they work in the field will make the problem of nonrandom error less serious. This is not true of another characteristic of theoretically oriented surveys: the large number of hypotheses that are formulated after examination of the data. The typical experiment is designed to gather data on a small number of variables in order to study a few hypotheses; it usually does not gather data that would allow many other hypotheses to be studied. In the typical survey the overhead costs are so high and the marginal cost of adding a question so low that dozens or even hundreds of variables are included. Although some hypotheses may be stated in advance, it would be a deplorable waste of scarce resources to limit a questionnaire to the data necessary to test these few hypotheses: such a limitation would also preclude much elaboration of the relations under study.

Trouble enters when one begins to test hypotheses that were not stated before inspecting the data.[45] Consider first the cognate situation of hunting through a table of random numbers until one finds a "nonrandom" sequence striking enough to test. Thus the probability that the next ten random digits I examine will all be odd is $(\frac{1}{2})^{10}$, or $1/1024$. Everyone will agree that this is a valid computation. However, suppose that I first scan the columns of random digits until I came across a sequence of ten odd digits. May I compute the probability of finding this

---

[44] Even in large research organization such data are not easy to come by. As Stephan and McCarthy point out, they require specially designed investigations. Frederick F. Stephan and Philip J. McCarthy, *Sampling Opinions* (New York: John Wiley & Sons, Inc., 1958), Part II.

[45] For a fuller discussion of this and related problems, see Selvin and Stuart, *op. cit.*

sequence? Of course not! This sequence was found by "hunting." The longer one hunts, the more likely is a sequence of odd digits—ten or a hundred or a thousand!

In this situation the error is obvious, because there are no substantive or theoretical considerations to divert one from the meaning of the probability calculations. When the survey investigator rummages through a pile of tables from a real survey, he has many other things on his mind in addition to the tests of significance; it is perhaps understandable that he computes meaningless figures. But the two situations are formally the same, and so is the moral to be drawn from them: it is meaningless to perform tests of significance (or to compute confidence intervals) on the same data that were used to suggest the hypothesis being tested (or the parameter being estimated). Under these circumstances a valid test or interval estimate requires an independent body of data.

In the unlikely event that one knows in advance how many hypotheses are to be found and tested (or, equivalently, if one agrees to stop hunting after arriving at some predetermined number), then it is possible to reserve *in advance* a properly selected subsample of the data on which to test the hypotheses found in the rest of the data. However, if there are many hypotheses, the subsample would have to be too large to be economical.

In the usual survey situation, the only valid way to test a series of hypotheses discovered by hunting through the data is on a new body of data. Now if one had to design and conduct an entirely new survey specifically for this purpose, the rate of valid tests of significance would be very slow indeed. However, if one is working in an area in which published data are abundant, as they were for suicide in Durkheim's time, then the hypotheses can be readily tested. For most of the problems that sociologists study, such data are not available, or, if they are available, the form of the published results is often not the form that is needed.

All this has been changed by the development of "libraries" of survey data. Since these "libraries" catalog their material by the individual question, it should be the work of a few minutes to find a body of data with the two or three variables of the hypothesis to be tested and to run the appropriate tables. In short, these "libraries" make it possible to test most survey hypotheses by means of external replications, and the cost of performing these tests by mail may be no more than the cost of computations required for the conventional test on the data at hand.[46]

The simplest statistical procedure for using replications to test hy-

---

[46] Here is a new field of application for libraries of survey data. Is it far-fetched to envisage a service that would test statistical hypotheses at a moderate fee?

potheses is the *sign test,* which is explained in most elementary statistics texts. The investigator chooses the level of significance and then examines the appropriate independent replications. Thus if five replications all turn out to be in the same direction as the original relation, the level of significance is $(\frac{1}{2})^5$ or about 3 per cent. Similarly, a test at the 1 per cent level requires seven replications.

A more difficult statistical problem is to choose the right kind of replication: should it be an internal replication, a stratified external replication, or a series of unstratified external replications? It is now clear that internal replications cannot serve this function.[47]

Suppose, for example, that the correlation between two variables in a sample is 0.30. The corresponding statistical hypothesis is to be tested by examination in five subsamples of the original sample, determined either by stratification or by some random procedure. The five correlations thus obtained all come from a "population" (the original sample) whose correlation is known to be 0.30; they thus provide no information about the population from which the original sample was drawn—in particular, they have nothing whatever to do with the hypothesis that the correlation in this population is zero or any other specified value.

The best procedure for testing statistical hypotheses appears to be a stratified external replication in which the strata are determined by some random procedure (perhaps based on the serial numbers of the respondents). The value of random division lies in its ability to deal with nonrandom errors that may appear if some other principle of division is used. For example, suppose that one wanted to replicate the relation between social class and political party preference by dividing the replicative sample according to the areas of the city in which the respondents lived. Many nonrandom errors would be correlated with this geographical division, notably sampling bias, nonresponse bias, and interviewer bias. Dividing the sample randomly into subsamples turns all these nonrandom errors into random errors, exactly as in a randomized experiment, and

---

[47] The earlier version of this paper argued strongly for the efficacy of internal replications as approximations to tests of significance. I am indebted to Travis Hirschi for recognizing the fallacy in this argument and persuading me that I had been wrong— not only in the earlier paper but also in *The Effects of Leadership, op. cit.,* where the procedure was called *homogeneous subgroup analysis.* See also the "method of matched comparisons" in Samuel A. Stouffer, *et al., The American Soldier* (Princeton, N.J.: Princeton University Press, 1948), Vol. I, pp. 92-95, and Samuel A. Stouffer, "Quantitative Methods," in Joseph B. Gittler (ed.), *Review of Sociology* (New York: John Wiley & Sons, Inc., 1957), pp. 45-46. Stouffer's discussions might be interpreted as a plea for stratified external replications except for his failure to require that the data for the replications be different from the data on which the original hypothesis was based.

makes the replication more nearly adequate as the basis for a test of significance.[48]

Another procedure used by Durkheim appears at first glance to be a form of unit replication. In demonstrating that the relation previously found between time of day and the suicide rate really depends on the "intensity of social life," he musters a variety of indicators of social activity—accidents, rail travel, and express receipts.[49] Social activity and suicide turn out to be highly associated, thus supporting his interpretation of the time-of-day relation. Although this seems to be another type of replication, serving the same ends as those already discussed, this *item replication* lacks one essential element of the unit replications: independence of observations. In unit replications each respondent appears only once, no matter how many strata are included, but in item replications the entire sample is used to study the relations between items. Item replications help to demonstrate that an indicator is valid—in other words, that it means what the analyst says it means. The greater the variety of indicators of social activity that Durkheim can relate to suicide, the greater his assurance that social activity—and not some accidental correlate of it—is what accounts for the variations in suicide.[50]

Each of the four types of replication discussed in the preceding sections —internal replication, unstratified and stratified external replication, and item replication—serves a distinct function. Although Durkheim could not have envisaged the ways in which research is conducted today, it is noteworthy that he, too, used each type differently. In all likelihood, further study of his use of replications will reveal still other problems and some valuable clues to their solution.

A PROBLEM IN DESCRIBING GROUPS

The first section of the chapter on anomic suicide begins: "It is a well-known fact that economic crises have an aggravating effect on the suicidal

[48] It is necessary to be cautious here, since the random division of the sample used in the replication randomizes only those factors associated with the division into strata; it obviously cannot turn the original survey into a randomized experiment.

[49] *Suicide, op. cit.,* pp. 118-20.

[50] Item replication is, in a sense, the inverse of scaling. In item replication, one begins with a concept and seeks a variety of indicators to clarify its meaning. In scaling, one begins with a set of items and asks whether there is a single underlying concept that accounts for them.

tendency." [51] Durkheim then establishes that poverty is not the link between economic crises and suicide. He argues that poverty "tends rather *to produce the opposite effect.* There is very little suicide in Ireland, where the peasantry leads so wretched a life. Poverty-stricken Calabria has almost no suicide; Spain has a tenth as many as France." [52] Here is an association between groups (countries) and individual behavior, in which the relationship is attributed to one property of the groups—their poverty. But Calabria, Ireland, and Spain are not only poorer than France; they are also more Catholic than France and, as Durkheim was at pains to show in his analysis of egoistic suicide, less educated. There is no necessary reason why poverty should be singled out as *the* cause of the lower suicide rate in these countries. Religious or educational differences would have accounted equally well for the variations in suicide.

The source of this difficulty is clear. It is the oversimple description of a group according to a single variable. What can be done to avoid such problems? One answer is to hold the other group characteristics constant by cross tabulation, just as one does with individual characteristics. To study the influence of poverty on suicide, Durkheim would have had to find areas that were alike on other variables, such as religion, urbanization, and education, and different only in relative wealth. As a practical matter, this is impossible. Murdock's cross-cultural comparisons are based on as many as 250 different cultures, but even this number is too small to allow more than one variable to be held constant in any table. [53] The smaller the groups, the easier such statistical manipulation of group variables becomes, at least in principle. But surveys of the joint effects of group and individual characteristics on behavior seldom have the resources to include the hundreds of groups that would be necessary if group characteristics were to be manipulated by cross tabulation.

If groups differing in only a single characteristic are practically impossible to find in survey research and if large numbers of groups are impossibly expensive, is there any alternative? The most attractive alternative —perhaps the only one—is to abandon the attempt to deal with one group characteristic at a time and to describe the groups with as many variables as necessary. Where the number of groups is too small for cross tabulation, they should be described in terms of a multivariate typology. [54] In the first example above, for instance, Calabria, Ireland,

[51] *Suicide, op. cit.,* p. 241.

[52] *Ibid.,* p. 245; italics added.

[53] George Peter Murdock, *Social Structure* (New York: The Macmillan Company, 1949).

[54] Allen H. Barton, "The Concept of Property-Space in Social Research," in Lazarsfeld and Rosenberg, *op. cit.,* pp. 40-53.

and Spain would have been described as *poor, Catholic, and having a low level of education.* Theoretical simplicity is thus sacrificed for theoretical and empirical accuracy. These countries would differ from France on three or more independent variables instead of one, but they would be described in all their relevant aspects.

Durkheim seems to have had something like this in mind in his chapter entitled "How to Determine Social Causes and Social Types" (Book II, Chap. 1). He argues for the classification of suicides according to "morphological types" determined by the psychological and other characteristics of each suicide. Only because the necessary data were not available was he compelled to use his "etiological types." The same logic and the greater ease with which group data may now be gathered suggest that groups be described as multivariate types rather than by a single variable.[55]

Despite its occasionally archaic language ("suicidogenic current"), the empirical analysis in *Suicide* is as vital today as it was in 1897—perhaps more so, since the quantitative approach that Durkheim pioneered has since become widely accepted among sociologists. But overemphasis on the quantitative aspects of *Suicide* would be as dangerous as total neglect, if it furthered the current tendency to substitute technical virtuosity for hard thinking about empirical data, thinking that is guided by theory and directed toward enriching theory. This, after all, is the essential message of *Suicide:* that methodology is valuable insofar as it springs from the needs of theory and that theory is most fruitful when it is continually tested and refined in methodologically adequate research.

[55] With the aid of modern statistical techniques and computing machinery Warren O. Hagstrom and I have developed a procedure for the multivariate description of groups. See Hanan C. Selvin and Warren O. Hagstrom, "The Empirical Classification ol Formal Groups," *American Sociological Review,* XXVIII (1936), 399-411, and the exchange between James A. Davis and us in the October 1964 issue of the same journal. Although all of the components of our procedure had been used previously in sociology, the combination we developed appeared to be new. However, we have since learned that our procedure is one of a number worked out by taxonomists in biology and other fields; see Robert Sokal and Peter H. A. Sneath, *Principles of Numerical Taxonomy* (San Francisco: W. H. Freeman Company, 1963).

DURKHEIM'S FUNCTIONAL
THEORY OF RITUAL

HARRY ALPERT

FUNCTIONALISM IN SOCIOLOGY is seen at its best, perhaps, in Durkheim's analysis of ceremony and ritual. The French sociologist inquired into the nature and functions of ceremonial and ritualistic institutions in Book III of *Les Formes élémentaires de la vie religieuse*. His mode of analysis here follows his general theory of religion which he perceives as an expression, in symbolic form, of social realities. He first determines the religious functions of ceremonial and ritualistic behavior and then tries to get behind the symbolic beliefs and behavior to the social realities which they are purported to express. In thus "substituting reality for symbol," he brings religion down to earth, so to speak, and hence is able to ascertain the social functions of the religiously symbolic conduct.

A study of the proscribing rites—i.e., taboos and interdicts ("the negative cult")[1]—and of the prescribing ones—such as sacrificial, imitative, commemorative, and piacular rites ("the positive cult")[2]—reveals that ritualistic institutions have a number of vital social functions which vary, of course, with the nature of the particular ceremony being performed. The following are four social functions of ritual to which Durkheim pays special attention.[3]

1. *A disciplinary and preparatory function.* Ritual prepares an individual for social living by imposing on him the self-discipline, the "disdain

From *Sociology and Social Research*, XXIII (1938), 103-108. Reprinted by permission of the author and the publisher.

[1] *Les Formes élémentaires de la vie religieuse*, 2nd ed. (Paris: Alcan, 1925), Book III, Chap. 1.

[2] *Ibid.*, Book III, Chaps. 2-5.

[3] We list them without regard to the specific rites which especially foster each. Durkheim, we feel, tends to classify as separate rites what are in a sense only elements found in varying degree and with varying frequency in almost all ceremonies. Thus a "piacular rite," such as mourning, is frequently not devoid of sacrificial, commemorative, or imitative elements; nor is the taboo aspect entirely absent.

for suffering," the self-abnegation without which life in society would be impossible. Social existence is possible only as individuals are able to accept constraints and controls. Asceticism is an inherent element in all social life.[4] Ritual, being formal and institutional and, hence, to some degree prohibitive and inhibitive, is necessarily ascetic. Durkheim observes:

> In fact, there is no interdict, the observance of which does not have an ascetic character to a certain degree. Abstaining from something may be useful or from a form of activity, which, since it is usual, should answer to some human need, is, of necessity, imposing constraints and renunciations.[5]

But abstinences, he adds,

> . . . do not come without suffering. We hold to the profane world by all the fibers of our flesh; our senses attach us to it; our life depends upon it. It is not merely the natural theater of our activity; it penetrates us from every side; it is a part of ourselves. So we cannot detach ourselves from it without doing violence to our nature and without painfully wounding our instincts. In other words, the negative cult cannot develop without causing suffering. Pain is one of its necessary conditions.[6]

Moreover, the positive cult is possible "only when a man is trained to renouncement, to abnegation, to detachment from self, and consequently to suffering.[7] Ascetic practices, therefore, are "a necessary school where men form and temper themselves, and acquire the qualities of disinterestedness and endurance without which there would be no religion." [8] Substitute, in the above quotations, *social rule* for *negative cult, social life* for *positive cult,* and *society* for *religion,* and one has a clear picture of the disciplinary function of social ritual.

2. *A cohesive function.* Ceremony brings people together and thus serves to reaffirm their common bonds and to enhance and reinforce social solidarity: "Rites are, above all, means by which the social group reaffirms itself periodically." [9] Ceremonial occasions are occasions of social communion. They are necessitated by the inevitable intermittency of social life.[10] The workaday, immediate, private, and personal interests of an individual occupy much of his everyday life. His social

---

[4] *Les Formes élémentaires, op. cit.,* p. 452.
[5] *Ibid.,* p. 444.
[6] *Ibid.,* p. 446.
[7] *Ibid.,* p. 451.
[8] *Ibid.,* pp. 451-52.
[9] *Ibid.,* p. 553.
[10] *Ibid.,* p. 493.

ties to his fellow men, their common pool of values, tend to become obscure, indistinct, and even to lapse from consciousness. But since society is a necessary condition of human civilized living, it is imperative that this condition be remedied, that periodically at least man be given the opportunity to commune with his fellow social beings and to express his solidarity with them. Ceremonial institutions afford just such opportunities. Whatever their stated purpose, "the essential thing is that men are assembled, that sentiments are felt in common, and that they are expressed in common acts." . . . [11]

3. [A] *revitalizing function.* If society is to be kept alive, its members must be made keenly aware of their social heritage. Traditions must be perpetuated, faith must be renewed, values must be transmitted and deeply imbedded. In this task of vitalizing and reanimating the social heritage of a group, ceremony and ritual play an important part. Men celebrate certain rites in order to "remain faithful to the past, to keep for the group its moral physiognomy." [12] A large number of ceremonies include rites whose object it is "to recall the past and, in a way, to make it present by means of a veritable dramatic representation." [13] These rites serve to sustain the vitality of the social heritage and to keep its essential parts from lapsing from memory and consciousness. In short, they "revivify the most essential elements of the collective consciousness." Through them, "the group periodically renews the sentiment which it has of itself and of its unity; at the same time individuals are strengthened in their social natures." [14] Ceremony functions, then, "to awaken certain ideas and sentiments, to attach the present to the past, the individual to the group." [15] Since it aids in transmitting the social heritage, it may also be said to have an educational function. . . .

4. *A euphoric function.*[16] . . . [Ceremony and ritual also] serve to establish a condition of social euphoria, i.e., a pleasant feeling of social well-being. This function takes on special significance when a group is faced with an actual or a threatened condition of dysphoria. All societies are subject to crises, calamities, disappointments, losses of particular members, and other dysphoric experiences. In certain cases the very existence of the group may be in jeopardy. These socially adverse conditions tend to disrupt the smooth functioning of the group; they threaten its

[11] *Ibid.,* p. 553.
[12] *Ibid.,* p. 530.
[13] *Ibid.,* p. 531.
[14] *Ibid.,* p. 536.
[15] *Ibid.,* p. 541.
[16] *Cf. ibid.,* pp. 591, 613.

sense of well-being, its feeling that all's right with the world. The group attempts, therefore, to counterbalance the disturbing action of these dysphoric situations; and in smoothing its way through crises and adversities, ceremony and ritual are of invaluable service.[17] They perform this function by requiring individuals to have and to express certain emotions and sentiments, and by making them express these sentiments and feelings together.

Consider, for example, the mourning ceremonies: "When a society is going through circumstances which sadden, perplex, or irritate it, it exercises a pressure over its members to make them bear witness, by significant actions to their sorrow, perplexity, or anger." [18] Thus, in the face of a dysphoric experience such as the loss of a member through death, a group exerts moral pressure on its members to make their sentiments harmonize with the situation. They must show that they have been duly affected by the loss. In any case, the group cannot allow them to remain indifferent . . . :

> [T]o allow them to remain indifferent to the blow which has fallen upon it and diminished it would be equivalent to proclaiming that it does not hold the place in their hearts which is due it; it would be denying itself. A family which allows one of its members to die without being wept for shows by that very fact that it lacks moral unity and cohesion; it abdicates, it renounces its existence.[19]

When someone dies, then,

> the family group to which he belongs feels itself lessened, and to react against this loss, it assembles. . . . Collective sentiments are renewed, individuals consequently tend to seek out one another and to assemble together.[20]

This coming together of individuals, this entering into closer relations with one another, and this sharing of a like emotion give rise to "a sensation of comfort which compensates the original loss." Since the individuals weep together,

> they hold to one another, and the group is not weakened. . . . Of course they have only sad emotions in common; but communicating in sorrow is still communicating; and every communion of mind, in whatever form it may be made, raises the social vitality.[21]

---

[17] Symbols and slogans are also effective, as the Lynds have well illustrated in *Middletown in Transition.*

[18] *Les Formes élémentaires, op. cit.,* p. 589.

[19] *Ibid.,* p. 571.

[20] *Loc. cit.*

[21] *Ibid.,* p. 574.

We see then that ritual and ceremony in general serve to remake individuals and groups morally.[22] They are disciplinary, cohesive, vitalizing, and euphoric social forces.

The above summary sketch of Durkheim's analysis of the social functions of ceremony and ritual can do justice neither to its profundity nor to its wisdom. Durkheim may have been mistaken in his interpretation of certain Australian ceremonies and in his sharp differentiation between magic and religion,[23] and no doubt he erred in considering only religious rites to the practical exclusion of secular ritual [24] and in neglecting in general to give due attention to those phenomena that are social but nonreligious.[25] His functional analysis of ceremonial and ritualistic institutions, nonetheless, remains, we believe, a major contribution to sociology.

[22] *Ibid.,* p. 529.

[23] See W. L. Warner, "The Social Configuration of Magical Behavior," in *Essays in Anthropology Presented to A. L. Kroeber* (Berkeley: University of California Press, 1936).

[24] *Cf.* Dr. Benedict's remarks: "The contention of Durkheim and many others that religion arises from ritualism as such must be challenged, for the most extreme ritualistic formalism does not convert the council of elders or affinal exchange into an aspect of the already existing religious complexes. Durkheim's theoretical position is untenable once it is recognized that ritual may surround any field of behavior and of itself does not give birth to religion any more than it gives birth to art or to social organization." R. Benedict, "Ritual," *Encyclopedia of the Social Sciences,* Vol. XIII, 1934, p. 396.

[25] *Cf.* A. A. Goldenweiser: "In economic pursuits and in industry, in the ideas and customs clustering about the family or kinship, social factors figure at least as prominently as individual ones, without, however, assuming a halo of sanctity." *Anthropology* (New York: Appleton-Century-Crofts, Inc., 1937), p. 220.

DURKHEIM'S ETHICAL THEORY

MORRIS GINSBERG

IT IS USUAL NOWADAYS to classify ethical theories as "naturalistic" and "nonnaturalistic." Durkheim's views do not fall readily into either category. It is true that he sets out to study morality *"d'après la méthode des sciences positives."* But this does not mean that he proposes to reduce moral judgments to expressions of subjective desires or preferences either of the individual or the group. It is true again that in his view moral rules come from society and have society for their object. But society is not to be interpreted naturalistically. It is the home of ideals and these have a reality of their own different from the reality of the facts with which the natural sciences are concerned. Again and again he explains that he does not propose to "derive morality from science but to make a scientific study of morality, which is quite another matter." [1] Such a science is not confined to a study of the means or techniques by which human ends are achieved. It must deal, he tells us, with the ends themselves and with the basis of the obligations they impose. It has thus a double task, first to describe the facts of the moral life and discover their conditions and consequences, and secondly, by eliciting the ideals which in a confused manner they embody, to afford guidance for future conduct. The method is "positive" in the sense that the ideals are not to be laid down a priori but to be "disengaged" from the "facts" of the moral life.

That ethical theory must begin with the facts—that is to say, with the moral judgments actually found in societies—will hardly be disputed. That it is legitimate to study the conditions, psychological and social, in which they arise, change, or decay and the influence they exert on conduct or social institutions, is again not open to doubt. The problem

From Morris Ginsberg, *On the Diversity of Morals* (London: William Heinemann, Limited, 1956). Reprinted by permission of the publisher.
[1] *De la division du travail social*, p. xxxvii.

remains, however, in what ways the ideals implicit in actual moral codes can be "elicited" and by what methods or criteria their validity can be tested. Durkheim insists that we must not begin, in the manner attributed by him to the philosophers, by assuming a single moral principle which can be intuitively grasped and then applied to particular situations. Actual morality, as we find it in any given society, consists of collections of special rules which prescribe the conduct regarded as fitting in each of the spheres of human life: e.g., the domestic, the professional, the political. These do not form a unified system deducible from a single principle. The moralities prevailing in the different spheres do not always keep pace in their development and, on examination, reveal different degrees of coherence and consistency. We must begin then with the rules actually found, whether enunciated in codes, or in popular aphorisms, or in current opinion. One would expect Durkheim to start by giving a description of these and then proceed to "explain" them by disclosing their functions: i.e., the ways in which they fulfill the needs of the society. But this is not what he does. Having given a few perfunctory examples, he adopts what is in effect the Kantian manner. He asks, in short, what is implied in the fact that there is such a thing as morality, and it is the implications thus elicited that constitute for him "the distinctive characteristics of the moral fact." This may or may not be sound procedure, but it cannot, as he claims, be rightly described as empirical. This will become clear when we have considered what these characteristics are.

In the first place, he argues, moral rules, whatever their specific content, imply the notion of obligation—that is, they are invested with a special authority in virtue of which they are obeyed out of respect for them and for no other reason. They imply the acceptance of duty for duty's sake. It is difficult to see how this can be an empirical generalization. It may be possible to show that in all societies there is a recognition that there must be rules, that complete anarchy cannot be allowed, and that the individual is expected to obey the rules without stopping on each occasion to calculate the probable consequences of his act. But that only those acts are universally assigned moral quality which are performed from the motive of duty alone is not a proposition which Durkheim has established empirically.

In proceeding to the second characteristic of moral acts Durkheim, in fact, himself makes this clear. It is not possible, he says, that we should perform an act merely because we are commanded to do so. The act must appeal to our sensibility as desirable. Moral acts can, he thinks, be shown to involve, in addition to constraint, the quality of attraction. They cannot be performed without effort or sense of difficulty, but at the same time they appeal to the agent as in a measure satisfying or satisfactory. In other words, duty and good are two characteristics which are found in all moral acts, though they may be combined in different proportions in different cases. These characteristics constitute the formal elements of morals. The next step is to inquire what sort of acts are regarded as moral: i.e., as at once obligatory and desirable.

An empirical survey would necessitate an examination of the moral rules which are found in our society or some other society. This is not attempted. Instead he appeals to the "conscience of contemporary man," and claims that the answers thus obtained would be confirmed by a study of the moral systems of all known societies. He adopts from Wundt, without further inquiry, a classification of ends as "personal" and "impersonal." By the former he understands ends which concern the agent only; by the latter, ends which relate to other individuals or groups of individuals, or to things. He then argues that moral quality is never predicated of acts directed to ends in the first category: acts which make for the preservation of the agent or even for his development are morally indifferent even if they may be considered prudent or sensible. It follows logically that acts which make for the preservation of other individuals or their development cannot have moral value either. If each individual taken in himself has no moral value, neither can a sum of individuals: "A sum of zeros can only equal zero. If any particular interest whether that of myself or others has no moral value the sum of such interests must also be of no moral value." From this it follows by exclusion that the only ends which have moral value are those which have a society as such as their object. If there is any morality it must have for its object a society "considered as a personality qualitatively different from the individual personalities of which it is composed." [2]

It is truly remarkable that Durkheim could have believed that these dialectical arguments could claim the support of experience. He offers no evidence that no people has ever regarded the efforts of an individual to develop his personality at the cost of immediate satisfaction as morally praiseworthy. Again, it is simply not true that we deny moral quality to acts which are directed at the relief of suffering or the promotion of good will between individuals. Durkheim offers no evidence at all for the view that these acts are regarded as morally valuable not in themselves but only because they make for the survival of the group as such. Patriotism

[2] *Sociologie et philosophie*, p. 53.

may be a virtue, but it is surely to fly in the face of all the evidence to say that it is the only virtue. Nor is it at all clear that patriotism implies the attribution to society of a personality which is qualitatively different from the members which compose it. This is a conclusion which Durkheim may or may not be justified in reaching on other grounds. But that such a view is implied in the moral judgments of our own or any other society he has certainly not succeeded in showing. A further point is relevant in this connection. In classifying moral acts Durkheim considers only the ends or goods at which they aim but neglects the distribution of the goods; in other words, he neglects the problem of distributive justice. Had he taken this into consideration he would have realized that justice is concerned, not only with the relations between the community as a whole and its component members, but also with the relations of the members to one another and, therefore, that to exclude interpersonal relations from the domain of morals, or to regard them as belonging to morals only indirectly and derivatively, is entirely unwarranted.

So far the conclusion reached by Durkheim is that all moral activity is directed toward society, consists in the service of or devotion to society for its own sake and not for the services that it renders to the individual. This accounts in his view for the formal characteristics of morality, the combination of obligatoriness and desirability. Society is desirable to the individual because it lives and acts in him and contributes all that is of value in his nature. In accepting it he accepts what is immanent in him. He cannot sever himself from it without severing himself from himself. It is part of his substance and, Durkheim thinks, the best part. Yet at the same time society transcends the individual. It is infinitely greater than the individual and therefore the rules that emanate from it come to him with authority and impose themselves upon him as obligatory. Two questions now arise. First, if morality comes from the group and is obligatory for that reason, has then the individual no right to criticize it? Must he accept as binding every demand that society at any time makes upon him? Second, if Durkheim's account of obligation answers the question of fact, does it also answer the question of jurisdiction? Ought we to obey the commands of society merely because they are commands? A command requires justification, and this must apply to society as to others who claim authority. To both these questions Durkheim offers answers, but they fail, I think, to carry conviction.

With regard to the first point, Durkheim explains that when he maintains that the demands of society are morally binding he is not advocating passive conformity. Current opinion may not reflect the real state of society. The prevailing code may contain survivals from a former state of society and may take no account of changing conditions. Socrates, he says, expressed more faithfully than his judges the morality which was appropriate for the society of his time. When the individual refuses to conform to the morality of his day he is justified in doing so if he possesses deeper insight into the state of society as it is or is tending to become. It is science rather than the individual reason that is the ultimate court of appeal. A science of morals can, it seems, draw attention to fundamental principles which, in the stress of a social crisis, may tend to be forgotten or rejected. It can go further perhaps and show that such principles are still required in existing conditions. In dealing with new moral tendencies, it can inquire how far they are necessitated by the changes which society is undergoing. It will be seen that, in all this, science does not go beyond what exists or is considered likely to come into existence.

The difficulty in all this is that Durkheim does not explain at all clearly how the relations between the conditions prevailing in a society and its needs are to be investigated. In his earlier writings and, to a lesser extent, in his later [ones] he laid great stress on the distinction between the normal and the pathological. He tended to identify the normal with the general and he repeatedly urges that what is general in a society must on the whole be adapted to its needs. But he points out himself that selection operates very crudely and that though it will eliminate the worst, it does not necessarily make for the emergence or prevalence of the best. Indeed he distinguishes between a *normalité en fait* and a *normalité en droit,* and this I think must mean that what is in fact general is not necessarily best suited to the needs of the society. The resort to the notion of the "conditions necessary for the existence of a society" or the "needs of a society" does not carry us much further. For the needs of the society are not what people actually want, but what in an ideal society would be wanted, and the conditions of existence are only necessary in an ideal sense, since it is clear from Durkheim's discussion that in existing societies they are far from being attained. In short, value judgments are implied which go beyond the given and are not shown to be deducible from actual social conditions or tendencies.

One or two illustrations may be given. In *De la division du travail social,* Durkheim seeks to show that the function of the division of labor is to bring about what he calls *organic solidarity.* In contrast with *mechanical solidarity,* this depends not on resemblances or uniformity but upon differences. Now the movement toward the organic need indicate no moral advance. Specialization of functions may be achieved in a manner which may impoverish rather than enrich social life. But Durkheim claims moral value for the organic type of society on the ground that it brings home to people their need of and dependence upon each other, and at the same time encourages individual diversity. He realizes that this moral function can only be fulfilled by the division of labor under certain conditions of freedom and equality. It is necessary in the first place that individuals shall be free to choose the occupation which corresponds to their capacity and that there shall be sufficient equality of conditions to insure that no individual shall be forced into contractual relations detrimental to his full development. In Durkheim's own time these conditions were certainly not present. The division of labor had brought about not concord but strife and a form of specialization which was not conducive to the realization of individual potentialities. In these circumstances,

> . . . it is necessary to put an end to this anomie, to find ways of making those organs work in harmony which at present clash in mutual discord, that is, to introduce more justice into their relations by removing the external inequalities which are the source of the trouble . . . *Notre premier devoir actuellement est de nous faire une morale.*[3]

But who imposes this duty upon us?—clearly not the existing society. The appeal is to a standard of justice, equality, and freedom in the light of which the existing social structure is to be remolded. All that sociology can do is to reveal the discrepancy between the existing conditions and the ideal and possibly to suggest methods for removing the discrepancy. But it cannot of itself define the ideal.

Similar considerations apply to Durkheim's discussion of the limits of the group in devotion to which, according to him, morality consists. He shows that in the history of humanity the units of social organization have steadily expanded in volume and have absorbed within themselves smaller units of all kinds, and that there is no reason for believing that this process has reached its limit. Is not our duty then to promote the highest and most inclusive ends, namely those of the whole of humanity? This conclusion Durkheim refuses to draw. Humanity is not yet an organized group, but *un être de raison,* an abstract term under which we bring together the sum of tribes, nations, and states which constitute mankind: *"Ce n'est pas un organisme social ayant sa conscience propre,*

---

[3] *De la division du travail social,* p. 406.

son individualité, son organization." [4] There cannot be any duties to this vague entity. But since this conclusion is repugnant to him Durkheim argues, in this respect agreeing with some of the Hegelians, that the solution is to be found in a more rigorous interpretation of the internal morality of the state. If states abandoned the policy of expansion at the expense of their neighbors and took for their ends the realization of justice within their own domains, there would be no occasion for rivalry between them and cosmopolitanism and patriotism would be reconciled. Admittedly there is thus a hierarchy of groups which claim our devotion in varying degrees, but the highest in the hierarchy so far developed is the nation-state. To the nation-state, therefore, we owe our fullest allegiance, provided only that each state gives up the pursuit of selfish ends and considers itself as one of the many organs which together are needed for the progressive realization of the idea of humanity. It is clear to me that here again Durkheim reaches this conclusion not on the basis of a scientific estimate of the direction in which states are moving but of a universalistic ethic accepted in advance and recognized as binding, whether it will in fact be accepted by states or not.

I turn next to the problem of validation. Morality, Durkheim tells us, can be approached from two points of view: we can try to know and understand it, and we can seek to "judge" it.[5] This latter task is, however, nowhere systematically attempted. In his book on *Moral Education* the essential elements of morality are taken to be three: discipline, attachment to a group, and individual autonomy. Durkheim shows that reasonable grounds can be given for all these. The respect for the moral imperative, the acceptance of discipline qua discipline is justified not only because without adherence to rules no society could maintain itself, but because it is essential to the integrity of the individual. Self-control is a primary condition of self-realization and of any freedom worthy of the name. Again, attachment to a group is justified on the ground that the society is the source of all values and of the best that the individual is capable of. Service to society is not a denial of self but a fulfillment of self: *"La meilleure partie de nous-même n'est qu'une émanation de la collectivité. Ainsi s'explique que nous puissions nous y attacher et même la préférer à nous"* (p. 83). These arguments are set out with much moving eloquence, but they suffer from the cloud of mystery which gathers round Durkheim's conception of *la société*. He admits, as we have seen, that not all societies are of equal moral worth. We have to

⁴ *L'Éducation morale*, p. 86.
⁵ *Sociologie et philosophie*, p. 49.

judge between their claims and we can only do so by reference to the ends or values or ideals which they embody. Society no doubt opens out to us all the goods of civilization, but also all the evils. The mere fiat of a particular society offers no ground for moral decision.

The problem comes to a head in Durkheim's discussion of the autonomy of the individual. Despite the fact that the individual depends on society and owes everything to it, he will not abandon the claim to autonomy. This claim to freedom or autonomy must be taken as a datum of the moral consciousness and is not to be dismissed as based on illusion. The Kantian explanation is rejected. Autonomy cannot consist in accepting the commands of reason. *"Tout prouve, au contraire, que la loi morale est investie d'une autorité qui impose le respect même à la raison. Nous ne sentons pas seulement qu'elle domine notre sensibilité, mais toute notre nature, même notre nature rationelle."* Moreover, Kant's view of reason implies too sharp a separation from sensibility and from nature and thus can have little bearing on freedom in actual life. Durkheim's solution is that freedom rests on knowledge. We learn to command external nature by the discovery of its laws. So we can learn to command human nature by a knowledge of its laws. *"C'est la pensée qui est libératrice de la volonté."* When we know the reasons for the laws of conduct we can obey them freely, without losing our respect for the authority with which they come to us. Whether this is an adequate theory of freedom is a question which will not here be discussed. But it is clear that Durkheim recognizes that the fact that moral rules come from society affords in itself no rational basis for moral obligation. "The developed conscience," he says elsewhere, "requires to know the reasons which justify the commands." [6] He adds that these reasons are at present unknown. *"Nous ignorons entièrement, je ne dis pas seulement les causes historiques, mais les raisons téléologiques qui justifient actuellement la plupart de nos institutions morales."* This applies, for example, to the family, marriage, the rights of property, whether in the form in which they exist now or in the new forms which are beginning to emerge. It seems then that what Durkheim offers is not an explanation of moral institutions but, rather, a program for explanation.

What is this explanation likely to yield? According to the account given in the *Règles de la méthode sociologique,* to explain a social fact is to trace the conditions in which it arises and to elicit its function, i.e., "to determine whether there is a correspondence between the general needs of the social organism and the social fact under consideration and in

[6] *Ibid.,* p. 109.

what this correspondence consists." But, as we have seen, there is an ambiguity in the use of such words as *functions, needs* or *necessary conditions of existence*. There are three different questions that may be asked with respect to the ends of social institutions: what ends do they in fact serve, what ends are they intended or believed to serve, and what ends ought they to serve? Now it is highly probable that if we had clearer knowledge of the ends actually achieved by, say, the criminal law, or property, or war and could compare them with the ends they are believed to achieve, our moral judgment regarding them might be seriously affected. But the moral judgment itself would still have to be made independently and could not be deduced without remainder from the psychological or sociological facts.

Durkheim returns to this problem in his essay on *"Jugements de valeur et jugements de réalité."* He rejects outright all subjectivist interpretations of value judgments which would reduce them to expressions of desires and preferences. Their claim to be objectively valid—i.e., to be independent of the subject making them—must be taken seriously and not dismissed as illusory. This holds good whether the subject in question be one or many. On the other hand, their validity is not safeguarded to any purpose if they are relegated to an ideal world beyond experience. For in that case they would be "immobilized," incapable of affecting action, and it would, moreover, be difficult to account for the fact that they vary in different societies. Durkheim's own solution is as follows. Value judgments express a relation between the things said to possess value and an ideal. It is the relation to the ideal and not any intrinsic quality in the things that gives them value, so that, for example, things may change in value or lose it entirely if the ideal changes. What then are the ideals? They are said to be *"tout simplement les idées dans lesquelles vient se peindre et se résumer la vie sociale telle qu'elle est aux points culminants de son développement"* (p. 136). In the creative periods of history there occurs an intensification of social activity, and a new synthesis of forces results which raises the level of the social consciousness and gives it new vitality. Ideals are then generated which thereafter serve to guide conduct. In describing these processes Durkheim uses highly metaphorical language. He speaks not only of society becoming aware of itself but of the collective ideals becoming aware of themselves (*prendre conscience d'eux-mêmes*). The question arises by what criteria we can decide when a society is at a culminating point of its development. The amount of social effervescence is surely no guide, since this may as easily lead to folly or worse as to grandeur. Durkheim nowhere undertakes the inquiry, the importance of which he repeatedly stresses, into the conditions in which ideals are generated, and no evidence is adduced to show that there is any sort of proportion between the intensity or range of social interaction and the relative worth of ideals. Sometimes, indeed, he seems to allow that the value of society is not in itself but in the fact that it is the birthplace of ideals or the "goods of civilization," but in general *la société* has an intoxicating effect on his mind, hindering any further reflection on the nature of the goods of which it is the condition.

What then emerges from this survey of Durkheim's attempt to study morals in accordance with the "method of the positive sciences"? First, he is clearly right in insisting that the study of morals must begin with the beliefs about conduct that men actually entertain in given societies. He is further right in holding that it is important to discover the conditions in which these beliefs are generated, to estimate the influence they have on conduct, to show how it happens that ideals which have remained latent for centuries may suddenly come to life with revolutionary fervor, or why it is that at certain ages the fabric of belief is shattered, while at others is taken for granted. These are matters for what might be called *the sociology of morals*. The question remains whether, in Durkheim's language, the ideals and principles of conduct can be "judged." Here there are possibilities which Durkheim hints at but does not explore. It may, for example, be possible (1) to show that men do not clearly understand the principles which they believe themselves to hold or that they do not realize their full implications; (2) to investigate the extent to which men's actions correspond to their principles and especially to what are, at a particular time, taken to be fundamental principles; (3) to examine how far the different principles which men believe themselves to hold or in accordance with which they in fact act are consistent with each other or might be made more consistent by mutual correction or adjustment; (4) to follow a similar procedure in relation to public policy as embodied in the institutions of given societies. Such a procedure applied, for example, to legal codes, or to sexual morality or to professional ethics would amount to a "judging" of them and might open the way to their rational reconstruction. The problems thus raised belong, however, not to social science, as Durkheim thought, but to philosophy. The principles of conduct must, as he says, be taken as given. But they refer not to what is given but to what ought to be. Their further clarification or systematization will not turn them into judgments of fact. Ideals, Durkheim tells us, are real "in their own way." This only means, however, that the human mind can come to know them, as it comes to know the real world. It does not follow that the only method available is that of the "positive" sciences. Durkheim's own procedure is, despite his frequent disclaimers, philosophical rather than scientific, though it is arguable that the philosophy would have been more convincing had the scientific foundations been more securely laid. On the philosophical side his work suffers from a failure to distinguish clearly between problems of origin and problems of validity and from too great a readiness to identify the impersonal with the collective, the pressure of society with objective validity. He set out to find an objective basis for moral obligation. He himself draws an analogy between his argument and Kant's. "Kant," he says, "postulates God, because without this hypothesis, morality would be unintelligible. I postulate a personality specifically distinct from individuals, because otherwise morality would have no object and duty no point of attachment" (p. 74). *"Entre Dieu et la société il faut choisir."* But he has not shown that morality implies reference to society conceived as possessing a personality distinct from the individuals that compose it or that, if there were such a being, its mere fiat would justify obligation. The argument would only be plausible if we first accepted the value judgment that society embodies the highest values we know. This is certainly Durkheim's view. *"Dans le monde de l'expérience, je ne connais qu'un sujet qui possède une réalité morale plus riche, plus complexe que le nôtre, c'est la collectivité"* (p. 75). In view of the way in which societies behave to each other, this is indeed a startling statement. But even if it were accepted, it would not follow that the basis of moral obligation is the fact that moral rules come from society but rather that society is the object which deserves the highest devotion. We should then have to determine what it is in society that we value and in which societies the highest values are embodied, and we should in fact be back at the point at which Durkheim started. To appeal to *la société* in general is thus to conceal the essential problems of moral philosophy.

DURKHEIM AND HISTORY

ROBERT N. BELLAH

HISTORY WAS ALWAYS of central importance in Durkheim's sociological work. Without understanding this a full appreciation of his contribution to sociology is impossible. And yet Durkheim is widely thought of as an ahistorical theorist. This impression seems to derive in part from some remarks near the end of Chapter V of *The Rules of Sociological Method*,[1] but more generally from the commonly held view that structural-functionalism, of which Durkheim is undoubtedly one of the founders, is incapable of accounting for social change and so uninterested in history.[2] Whether or not the structural-functional position is in fact incompatible with a theory of social change will be questioned in this paper. As for history, Durkheim, from his earliest to his latest work, urges the closest *rapprochement* between sociology and history.[3] In one of his earliest published papers[4] he stresses the importance of history for sociology and of sociology for history.[5] In the prefaces of Volumes I (1898)

From *American Sociological Review*, XXIV (1959), 447-61. Reprinted by permission of the author and the publisher. Revision of paper read at the Durkheim-Simmel Centenary Session of the annual meeting of the American Sociological Society, August 1958.

[1] (New York: The Free Press of Glencoe, Inc., 1950), pp. 115-120. See below for a discussion of this passage and the relevant sections of Chapter VI.

[2] This criticism often strikes an ideological note in accusing structural-functionalism of political conservatism, justification of the status quo, and so on. For an analysis of this argument see Robert Merton, "Manifest and Latent Functions," in *Social Theory and Social Structure* (New York: The Free Press of Glencoe, Inc., 1957), esp. pp. 37-38. Stemming from a quite different setting, the antihistorical polemic of Durkheim's English anthropological disciples, Malinowski and Radcliffe-Brown, has added currency to the notion of Durkheim as ahistorical.

[3] What Durkheim meant by *history* will, it is hoped, become clear during the course of this paper. At this point it may merely be noted that he was not committed to any special conception of history such as the "historical individual" of German historicism or the trait atomism of the "historical" anthropologists.

[4] "Introduction à la Sociologie de la Famille," *Annales de la Faculté des Lettres de Bordeaux*, X (1888), 257-81.

[5] *Ibid.*, pp. 262-65, and pp. 276-78.

and II (1899) of *L'Année Sociologique* he lays down the policy of including a large proportion of historical works among the books reviewed, a policy from which *L'Année* never deviated, and addresses his colleagues: "It has appeared to us that it would be useful to call these researches to the attention of sociologists, to give them a glimpse of how rich the material is and of all the fruits which may be expected from it." [6] In 1905 he calls to his students' attention the importance of history for the understanding of the sociology of education,[7] and in 1912 he speaks of the crucial importance of history for the sociology of religion.[8] And in his last paper, the "Introduction à la morale" of 1917, Durkheim once again notes the fundamental significance of history for the understanding of man.

SOCIOLOGY AND HISTORY:
METHODOLOGICAL CONSIDERATIONS

At several points Durkheim went so far as to question whether or not sociology and history could in fact be considered two separate disciplines. In the preface to Volume I of *L'Année* he quotes the great historian Fustel de Coulanges, who was his own master and to whom he dedicated his Latin doctoral dissertation, to the effect that "the true sociology is history." [9] Durkheim approves this saying on the condition that history be done sociologically; and in an article of 1903 he traces the tendency of history for the preceding fifty years to become in fact more and more sociological.[10] His most extreme statement on the subject was made in the course of a discussion held by the French Society of Philosophy in 1908 where, in reply to the statement of a distinguished historian, he said:

> In his exposition, M. Seignobos seemed to oppose history and sociology, as if they were two disciplines using different methods. In reality, there is nothing in my knowledge of sociology which merits the name, which doesn't have a historical character. . . . There are not two methods or two opposed conceptions. That which will be true of history will be true of sociology.[11]

[6] Preface, *L'Année Sociologique*, II (1899), v.

[7] *Education and Sociology* (New York: The Free Press of Glencoe, Inc., 1956), pp. 152-53.

[8] *The Elementary Forms of Religious Life* (New York: The Free Press of Glencoe, Inc., 1947), p. 3.

[9] Preface, *L'Année Sociologique*, I (1898), iii.

[10] "Sociologie et sciences sociales," *Revue Philosophique*, LV (1903), 465-97 (with P. Fauconnet).

[11] Discussion of "L'Inconnue et l'Inconscient en Histoire," séance du 28 mai, 1908, *Bulletin de la Société Française de Philosophie*, VIII (1908), 229.

When reviewing some articles by Salvemini, Croce, and Sorel, however, he draws the distinction between the two fields that he held to more or less constantly: history is concerned with the particular, sociology with types and laws, that is, with comparative structure and analytical theory, studying things not for themselves but as examples of the general. But he adds that these are not two disciplines but two points of view which, far from excluding each other, support and are necessary for each other, although they should not be confused.[12]

But Durkheim did not merely preach. Almost all of his own researches draw heavily from historical and ethnological sources and are in fact organized in an historical framework. This is true, for example, of his sociology of the family,[13] his treatment of the division of labor,[14] his

[12] *L'Année Sociologique*, VI (1903), 123-25. The relevant passage is as follows: "It is necessary, then, to choose. History can only be a science on condition that it raise itself above the particular; it is true that then it ceases to be itself and becomes a branch of sociology. It merges with dynamic sociology. It can remain an original discipline if it limits itself to the study of each national individuality, taken in itself and considered in the diverse moments of its becoming. But then it is only a narrative of which the object is above all particular. Its function is to place societies in the state of remembering their past; this is the eminent form of the collective memory. After having distinguished these two conceptions of history, it is necessary to add further that more and more they are destined to become inseparable. There is no opposition between them, but only differences of degree. Scientific history or sociology cannot avoid direct observation of concrete facts and on the other hand national history, history as art, can only gain by being penetrated by the general principles at which sociology has arrived. For in order to make one people know its past well, it is still necessary to make a selection among the multitude of facts in order to retain those that are particularly vital; and for that some criteria which presuppose comparisons are necessary. Similarly, to be able with greater sureness to discover the way in which concrete events of a particular history are linked together, it is good to know the general relations of which these most particular relations are examples and applications. There are not then in reality two distinct disciplines, but two different points of view, which, far from excluding each other mutually presuppose each other. But this is no reason to confuse them and attribute to the one what is the characteristic of the other." (pp. 124-25)

[13] "Such are the general conclusions of the course: The progress of the family has been to be concentrated and personalized. The family becomes more and more contracted at the same time that relations take on a more and more exclusively personal character, along with the effacement of domestic communism. As the family loses ground marriage on the contrary is strengthened." "La Famille Conjugale," *Revue Philosophique*, LXL, p. 14. The material is drawn from classical, ancient German, medieval, and modern sources. See also Georges Davy, *Sociologues D'Hier et D'Aujourd'hui* (Paris: Alcan, 1931), Part II, "La Famille et la Parenté d'après Durkheim," pp. 104-58.

[14] *The Division of Labor in Society* (New York: The Free Press of Glencoe, Inc., 1949). The concepts of mechanical and organic solidarity are developed from an essentially historical framework, and a wide range of historical material is presented as evidence.

theory of punishment,[15] his discussion of property and contract,[16] his sociology of education,[17] his sociology of religion, of his study of socialism.[18] Even *Suicide*,[19] which depends more on contemporary data than almost any other of his studies, derives its conceptual scheme in part at least from hypotheses about very long-term changes in the structure of solidarity in society.

If Durkheim was not an ahistorical theorist neither was he just another philosopher of history whose work stimulated little concrete historical research. Durkheim's profound influence on two generations of anthropologists and sociologists is well-known, but what is perhaps less well-known is his equally profound influence on cultural history—Hubert's work on the Celts, Granet on China, Harrison and Cornford on ancient Greece, Maunier on North Africa, and many others.[20] Of course, Durkheim advocated comparative historical studies relevant to problems of analytic theory, not a narrow historicism.

What is the theoretical groundwork of Durkheim's lasting concern with history in his sociological thought? His Latin thesis contains an early formulation of his position:

> There are two types of conditions which move social life. One is found in present circumstances such as the nature of the soil, the number of social units, and so on; the other is found in the historical past (*in praeterita historia*). And in fact just as a child would be different if it had other parents, societies differ according to the form of the antecedent society. If it follows a

[15] "Deux lois de l'évolution penale," *L'Année Sociologique*, IV (1901), 65-95. The laws are "The intensity of punishment is greater the less advanced the society and/or the more absolute the central power" (p. 65) and "Punishments which involve deprivation of liberty and of liberty alone, for periods of time variable according to the gravity of the crime, tend more and more to become the normal type of repression." (p. 78) Evidence is drawn from the ancient Near East, India, Greece, Rome, medieval and modern Europe.

[16] *Professional Ethics and Civic Morals* (New York: The Free Press of Glencoe, Inc., 1958), Chaps. 11-18.

[17] Especially his *L'Évolution pédagogique en France* (Paris: Alcan, 1938), 2 vols. This is a major work of Durkheim, unfortunately too little known. It is in fact nothing less than a history of the French spirit in its sociological setting. As his major essay in what might formally be called "history," the book is especially rich in implications for the relation between history and sociology.

[18] *Le Socialisme* (Paris: Alcan, 1928). This is the beginning of an unfinished *history* of socialism.

[19] (New York: The Free Press of Glencoe, Inc., 1951.)

[20] Most of the writers cited have worked on problems in connection with the emergence of early societies from a "primitive" background. The hypotheses put forward in "De Quelques Formes Primitives de Classification: Contribution à l'Étude des Représentations Collectives," *L'Année Sociologique*, VI (1903), 1-72 (with Marcel Mauss), and *Elementary Forms, op. cit.*, have been especially fruitful.

lower society it cannot be the same as if it had issued from a very civilized nation. But Montesquieu, having not known this succession and this kinship of societies, entirely neglected causes of this type. He didn't take account of this force from behind (*vis a tergo*) which pushes peoples and only paid attention to the environing circumstances (*circumfusa*).[21]

He then points out that Comte was equally mistaken in the opposite direction in thinking that placing a society in an historical series was in itself sufficient for sociological explanation.

The position maintained in the Latin thesis, however, was inherently unstable. In saying that both the historical past and the social milieu are causal factors in sociological explanation Durkheim seems to be adopting an eclectic "both/and" position which leaves the fundamental antinomy unresolved. But as early as in *The Rules of Sociological Method* he adopted a stable position which he maintained with consistency thereafter. In the *Rules* he decisively rejects both causal finalism, which seeks to account for the emergence of sociological phenomena in terms of the use or advantage which will result from them,[22] and historical determinism which explains sociological phenomena as the product of an inevitably operative sequence of stages.[23] In opposition to both of these types of explanation, Durkheim holds the position that only efficient causes are admissible in scientific explanation. Thus he maintains that only currently operative variables can account for the emergence of social phenomena and that neither a hypothetical sequence of past historical stages nor a hypothetical future utility can do so. Causes, then, are to be

[21] *Quid Secundatus Politicae Scientiae Instituendae Contulerit* (Bordeaux: Guonouil-hou, 1892), p. 69. A French translation of "The Contribution of Montesquieu to the Establishment of Social Science" is to be found in E. Durkheim, *Montesquieu et Rousseau: Précurseurs de la Sociologie*, edited and translated by Armand Cuvillier (Paris: Riviere, 1953). This translation is superior to that of F. Alengry, *Revue d'Histoire Politiques et Constitutionelle*, I (1937), 405-63. A similar formulation is to be found in *Professional Ethics and Civic Morals, op. cit.*, pp. 1-2: "The problem of the origin and the problem of the operation of the function must therefore form the subject matter of research. This is why the equipment of the method used in studying the science of morals and rights is of two kinds. On the one hand we have comparative history and ethnography, which enable us to get at the origin of the rule, and show us its component elements first dissociated and then accumulating by degrees. In the second place there are comparative statistics, which allow us to compute the degree of relative authority with which this rule is clothed in individual consciousnesses and to discover the causes which make this authority variable."

[22] Durkheim's reserved and cautious use of the concept of function eliminates at least nine tenths of the objections made to functionalism. See *The Rules . . . , op. cit.*, pp. 89-97.

[23] *Ibid.*, pp. 115-21. This is the fundamental ground of his opposition to any unilinear theory of social evolution.

found only in the currently operative social milieu, or, as we might say, in the social system, a position which some have taken as Durkheim's renunciation of history.[24]

Durkheim, however, had by no means renounced history. This is shown by his insistence that currently operative variables cannot be understood without a knowledge of their history, on the one hand, and his deepening understanding of those variables themselves, on the other. Again the preface of Volume II of *L'Année* is instructive. Immediately after having commended historical researches to the attention of sociologists he says:

> Perhaps, it is true, the busy sociologist will find this procedure uselessly complicated. In order to understand the social phenomena of today . . . , isn't it enough to observe them as they are given in our actual experience and isn't it a work of vain erudition to undertake research into their most distant origins? But this quick method is full of illusions. One doesn't know social reality if one only sees it from outside and if one ignores the substructure. In order to know how it is, it is necessary to know how it has come to be, that is, to have followed in history the manner in which it has been progressively formed. In order to be able to say with any chance of success what the society of tomorrow will be . . . , it is indispensable to have studied the social forms of the most distant past. In order to understand the present it is necessary to go outside of it.[25]

Durkheim repeatedly warned that to study the present from the point of view of the present is to be enslaved by all the momentary needs and passions of the day.[26] It is necessary to go into the past to uncover the deeper lying forces which, though often unconscious, are so largely determinative of the social process. Durkheim compares this stricture with the necessity of studying the past of an individual in order to understand

[24] This interpretation of the passages under consideration has several times been put forward by M. Georges Davy, e.g., in "L'Explication Sociologique et le Recours à L'Histoire d'après Comte, Mill et Durkheim," *Revue de Metaphysique et de Morale,* LIV (1949), esp. 346-53; in the Introduction to *Professional Ethics, op. cit.,* esp. pp. xxix-xxx (first published in French in 1950); and in the Introduction to *Montesquieu et Rousseau, op. cit.* Nevertheless one of the clearest presentations of Durkheim's real position was put forward by M. Davy himself at a much earlier date; see *Émile Durkheim,* Choix de Textes avec Étude du systeme sociologique par Georges Davy (Paris: Louis-Michaud, 1911), esp. pp. 31-51.

[25] P. v. The application of this stricture to a great deal of contemporary sociological work is obvious. Don Martindale has recently given an example in showing how American urban sociology would have benefited from historical research in understanding some of its own chief problems. See his Introduction to Max Weber's *The City* (New York: The Free Press of Glencoe, Inc., 1958).

[26] Here again the contemporary application, in a day when "policy" considerations determine more than a little sociological research, is obvious.

the unconscious forces at work in him, thus urging a sociological analogue to the psychoanalytic method.[27]

But history is not only essential to the understanding of the present. History is central to sociology by the very nature of the sociological method; namely, that it is comparative. This is precisely the point that Durkheim makes in Chapter VI of the *Rules*. There he argues that the comparative method is above all the appropriate method for sociology and, more specifically, within the general logic of comparative analysis, the method of concomitant variation[28]—a position which the subsequent history of sociology has largely borne out. But Durkheim was always acutely aware of the problems of analysis and definition in sociological work. He therefore criticizes those sociologists and anthropologists who understand the comparative method to consist in the indiscriminate collection of facts and who believe that the sheer weight of documentation can prove anything. Durkheim, rather, insists that comparison can only be meaningful when the facts compared have been carefully classified in terms of a systematic and theoretically relevant typology. This means for him especially the typological classification of whole societies or what he calls *social species*.[29] Durkheim's work in this area, while far from defini-

[27] E.g.: "But we know today that in order to know ourselves well, it is not enough to direct our attention to the superficial portion of our consciousness; for the sentiments, the ideas which come to the surface are not, by far, those which have the most influence on our conduct. What must be reached are the habits, the tendencies which have been established gradually in the course of our past life or which heredity has bequeathed to us; these are the real forces which govern us. Now, they are concealed in the unconscious. We can, then, succeed in discovering them only by reconstructing our personal history and the history of our family. In the same way, in order to be able properly to fulfill our function in a scholastic system, whatever it may be, it must be known, not from the outside, but from within, that is to say, through history. For only history can penetrate under the surface of our present educational system; only history can analyze it; only history can show us of what elements it is formed, on what conditions each of them depends, how they are interrelated; only history, in a word, can bring us to the long chain of causes and effects of which it is the result." *Education and Sociology, op. cit.*, pp. 152-53. See also *L'Évolution Pédagogique en France, op. cit.*, Vol. I, pp. 15-19.

[28] *The Rules* . . . , *op. cit.*, pp. 129-36.

[29] Durkheim's insistence on taking the total society as his theoretical frame of reference was one of his major contributions, as Talcott Parsons has recently pointed out with respect to mechanical and organic solidarity in "Durkheim's Contribution to the Theory of Integration of Social Systems," forthcoming. On this point the Latin thesis contains some valuable observations: "Montesquieu follows one rule of method which present social science must retain. . . . [He] has well seen that all the elements form a whole of a sort that when they are taken separately and apart from others they cannot be understood; that is why he doesn't separate law from morality, from religion, from commerce, and so on, nor above all from the form of the society which extends its influence to everything social. Different though they are all the facts express

tive, did lay down some of the essential guidelines. His basic principle of classification, that of morphological complexity, as he plainly saw, has both analytical and genetic implications. The arrangement of social types or species show a rough sequence, in that the more complex types emerge from the simpler. But there is no suggestion of "inevitable stages": the genetic concept was not tainted with unilinear evolutionism.[30]

How, then, is the comparative method to be applied in sociology? It can, according to Durkheim, be used in a single society "when absolutely necessary" if certain conditions obtain; namely, when there are data for a considerable period of time and when the data themselves reveal extensive systematic variation, as in the case of suicide.[31] Results obtained from several societies of the same species are desirable in confirming the generalizations reached on the basis of a single case. But by far the best use of the comparative method, from Durkheim's point of view, is its application to an extended series of social types, involving a wide range of historical and ethnographical material.

> To explain a social institution belonging to a given species, one will com-
> pare its different forms, not only among peoples of that species but in all
> preceding species as well. . . . This method, which may be called *genetic,*
> would give at once the analysis and the synthesis of the phenomenon. For,
> on the one hand, it would show us the separate elements composing it, by
> the very fact that it would allow us to see the process of accretion or action.
> At the same time, thanks to this wide field of comparison, we should be in a

---

the life of one and the same society; they correspond to diverse elements or organs of the same social organism. If one refrains from seeking how they realize their harmony and their reciprocal influence one cannot determine the function of each. Indeed one lets their nature escape completely, because they seem to be realities endowed with their own existence while they are only elements of a whole." *Montesquieu et Rousseau, op. cit.,* pp. 102-104. We are still far from having learned this lesson.

[30] A satisfactory typology of societies remains to be achieved, though it is one of the first tasks of sociology as Durkheim clearly saw. All comparative work which does not use at least an implicit typology is severely limited. This stricture applies to at least some of the cross-cultural survey studies which use, say, "400 societies," but where we have no idea how comparable these societies in fact are in terms of structural types. It is safe to say that an adequate typology will be based on the most *generally* applicable concepts of sociological theory *and* will be genetically valid. It is in the work of Max Weber rather than Durkheim that the most fruitful beginnings of a satisfactory typology are to be found.

[31] "For example, when comparing the curve which expresses the trend of suicide during a sufficiently long period of time with the variations which the same phenomenon presents according to provinces, classes, rural or urban areas, sex, age, social status, and so on, one can arrive, even without extending one's researches beyond a single country, at establishing genuine laws, although it is always preferable to confirm these results by other observations made on other peoples of the same species." *The Rules,* p. 136.

much better position to determine the conditions on which depend their formation. *Consequently, one cannot explain a social fact of any complexity except by following its complete development through all social species.* Comparative sociology is not a particular branch of sociology; it is sociology itself, insofar as it ceases to be purely descriptive and aspires to account for facts.[32]

Here as so often Durkheim overstates his case. There are clearly some problems for which the historical and comparative method is less relevant than others. Still it is important to remember that most of his empirical work was carried out in terms of just such a method of extended comparison, and that the great theoretical advances which have inspired so much valuable work in anthropology, history, and sociology directly emerged from the use of that method.

Thus, although Durkheim stresses that only currently operative variables can be accepted as causes of social phenomena, he insists with equal vehemence that such variables can only be understood by a comparative analysis involving a recourse to history. So in Durkheim's mature view there are not two alternative modes of explanation of social phenomena, one in terms of sociological function, the other in terms of the historic past. There is only one method of explanation, at once both sociological and historical.

We may now turn to an analysis of the chief types of social cause with which Durkheim worked, an analysis which will take us even more deeply into Durkheim's conception of the role of the historical in sociology. For here Durkheim went quite far in the direction of developing a theory of social change—which, presumably, static functionalists are not allowed to do.

In the early period, roughly from *The Division of Labor* through *Suicide,* Durkheim gives primary emphasis to morphological variables in the explanation of social causes. Schnore has recently published an excellent analysis of Durkheim's views on morphology and structural differentiation; only the briefest summary is necessary here.[33] Durkheim isolates two especially important morphological variables: the number of social units or the "size of a society"; and the degree of interaction taking place between the units of the system, which he calls "dynamic" or "moral" density. In general, as size and dynamic density increase, competition

---

[32] *Ibid.,* pp. 138-39. Italics in the original.

[33] Leo F. Schnore, "Social Morphology and Human Ecology," *American Journal of Sociology,* LXIII, 63 (May 1958), 620-34. I wish to underscore Schnore's conclusion as to the importance of Durkheim's theory of structural differentiation and the necessity of developing structural taxonomies, adding that these are crucial not for ecology alone but for general sociology.

between unspecialized units engaged in the same activities also increases. Structural differentiation is then seen as an adaptive response to this increased competition: by specializing in different activities the units no longer come in conflict. Although his conception is schematic and over-simplified, Durkheim is unquestionably correct in seeing structural differentiation in response to adaptive exigencies as a major aspect of social change.[34] This concern with structure, far from obscuring the problem of change, actually illuminates it.

Durkheim saw that the focus of structural differentiation is economic organization, but he also saw that it had a profound effect on the total society and that it always involved important elements which were in no immediate sense economic. Examination of some of these noneconomic aspects of structural differentiation provides better understanding of Durkheim's conception.

FAMILY, INDIVIDUAL, AND DIFFERENTIATION

In Durkheim's conception the starting point of the process of structural differentiation is the undifferentiated segment that he tends to identify with a "diffuse clan." This is the beginning of the development of the family as an institution.[35] The diffuse clan has economic, political, religious, and other functions, as well as functions which, on the basis of our form of family (which Durkheim called *conjugal* and we sometimes call *nuclear*), are today often referred to as *familial*. Durkheim therefore believes that it is somewhat confusing to name the diffuse clan a "family" since by that term we mean something so different. He does recognize the existence of the nuclear family within such a unit but finds it weak in structural differentiation and institutional legitimacy compared with the

[34] Durkheim, *The Division of Labor, op. cit.*, Book II, Chap. 2; *The Rules*, pp. 92-93, 112-15. Parsons and Smelser have recently pushed the theory of structural differentiation considerably forward. See Talcott Parsons and Neil J. Smelser, *Economy and Society* (New York: The Free Press of Glencoe, Inc., 1956), Chap. 5; and esp. Neil J. Smelser, "Revolution in Industry and Family: An Application of Social Theory to the British Cotton Industry, 1770-1840" (unpublished Ph.D. dissertation, Harvard University, Cambridge, Mass., 1958). In the latter work Smelser treats certain social movements as reactions to strains generated in the process of social differentiation, a point which Durkheim anticipated in his *Le Socialisme, op. cit.*

[35] Durkheim's lectures on the family (discussed by M. Mauss in "In Memoriam, L'Oeuvre inédite de Durkheim et de ses collaborateurs," *L'Année Sociologique,* new series, I, pp. 7-29) unfortunately were never published. His sociology of the family therefore must be reconstructed from the items mentioned in notes 3 and 13 above, from his "La Prohibition de L'Inceste et ses Origines" *L'Année Sociologique,* I (1898), 1-70, and from scattered remarks in other works. See esp. the article by Davy cited in footnote 13 above.

family in our society. As the process of division of labor proceeds Durkheim sees the successive differentiation of religious, political, and economic functions away from the kinship unit itself. But together with these external changes there are also internal changes. As familial relations become disentangled from relations to property, political authority, and the like, they become more personalized. The external environment reaches into the family in the form of the state, which affords protection from abuse even within the family. Under these circumstances the conjugal family in modern society is enabled to carry out its indispensable functions; namely, the moral training of children or, as we would say, "socialization," and the provision of moral and emotional security for all family members.[36] So brief a summary gives no idea of the richness of the comparative material which Durkheim presents in support of his argument. But the essential position is that in the process of structural differentiation the family does not merely lose functions but becomes a more specialized unit playing a vital role in more complex societies, although not the same role as in simpler societies. Not only does this analysis increase our understanding of the family, it adds an important principle to the theory of structural differentiation—namely, that when in the course of differentiation a unit appears to lose important functions, it is not necessarily a weakened version of its former self; it may be a new, more specialized unit, fulfilling important functions at a new level of complexity in the larger system.

A similar conclusion may be drawn from the consideration of Durkheim's views on the changing position of the individual in society as the result of structural differentiation. This is a subject to which Durkheim devoted considerable attention, references to it being found in a great many of his books and articles. Taken as a whole, his work on this subject

[36] Davy, in summarizing Durkheim's views on the conjugal family, writes: "It is not only the framework which socially sustains the individual and constitutes the organized defense of certain of his interests. It is also the moral milieu where his tendencies are disciplined and where his aspirations toward the ideal are born, begin to expand, and continue to be maintained . . . in providing a place of refreshment where effort may be relaxed and the will reinvigorated; in fixing for this will and this effort, established in the nature of the species, an end which goes beyond egoistic and momentary enjoyments; in forming, finally, a refuge where the wounds of life may find their consolation and errors their pardon, the family is a center [foyer] of morality, energy and gentleness, a school of duty, love and work, in a word, a school of life which cannot lose its role." *Sociologues D'Hier et D'Aujourd'hui, op. cit.*, pp. 153-54. Parsons and Bales in seeing the modern type of family as the result of a process of specialization and its main functions as those of "pattern maintenance" and "tension management" are very close to the Durkheimian view. See Talcott Parsons and Robert F. Bales, *Family, Socialization and Interaction Process* (New York: The Free Press of Glencoe, Inc., 1955), Chap. 1.

constitutes an important contribution to the "sociology of personality," or, as it may be put, a historical and comparative social psychology.[37] Durkheim's great problem in this area is to explain the emergence of individualism on a sociological basis, avoiding both the abstract philosophical and purely psychological analyses of his predecessors.

The core of the problem is touched in *The Division of Labor*. Individuality is at its minimum in the undifferentiated segment characterized by mechanical solidarity; here a single *conscience collective* guides all individuals alike. In a differentiated society where the division of labor and organic solidarity have become important, the sphere of the *conscience collective* has shrunk and individual differences are not only tolerated but encouraged. How does this occur? In the first instance, Durkheim cites a number of morphological factors. One aspect of the increase of dynamic density (the degree of interaction between units in a social system) is increased physical mobility. As individuals move away from their place of origin the hold of the older generation, defenders of tradition (itself the stronghold of the *conscience collective*), is weakened and consequently individual differences more easily can occur—especially in the process of urbanization.[38] Another aspect of urbanization allowing greater individual variation is the anonymity afforded by large population aggregates, which renders the individual less subject to rigid traditional controls.[39] In addition to these rather negative causes Durkheim adduces certain important positive factors. One of these is the emergence of the state, which he sees as an essential prerequisite for the emancipation of the individual from the control of the undifferentiated segment. The state, seeking to extend its own influence at the expense of the primary and secondary groups which immediately envelop the individual, operates to secure the rights of individuals against such groups. If the state destroys the secondary groups, however, it becomes even more op-

[37] To cite only some of the chief references on this subject: *The Division of Labor in Society, op. cit.,* esp. pp. 283-303, 345-50, 386-88; *Suicide, op. cit.,* esp. pp. 152-276; "Deux lois de l'évolution pénale," *op. cit.; L'Éducation Morale* (Paris: Alcan, 1925); *Professional Ethics and Civic Morals, op. cit.,* pp. 55-75. Durkheim's works on the sociology of the family and of religion are also relevant. Marcel Mauss in a brilliant essay carried forward Durkheim's work in this area by undertaking an historical and comparative analysis of the concept of the "self" as found in the following societies: the Pueblos, the Indians of Northwest America, Australia, India, China, and Rome; and as the concept is treated by Stoics, Christians, and modern European philosophy. See "Une categorie de l'esprit humain: La Notion de personne, celle de 'Moi,'" in M. Mauss, *Sociologie et Anthropologie* (Paris: Presses Universitaires de France, 1950), pp. 331-62.

[38] *The Division of Labor in Society,* pp. 291-97.

[39] *Ibid.,* pp. 297-301.

pressive than they were. Durkheim sees a dynamic balance between the state and secondary groups as maximizing individuality.[40] As society becomes more voluminous it tends to become more universalistic—and here is another positive factor. Law, for instance, when it must apply to a vast empire must be more generalized than are the local customs of a petty hamlet. Religion too, if spread over a wide area, must have a universal appeal and not be restricted by narrowly local and particularistic concerns. But a more generalized and abstract law and religion will bind the individual less closely than the minutely specific customs of the undifferentiated segment.[41] Implicit throughout *The Division of Labor* is the notion that the performance of complex differentiated functions in a society with an advanced division of labor both requires and creates individual variation, initiative, and innovation, whereas undifferentiated segmental societies do not.[42]

These more or less morphological hypotheses may serve as an introduction to Durkheim's sociology of the individual. His understanding of this problem was greatly deepened as he became aware of a second main type of causal variable, noted below. The foregoing discussion, however, is sufficient to indicate that Durkheim not only introduced a series of stimulating hypotheses about the role of the individual, but also added further important corrolaries to the theory of structural differentiation. One of the most important of these is what Talcott Parsons calls "institutionalized individualism."[43] This is the notion that the emergence of individuality involves the shift from one kind of social control to another, not the weakening of social control itself. Durkheim, then, stressing the necessity of conformity in some sense for social order, turns our attention from the false issue of conformity versus nonconformity to a considera-

---

[40] *Professional Ethics*, pp. 55-64.

[41] *The Division of Labor in Society*, *op. cit.*, pp. 287-91. Here Durkheim seems to be getting at a very important aspect of normative systems, namely their level of generality, whether or not his overly simple morphological explanation of the problem is acceptable. See Howard Becker, "Current Sacred-Secular Theory and Its Development" in H. Becker and A. Boskoff (eds.), *Modern Sociological Theory in Continuity and Change* (New York: Dryden, 1957), Chap. 6. Becker's distinctions between proverbial and prescriptive, on the one hand, and principial, on the other, seem to be concerned with what Durkheim is here discussing.

[42] Recent work by Morris Janowitz on long-term changes in military organization tend to bear out some of Durkheim's ideas. As military units change from the old undifferentiated infantry to the complex organization geared to the use of modern weapons, control of individuals becomes less formal and rigid and involves more participation and initiative. His finding that repressive corporal punishment tends to diminish in modern armies supports Durkheim's contention in "Deux Lois."

[43] Parsons, "Durkheim's Contribution," *op. cit.*

tion of various types of conformity, including, of course, the pathological possibility of overconformity.

For our purposes, however, the point of special interest in Durkheim's views on the family and the role of the individual, for example, is that the basic analytic concepts of morphology[44] and social differentiation, which supply the basis of so much of Durkheim's work, apply, as he uses them, both to current functioning and to long-term historical change. Here are concrete examples of that method of extended comparison which Durkheim advocated. If the concepts which have emerged from these comparisons—the types of solidarity, the types of suicide, and so on—have proven useful in the analysis of the functioning of social systems, these same concepts when organized around the master idea of structural differentiation have made very important contributions to our understanding of social change.

RELIGION, COLLECTIVE REPRESENTATIONS, AND SOCIAL CHANGE

The second major type of social cause which Durkheim isolated, and which occupied him increasingly in his later years, is the *representation collective*. As is well-known, Durkheim's interest turned increasingly to religion, especially primitive religion, and it was in relation to this interest that the idea of collective representation takes on prominence.[45] It seems likely that Durkheim's concern with problems of structural differentiation turned his interest to religion. At any rate, his work on religion is closely related to that earlier concern, as indicated by the following remarks from the preface of Volume II of *L'Année:*

> At the head of these reviews one will find this year, as last, those which concern the sociology of religion. The kind of primacy we have accorded to this sort of phenomena is astonishing; but they are the germ from which all the others, or at least almost all the others, are derived. Religion contains in itself, from the beginning, but in a diffused state, all the elements which in

[44] See Durkheim's introductory note on "Morphologie Sociale," *L'Année Sociologique* II (1899), 520-21, where he points out that morphology cannot be a static science and that history and comparative ethnography are essential to it.

[45] According to Davy: ". . . he undertook the study of religious phenomena only after having written the *Division* and *Rules* and it is this new study which revealed to him the importance of ideal factors." *Émile Durkheim, op. cit.,* p. 44. Actually Durkheim's interest in religion is already clearly in evidence in *Division;* and even in one of his first articles, "Les Études de Science Sociale," *Revue Philosophique,* XXII (1886), 61-80, there is a long and interesting discussion of Spencer's theory of religion. Nevertheless Davy is almost certainly right that religion became a central concern of Durkheim only from the late 1890's.

dissociating, determining and combining with each other in a thousand ways, have given birth to the diverse manifestations of the collective life. It is from myths and legends that science and poetry have separated; it is from religious ornamentation and cult ceremonies that the plastic arts have come; law and morality were born from ritual practices. One cannot understand our representation of the world, our philosophic conceptions about the soul, immortality, and life, if one doesn't know the religious beliefs which were their first form. Kinship began by being an essentially religious tie; punishment, contract, the gift, homage are transformations of sacrifice, be it expiatory, contractual, communal, honorary, and so on. At most it will be asked if economic organization is an exception and derives from another source; although we don't think so, we will allow this question to be reserved. The fact remains nonetheless that a multitude of problems completely change their aspect from the day we recognize their relation to the sociology of religion.[46]

Thus Durkheim is interested to discover in religion, especially primitive religion, that undifferentiated whole from which the elements of social life gradually differentiated. (Durkheim twice speaks of this phenomenon in connection with the importance of the discovery of the unicellular organism in biology.[47]) It is in this context, then, that we can understand why Durkheim came to devote so much attention to religion in the Australian clan, attention that led to the production of his greatest work, *The Elementary Forms of the Religious Life*. As early as the 1880s, Durkheim had seen what he called the *diffuse clan* as the simplest form of kinship structure. By 1898 he had come to view the clan as more fundamentally a religious group than a consaguineal one. With the example of the Australian clan and its religious life, he undertook to analyze the social analogue of the unicellular organism, the basic structural type from which all other social structures have differentiated.[48]

[46] *L'Année*, II (1899), iv-v. Durkheim actually undertook research on most of the problems mentioned in this paragraph. He shows the relation between kinship and religion in "La Prohibition de L'Inceste," *op. cit.* (1898), between punishment and religion in "Deux Lois," *op. cit.* (1901), between categories of thought and religion in "De Quelques Formes," *op. cit.* (1903), between property, contract, and taxation and religion in *Professional Ethics . . . , op. cit.,* pp. 145-95, and in the *Elementary Forms . . . , op. cit.,* provided a summary of the whole problem, including the religious source of morality.

[47] *Elementary Forms . . . , op. cit.,* pp. 3-4; *Pragmatisme et Sociologie* (Paris: Vrin, 1955), pp. 191-92. The relevance of this point was first pointed out to me by Talcott Parsons in the summer of 1954.

[48] Of course, Durkheim did not view the Australian clan as a fossilized survival of the exact structure from which all other structures differentiated. Rather, in line with some of his ideas discussed above, he considered the Australian clan to be an example of a social *type*. Taking his results at a sufficient level of generality, then, we find them validly applicable to the "single-celled" type of society—all more complex societies

For fifteen years Durkheim used Australian totemism as a "laboratory" in which to study with minute precision the relations between religion, social structure, and personality. During that time he mastered the concrete empirical data to such an extent that *The Elementary Forms* anticipated discoveries made by Australian field workers only several years later, and profoundly influenced subsequent work in this field.[49] And it was during these long and painstaking experiments on Australian totemism that Durkheim made some of his most fundamental sociological discoveries, concerning the symbolic nature of the sacred, the theory of ritual, the role of religion in the internalization of values, and so on. It is impossible here to give even a superficial summary of *The Elementary Forms*. We can only cite a single point of method and discuss the major contribution to the theory of social change—our theme—which emerged from Durkheim's study of primitive religion.

Durkheim clearly regarded *The Elementary Forms* as a vindication of his genetic method. He said on one occasion that he understood the Australian primitives better than he did modern France.[50] He found the fundamental facts simpler and the relations between them easier to grasp

---

must have descended from some society of this type. Further, although Durkheim held that the Australian social structure was in certain key morphological respects simple, he was well aware of the considerable complexity of this system, especially as to kinship. Lévi-Strauss, in this regard, refers to ". . . Durkheim's important article 'La prohibition de L'Inceste' where anthropologists may find a remarkably clear interpretation of the genesis of the Australian eight-class systems through the cross-cutting of a matrilineal dichotomy based on filiation, and a patrilineal fourfold division based on residence." (C. Lévi-Strauss, "French Sociology," in G. Gurvitch and W. E. Moore [eds.], *Twentieth Century Sociology* [New York: Philosophical Library, 1945], p. 517.) In general, moreover, Durkheim understood that "simple" structures are in their own way complex: "When Spencer states that the universe goes 'from homogeneity to heterogeneity,' this formula is inexact. That which exists at the origin is also heterogeneous, but it is a diffuse state of heterogeneity. The initial state is a multiplicity of germs, modalities and different activities, not only mixed but, so to say, lost one in another, in such a way that it is extremely difficult to separate them: they are indistinct from one another. Thus in the cell of unicellular beings all the vital functions are gathered together: all are found there only they are not separated; the functions of nutrition and the functions of relation [integration?] seem blended and it is difficult to distinguish them. . . . In social life this primitive state of undifferentiation is even more striking still." *Pragmatisme et Sociologie, op. cit.*, p. 191. This passage dates from 1914 and indicates that Durkheim was aware of relatively recent developments in biology, the complex functions of unicellular organisms becoming well-known only in the early years of the century.

[49] See Lévi-Strauss, *op. cit.*, pp. 521-22, 536. Such distinguished Australian fieldworkers as Radcliffe-Brown, A. P. Elkin, and W. L. Warner have acknowledged Durkheim's remarkable contributions to the Australian field. Most anthropologists who have criticized Durkheim for being an armchair ethnologist have never set eyes on Australia.

[50] "L'Inconnu et l'inconscient en histoire," *op cit.* M. Seignobos found this assertion quite incredible.

than in a more complex society.[51] Unfortunately he was unable to carry out his method extensively, that is, by a series of studies of religion in societies of successively more complex types. He did give some suggestions along these lines, however, some of which are noted below.

Turning to the main contribution to the theory of social change emerging from his work on religion we must consider the idea of *collective representations*. This idea appears in 1898—when Durkheim was deeply concerned with the sociology of religion. One of the earliest uses of the concept is in "La Prohibition de L'Inceste," an article which appeared in that year, and is the first paper drawing heavily on Australian sources. Both in this paper and in another publication in 1898, "Individual and Collective Representations," the fundamental point is made that while collective representations (which Durkheim later called *ideals* and which we might call *values*—although the original conception was broader than these terms suggest) arise from and reflect the "social substratum" (the morphological variables of the earlier period) they are, once in existence, "partially autonomous realities" which independently influence subsequent social development. Thus Durkheim, in the concept of collective representations, made the fundamental discovery of culture as an element analytically independent of social system,[52] al-

---

[51] *Elementary Forms . . .* , *op. cit.,* pp. 6-7. Although Durkheim's method was "genetic," he was not a victim of the genetic fallacy. He never lost sight of his rule that social causes could only be understood in terms of current functioning. He knew that structures inherited from simpler societies might have quite different functions in more complex ones. As an example of his clarity on this fundamental point see his "La Prohibition de L'Inceste," *op. cit.,* pp. 66-70.

[52] This point is so crucial that we quote the relevant passage from "Individual and Collective Representations": "Also, while it is through the collective substratum that collective life is connected to the rest of the world, it is not absorbed in it. It is at the same time dependent on and distinct from it, as is the function of the organ. As it is born of the collective substratum the forms which it manifests at the time of its origin, and which are consequently fundamental, naturally bear the marks of their origin. For this reason the basic matter of the social consciousness is in close relation with the number of social elements and the way in which they are grouped and distributed, and so on—that is to say, with the nature of the substratum. But once a basic number of representations has been thus created, they become, for the reasons which we have explained, partially autonomous realities with their own way of life. They have the power to attract and repel each other and to form amongst themselves various syntheses, which are determined by their natural affinities and not by the condition of their matrix. As a consequence, the new representations born of these syntheses have the same nature; they are immediately caused by other collective representations and not by this or that characteristic of the social structure. The evolution of religion provides us with the most striking examples of this phenomenon. It is perhaps impossible to understand how the Greek or Roman Pantheon came into existence unless we go into the constitution of the city, the way in which the primitive clans slowly emerged, the organization of the patriarchal family, etc. Nevertheless the luxuriant

though the full significance of this insight remained somewhat obscured by his use of the word *social* to apply to both elements.

With the creation of the concept of collective representations, Durkheim made a twofold contribution to the theory of social change. First and better known, he greatly increased our understanding of how collective representations arise by showing their relation to morphological features. (In this, incidentally, he anticipated Mannheim by more than twenty years.) The greatest impact of *The Elementary Forms* on the study of primitive religion and on early societies in the ancient Mediterranean, the Far East, and elsewhere, was of this sort. But Durkheim, never a devotee of one-way determinism,[53] also saw clearly that collective representations have a reciprocal influence on social structure and are independent variables in the process of social change. This is stated explicitly as early as 1898[54] and receives something like a theoretical formulation in 1911.[55] But the richest and most exciting elaboration of this

---

growth of myths and legends, theogonic and cosmological systems, etc., which grow out of religious thought, is not directly related to the particular features of social morphology. Thus it is that the social nature of religion has been so often misunderstood." (*Sociology and Philosophy* [New York: The Free Press of Glencoe, Inc., 1953], pp. 30-31.) This passage deserves the closest study; in itself it is enough to acquit Durkheim of the charge of "sociologism."

Apart from the two papers cited above one other occurrence of the term *collective representation* may date as early as 1898, namely *Professional Ethics* . . . , *op. cit.*, pp. 48-50, which was drafted, according to Mauss, between November 1898 and June 1900. I have not found the term used before 1898, although there are various foreshadowings, e.g., in the discussion of religion in *Suicide, op. cit.*, pp. 157-60. Durkheim's discussion of Montesquieu's idea that different social types have different integrating ideals (e.g., "virtue" in the ancient city, "honor" in the monarchy, and "fear" in despotism), which occurs in the Latin thesis, may be a forerunner. The treatment of socialism in *Le Socialisme*, written in 1895-96, seems to move in the same direction, but the term 'collective representation' is not used. Durkheim's fullest treatment of what is in fact his theory of culture is in the core passage of the *Elementary Forms* . . . , *op. cit.*, Book II, Chap. VII, pp. 205-39. Lévi-Strauss believes that even in this passage Durkheim is not quite fully aware of the analytical independence of symbolism: "Society cannot exist without symbolism, but instead of showing how the appearance of symbolic thought makes social life altogether possible and necessary, Durkheim tries the reverse, i.e., to make symbolism grow out of society." *op. cit.*, p. 518. I would question Lévi-Strauss's view but to explain my reasons would require a more extended analysis of the passage in question than is possible here. It is shown below that Durkheim did use morphological (social) and representational (cultural) elements as independently variable in a number of instances.

[53] The old chicken and egg problem concerning material and ideal factors was never an issue for Durkheim at a time when it was agitating many lesser minds. On the reciprocal nature of causation see the references cited in *Pragmatisme et Sociologie, op. cit.*, p. 196, note 1.

[54] "La Prohibition de L'Inceste," *op. cit.*, p. 69.

[55] "Value Judgments and Judgments of Reality," *Sociology and Philosophy, op. cit.*, pp. 80-97.

view appears in that little known but extremely important book, published twenty years after Durkheim's death, *L'Évolution Pédagogique en France*, composed of lectures written in 1904 and 1905.

In this work Durkheim takes the history of French education as an index to the history of the French spirit and of the social and cultural framework out of which it arose: here is an intricate and sensitive analysis of the interplay of morphological and representational factors in the development of French culture from the early middle ages to the nineteenth century. In accordance with his penchant for origins, he begins by showing that French education first appeared in the church. He demonstrates how certain fundamental features of the Christian world view colored the conception of the school as a place for the education of the total personality, a conception which still survives. Here a representational element is used as a fundamental point of reference without any attempt to explain it morphologically.[56] There follows an interesting discussion of how the morphological factors involved in the political unification of Charlemagne and the religious unification of the high Middle Ages are related to the structure of the school system and to the predominance first of grammar and then of logic in the curriculum, although in this analysis he takes full account as well of cultural factors.[57] Subsequently, the changes in social structure involved in the breakdown of the medieval system and the several cultural tendencies of the Renaissance are considered as alternative answers to the problems raised by that breakdown.[58] The analysis of the factors involved in the French cultural synthesis of the seventeenth century is especially brilliant; and since the spirit of modern French culture derives from that period this discussion is helpful in understanding the France of today as well as Durkheim's thought.[59] A final example—there are many others—of Durkheim's his-

---

[56] *L'Évolution*, Vol. I, Chaps. 2 and 3.

[57] *Ibid.*, Chaps. 4-13.

[58] *Ibid.*, Vol. I, Chap. 14; Vol. II, Chaps. 1-4.

[59] *Ibid.*, Vol. II, Chaps. 5-8. He mentions the important morphological element of the political centralization under Louis XIV as one important factor. However, he pays especial attention to the brand of humanism being taught in the Jesuit schools which monopolized current education. He shows how it resulted in a kind of abstract and universalized rationalism which conceived of human nature only "as a sort of eternal reality, unchangeable, invariable, independent of time and place since the diversity of times and places does not affect it." (Vol. II, p. 128.) This attitude, he notes, is represented in the literature of the time, especially the dramatic literature, which deals with generalized human emotions and virtues. He also finds French political thought in the eighteenth century, with its tendency to speak not for France but for mankind, as representing this same syndrome. (Can we not see in the tendency to identify French culture with human culture, a trait whose origins Durkheim so carefully studied, one source of France's recent colonial problems?) Durkheim also

torical sociology in this work is his analysis of the relation between Protestantism and the rise of "realistic education," especially the teaching of science. In linking the orientation of Protestantism to science Durkheim independently reached a conclusion better known from the studies of Weber and Merton.[60]

Two general conclusions may be drawn from Durkheim's treatment of such problems, which have reference to the theory of social change. One is his insistence that collective representations (might we say, in this case, *values?*), once institutionalized, are capable of exerting an influence over an exceptionally long period of time and in the face of many social and cultural changes. He held, for example, that even modern secular ideas of duty, morality, and the like were derived from fundamentally Christian ideas since Christianity was the chrysalis of Western culture itself, and that these ideas are quite different from the ethical views of the classical pagan world. Again, he maintained that the Cartesian spirit held a certain cultural dominance in France in spite of the tremendous political and economic revolutions which occurred after its formulation. The second general conclusion is that as long as the social system is running smoothly the accepted system of collective representations will not be questioned. Only when the old system is breaking down, when there is a great deal of turmoil and social ferment, new systems of ideals become formulated, and then contribute to the establishment of a newly stabilized social system.[61] Durkheim's conclusions about the role of collective representations in social process together with his conception of structural differentiation, I believe, provide the outlines of a fruitful theory of social change and suggest the direction of future work in the development of such a theory.

---

points out changes in the French language in this period and traces the French insistence on clarity and precision to the same concern for the general and the abstract which held the day. Descartes is the veritable *representation collective* of these cultural tendencies: Durkheim sees the French spirit as essentially Cartesian. This summary is inadequate, but I believe that Durkheim's grasp of the "cultural whole" of French seventeenth century culture was as subtle as Ruth Benedict's treatment of the Zuni or the Japanese cultures.

[60] *Ibid.*, Vol. II, Chap. 9.

[61] This conclusion was anticipated in *Suicide, op. cit.*, pp. 157-160, and esp. in *Le Socialisme, op. cit.*, pp. 348-52, where Durkheim finds socialism, religious revival, sociology, and the historical method, diverse though they are, all reactions to the great social changes brought on by the Industrial Revolution and all in one way or another attempts to understand and cope with the new situation. The relation between this view and Weber's idea of charismatic revolution should not be overlooked—Durkheim stresses the features of social disturbance, Weber the charismatic response, but they are two sides of the same process.

THE CURRENT RELEVANCE OF DURKHEIM

So far the discussion has been carried on largely in Durkheim's terms. These concluding remarks suggest how the historical dimension, as Durkheim understood it, is related to current interests and problems.

Every research problem involves a time dimension and thus involves history. But the extent of the relevant time dimension varies with the type of problem under study. For example, if the focus of interest is the attitudes of individuals, the relevant time dimension is short—no longer than the life span of the individuals and usually much less. If the study is concerned with primary groups, such as friendships, delinquent gangs, nuclear families, or work groups, the relevant time dimension remains quite short for the duration of the groups is brief. If the interest is in complex associations, such as medical schools, armies, governmental bureaus, public school systems, and the like, the time dimension involved is considerably longer. The study of institutions (patterned sets of norms governing behavior)—such as legal norms, norms governing family life, and the normative patterns of economic and political life—involves a still longer time span. And the study of national societies implies an even longer time dimension. (Even the study of individual attitudes and primary groups, if related to variable structural settings, may involve very long time periods.)

Perhaps this way of looking at the problem helps to explain Durkheim's peculiar insistence on the importance of history. For Durkheim, sociology as the science of human society, involves a time span unlimited by the life duration of individuals or groups or even nations. It involves nothing less than the total life span of human society. For him there could be no opposition of history and science: the history of social forms is as central to sociology as is the history of life forms for biology, and for much the same reasons.[62]

One final word on a subject which must trouble any student of Durkheim. As noted above, while Durkheim distinguished between what we currently term *culture* and *social system* he did not systematically work out the interrelations between the two, and by referring to both levels as *social* he created a certain amount of confusion. The famous formula

[62] In spite of long-standing opposition to this position, I agree with Durkheim that the problem of evolution, including even social origins, is central for sociology as a science. To be convincing, this view must be backed by research—a challenge not to be evaded. This paper, however, is limited to a consideration of the concern for evolution in the work of Durkheim himself.

)

"society equals God," which perhaps doesn't mean quite what it often seems to mean, even in *The Elementary Forms*[63] where the fusion of clan and religion might to some extent justify the identification, presents grave problems to the serious student today. For Durkheim himself, who certainly lived *la vie serieuse,* this was indeed a problem. Unfortunately Durkheim never undertook a full-scale study of the place of religion in modern society. He believed that traditional religion was on its way out, essentially because it conflicts with science. But the concept of the sacred would remain: without this basis of moral respect society itself is impossible. But what would be the referent to which sacred symbols refer? Durkheim replied "society," and as the most comprehensive functioning society, "the nation." However, Durkheim was keenly aware of the danger of demonic nationalism. And his "social" includes, as we have seen, more than the concrete existing society: it included ideals. Thus Durkheim held that that which is sacred for us is the nation *insofar as* it embodies the ideal of humanity.[64] In his wartime pamphlet, *Germany over All,*[65] when he was faced with the full implications of taking the nation state as an ultimate, in a brilliant analysis of the German nationalist historian Treitschke, Durkheim states categorically that morality stands above both the state and individuals.

In the last years of his life Durkheim faced another challenge in the form of an alien doctrine, American pragmatism. Durkheim's sociological epistemology was apparently being interpreted by some of the younger men as supporting a radical brand of pragmatism which made truth relative and variable—more or less whatever suits individual needs at the moment. While admiring certain features of pragmatism, especially in the thought of Dewey, Durkheim considered this extreme interpretation (attributable to James rather than Dewey) as not only a threat to the great tradition of philosophic rationalism but to French culture itself of which rationalism is an important part.[66] In the face of this threat, Durkheim

[63] Armand Cuvillier, in his introduction to *Pragmatisme et Sociologie,* cites several passages in the *Elementary Forms* where it seems clear that society is not to be viewed an end in itself but has its exalted place because it is a superior medium for the manifestation of *reality* (a third term beyond individual and society) when compared with the individual consciousness. *Pragmatisme et Sociologie, op. cit.,* pp. 13-14.

[64] *Professional Ethics . . . , op. cit.,* pp. 65-75; *L'Education Morale, op. cit.,* pp. 73-90.

[65] *L'Allemagne au-dessus de tout: la Mentalité allemande et la guerre* (Paris: Colin, 1915).

[66] "There is further, a *national* interest. All our French culture is at bottom essentially rationalist. Here the eighteenth century prolongs Cartesianism. A total negation of rationalism would constitute then a danger: it would be the destruction of all our national culture. The whole French spirit would be transformed if this form of irrationalism which Pragmatism represents were to be admitted." *Pragmatisme et Sociologie, op. cit.,* p. 28.

declares that thought can know reality and that truth has an objective character which imposes itself on us as well as a moral character in that we feel that we ought to seek the truth.[67]

In both of these instances, concerning religion and nationalism and pragmatism, we can see the essential qualities of the man as well as the scientist. If he did not work through the metaphysical implications of all of his views with complete rigor, Durkheim at least cannot be thought to have irresponsibly deified society. As a man of science, he was in fact a model of responsibility for his nation,[68] for his culture, including his science, and for mankind. It was his fervent hope that sociology, born of the disturbances following the Industrial Revolution,[69] might help to contribute to the solution of those disturbances, in the midst of which we are still living. But he was also committed to the stern and austere discipline of science, which cannot be hurried however grave the crisis. Between these two loyalties, he lived a richly productive and morally committed life.

The greatest tribute to Durkheim, of course, is the fact that his work remains a living force. It still has much to teach us, although it would have been Durkheim's hope that we soon surpass him. Here I have stressed only one important aspect of his work, though one close to Durkheim's heart—namely, the belief that history is a primary field of sociological research and that structural functional theory provides the variables for an adequate theory of social change.[70] But let Durkheim's own statement from his last essay have the final word:

[67] "We perceive at once that [truth] is related:

1. to a *moral obligation*. The truth is not separable from a certain moral character. In all times men have been persuaded that they *should* seek the truth. There is in the truth something to be respected, a moral power before which the mind feels itself rightly obliged to incline;

2. to a necessitating power of fact. There is an impossibility in some way physical of not recognizing the truth. When a true representation is offered to our mind we feel that we cannot but declare it true. The true idea *imposes* itself on us. It is this characteristic which the old theory of *evidence* expresses: from the truth emanates a light which is irresistable." *Ibid.*, p. 153. Italics in the original.

[68] Durkheim's long-term concern to improve the integration of modern society in the sphere of economic institutions is well known. Many intermediate mechanisms have been worked out since Durkheim's day and to some extent have ameliorated the disturbed conditions which concerned him. Edward A. Shils in his *Torment of Secrecy* (New York: The Free Press of Glencoe, Inc., 1956), strikes a Durkheimian note decrying the weakness of organizations intermediary between state and family in the United States.

[69] *Le Socialisme, op. cit.,* pp. 349-50.

[70] The other great founder of structural functional sociology, Max Weber, was equally convinced of the importance of history as a field of sociological research and equally concerned with social change. Since the generation of Weber and Durkheim macroscopic problems involving comparative and historical research have been somewhat

. . . history is not only the natural framework of human life, man is a product of history. If one takes him out of history, if one tries to conceive him outside of time, fixed, immobile, one distorts him. This immobile man is not man.[71]

---

slighted as microscopic research based on new methods and instruments has come to the fore. Not only general sociology, but microsociology itself, would suffer if this imbalance were to go too far. Merton, for example, has recently stressed (*op. cit.,* pp. 306-307) the importance of comparative research in a wide variety of social structural types as indispensable for the development of reference group theory.

[71] "Introduction à la morale," *Revue Philosophique,* LXXXIX (1920), 89.

SELECTED BIBLIOGRAPHY
WORKS BY ÉMILE DURKHEIM

COMPREHENSIVE bibliographies of Durkheim may be found in Harry Alpert, *Émile Durkheim and His Sociology* (New York: Columbia University Press, 1939; new printing, New York: Russell and Russell, Inc., 1961); and in *Émile Durkheim, 1858-1917*, edited by Kurt H. Wolff (Columbus, Ohio: The Ohio State University Press, 1960). In these two excellent volumes the reader will find not only a listing of Durkheim's own works but of many works on Durkheim. Harry Alpert's volume is to be commended for its pioneering bibliographic presentation of Durkheim as much as it is for its valuable explication of Durkheim's thought. It is a pleasure to cite still another comprehensive bibliography of Durkheim, unfortunately still unpublished: that of John M. Foskett, *Émile Durkheim and the Problem of Social Order* (Ph.D. dissertation, Department of Social Institutions, University of California, Berkeley, 1939). In the bibliography that follows I have confined listing to those works of Durkheim that have manifestly and directly influenced modern sociology and that have appeared in English translation. Following Professor Kurt Wolff's excellent precedent I have arranged them in two groups reflecting original French publication and later English translation. The French listing is by year of publication; the English listing is alphabetical.

Quid secundatus politicae scientiae instituendae contulerit (Bordeaux: Gounouilhou, 1892). A translation of this into French may be found in the volume, published posthumously, *Montesquieu et Rousseau, précurseurs de la sociologie* (Paris: Marcel Rivière, 1953).

De la division du travail social: Étude sur l'organisation des sociétés supérieures (Paris: Félix Alcan, 1893). The second edition, with its important new preface on occupational groups, was published, also by Alcan, in 1902.

Les Règles de la méthode sociologique (Paris: Félix Alcan, 1895).

Le Suicide: Étude de sociologie (Paris: Félix Alcan, 1897).

Les Formes élémentaires de la vie religieuse: Le système totémique en Australie (Paris: Félix Alcan, 1912).

(*Published Posthumously*)

Éducation et sociologie (Paris: Félix Alcan, 1922).

Sociologie et philosophie (Paris: Félix Alcan, 1924).

L'Éducation morale (Paris: Félix Alcan, 1925).

Le Socialisme: Sa définition, ses débuts, la doctrine Saint-Simonienne (Paris: Félix Alcan, 1928).

Leçons de sociologie: Physique des moeurs et du droit (Istanbul: L'Université d'Istanbul; Paris: Presses Universitaires de France, 1950).

Pragmatisme et sociologie (Paris: Librairie philosophique J. Vrin, 1955).

English Translations

The Division of Labor in Society, translated and with an Introduction by George Simpson (New York: The Macmillan Company, 1933).

Education and Sociology, translated and with an Introduction by Sherwood D. Fox (New York: The Free Press of Glencoe, Inc., 1956).

The Elementary Forms of the Religious Life: A Study in Religious Sociology, translated by Joseph Ward Swain (London: Allen & Unwin; New York: The Macmillan Company, 1915).

Montesquieu and Rousseau: Forerunners of Sociology, translated by Ralph Manheim (Ann Arbor, Mich.: University of Michigan Press, 1960).

Moral Education: A Study in the Theory and Application of the Sociology of Education, translated by Everett K. Wilson and Herman Schnurer (New York: The Free Press of Glencoe, Inc., 1961).

Professional Ethics and Civic Morals, translated by Cornelia Brookfield (London: Routledge & Kegan Paul, 1957).

The Rules of Sociological Method, translated by Sarah A. Solovay and John H. Mueller and edited by George E. G. Catlin (Chicago: University of Chicago Press, 1938; New York: The Free Press of Glencoe, Inc., 1950).

Socialism and Saint-Simon, translated by Charlotte Sattler; edited and with an Introduction by Alvin W. Gouldner (Yellow Springs, Ohio: Antioch Press, 1958).

Sociology and Philosophy, translated by D. F. Pocock (New York: The Free Press of Glencoe, Inc., 1953).

Suicide: A Study in Sociology, translated by John A. Spaulding and George Simpson; edited and with an Introduction by George Simpson (New York: The Free Press of Glencoe, Inc., 1951).

CONTRIBUTORS

ROBERT A. NISBET. Professor of Sociology, University of California, Riverside; Vice Chancellor and Dean, 1953-63. Past President of the Pacific Sociological Association. Author of *The Quest for Community;* contributing author to *Studies in Leadership, Sociology in Crisis, Sociology and History,* and other works.

HARRY ALPERT. Professor of Sociology and Dean of the Faculties, University of Oregon. Past President of the American Association for Public Opinion Research and of the Pacific Sociological Association. Author of *Émile Durkheim and His Sociology.* Contributing author of *Freedom and Control in Modern Society, The Behavioral Sciences Today,* and other works.

ROBERT N. BELLAH. Associate Professor of Sociology and Regional Studies, Harvard University. Fellow of the Center for Advanced Studies in the Behavioral Sciences (1964-65). Author of *Tokugawa Religion* and other works. Editor of *Religion and Progress in Modern Asia.*

MORRIS GINSBERG. Martin White Professor of Sociology, University of London and London School of Economics; Emeritus since 1954. Huxley Memorial Lecturer and Medalist, 1953. Herbert Spencer Lecturer, Oxford University, 1958. Author of *Essays on Sociology and Social Philosophy; The Psychology of Society; Moral Progress,* and many other works.

ROBERT K. MERTON. Franklin H. Giddings Professor of Sociology, Columbia University; also Associate Director, Bureau of Social Research, Columbia University. Past President of the American Sociological Association. Author of *Science, Technology and Society in Seventeenth Century England; Social Theory and Social Structure;* and many other works.

HANAN C. SELVIN. Professor Sociology and Chairman of the Department, The University of Rochester. Past National Science Foundation Fellow, at the London School of Economics and the Centre d'Études sociologiques, Paris. Author of *The Effects of Leadership* and other works.